PITCHING UP AT CHRISTMAS!

Deborah Aubrey

Copyright © October 2023 Deborah Aubrey

All rights reserved

The characters and events portrayed in this book are fictitious. Any similarity to real persons, living or dead, is coincidental and not intended by the author.

No part of this book may be reproduced, or stored in a retrieval system, or transmitted in any form or by any means, electronic, mechanical, photocopying, recording, or otherwise, without express written permission of the publisher.

ISBN-13: 9798865631743
ISBN-10: 1477123456

Cover design by: Art Painter
Library of Congress Control Number: 2018675309
Printed in the United States of America
Oct23

*Dedicated to everyone enduring Other
People this Christmas. Good luck.*

CHAPTER 1

20th December

Brian and Faye

Their son, Ollie, told them that Jennifer and the children would not be coming for Christmas back in June, as they sat having lunch in a pub garden watching the grandchildren in the play area. Jennifer's parents had suggested they go to them instead and maybe take it in turns from now on. Faye seemed to take it quite well at the time, Christmas was a long way off and she thought they'd probably change their minds by then – nobody made Christmas dinner like she did. And besides, what was Christmas without family? Unthinkable, so she didn't think about it.

Ollie mentioned it again in August and Faye brushed it off with a laugh, as if he'd made a joke. He brought it up in September, and Faye, distracted by Dylan, the youngest, who was sneaking biscuits out of the 'secret hiding place' in the kitchen, pretended not to hear.

At the beginning of December, after talking to them both on speakerphone, he said, "Now don't forget we're not coming for Christmas this year, mum, but we'll pop in – "

"What?" Faye gasped.

Brian rolled his eyes and suppressed a groan.

"We're spending Christmas with Jennifer's – "

"You could have mentioned this before, Ollie! I've got everything in!"

There was a pause. "Dad?"

1

"She's blocked it, son. It's okay."

"Is it?" Faye snapped. *"Is it?"*

"Mum, I told you back in summer!"

"Did you?"

"Yes!"

"He did," Brian said.

"Don't you take his side," Faye snapped.

"I'm not taking any side, I merely speak the truth."

"The truth, *pfff*. This is the first I've heard of it!"

Brian reached for the mobile on the coffee table and said, "We'll see you later, Ollie."

"Will it be safe?"

"Yes. I'll lock your mother in the basement."

"You don't have a basement, dad."

"I'll make one."

Brian hung up, took a deep breath, and looked across at Faye, perched on the edge of the sofa. Tears streamed down her face.

"What about all the presents?" she sniffed.

"They're popping in on the way to Jennifer's parents."

"Popping in?" She pulled a face. *"Popping in?"*

Brian moved from his comfy chair to sit next to her. "It's okay," he soothed, putting an arm across her shoulders and pulling her to his chest. "It's going to be okay, just different, quieter, more relaxing. It'll be fine."

"How is it going to be fine?" she wailed. "They're not coming! The grandkids aren't coming! Our Ellie's gone travelling with her boyfriend in South America – *South America*! How will having no family at Christmas be *fine*, Brian?"

"It'll just be us," he said cheerily, and Faye emitted a prolonged WAAAH sound. "You must have known this was going to happen at some point, lass."

"No, I didn't!"

"You must have thought about it!"

"Thought about what, being abandoned at Christmas by my *own children*?"

"Get a grip, woman!"

"I don't want to!" She held onto the last word and turned it into an *AAAAH!* noise in a perfect rendition of Lucille Ball.

"They come to us every year," Brian said.

"Of course they do, that's what families do, get together at Christmas."

"It's perfectly normal that Jennifer's family would want them to go there for a change."

"What about what I want, Bri?"

"It's fair to take turns, Faye. And think of the peace and quiet, think of all the fun we can have together, eh? We can run round the house completely naked and tear into the turkey with our *bare hands* if we want to."

"WAAAAH!" she cried, throwing herself to the other side of the sofa and burying her head in a cushion.

"Is the thought of just you and me so horrifying? I was joking about the nakedness … unless you fancy it?"

Faye lifted her angst-ridden face up and cried, "WAAAAH!"

Brian tried the firm approach. "Wife, you're overreacting. Pull yourself together and act like a grown-up."

"I don't want to be a grown-up, I want to be a wife and mother who has her family around her at Christmas!"

"It's going to be okay," he said.

"It's not going to be okay, Brian, it's going to be *horrible*." She sniffed and sat up straight. "I've got all this food in, what am I going to do with it all?"

Brian rubbed his belly. "I think I could help with that."

"And the television, there won't be any arguments about what to watch."

"That's a good thing, isn't it?"

"And the kids, running around, over-excited and pumped up to the eyeballs with excitement and sugar."

"I could do that if you want."

"What?"

"I'll wake up at three in the morning and run around the

house shouting and screaming, demolish the contents of several selection boxes, then throw some migraine inducing strops on the living room floor because I'm overtired and overwrought, how about that?"

Faye hesitated, clearly imagining Brian writhing and wailing on the floor. "It won't be the same," she eventually said.

"Nothing stays the same, Faye."

"Why not?"

"Because kids grow up and move on and make their own family traditions."

"What about *our* traditions?"

"We've had our time, Faye, let the kids have theirs."

She looked at him with her watery eyes for a long time. She seemed to be calming down. Then she stood up, wiped her nose, and started cleaning.

It wasn't a good sign.

Brian retreated to his ice box of a shed. The wooden door cracked as he opened it. This was his sanctuary, his safe space. And it *was* safe, until there came a knocking on the door late that afternoon.

"Who is it?" he asked.

"It's me," said Faye.

"What do you want?"

"Open the door."

"Why?"

"So I can come in."

"Again, why?" This was his domain, why did Faye want to invade his space? She'd never come in before, primarily because she was afraid of spiders – he encouraged the spiders.

"Open the door, Bri, it's bloody freezing out here."

"It's not much warmer in here."

"Open the door!"

He did, wearing a hangdog expression. Faye bustled in with a broom, a dustpan and brush, and a duster. Pump sprays bulged from the pocket of the apron she was wearing, the one that had 'Kiss the Cook' printed on it. Brian thought 'Kiss the

Grinch' would have been more appropriate.

"What do you want?" Brian asked, stepping back.

"I've done the house," Faye said, lifting up a hammer and polishing it. "I thought I'd make a start in here."

"In here?" Aghast, Brian snatched the hammer from her and clutched it to his chest, "But this is my stuff! Don't touch my stuff!"

She reached towards his socket set, pulling a spray bottle from her pocket. Panicked by her proximity to the cupboard where he kept his 'special magazines', Brian stood in her way and, using his enormity, backed her out of the shed. He took a gentle hold of her arm and guided her back into the house.

"Don't touch anything in here!" she cried, "I've cleaned *everything*, ready for Christmas, except ..." She sniffed. "... nobody's coming."

He eased her down onto the sofa. "Faye," he said, and the tone of his voice silenced her. "You look knackered."

"Thanks, Bri. You sure know how to make a girl feel special."

He stood over her as she fidgeted on the sofa, unable to keep still. She brushed a speck of dust off the coffee table and looked around for any other specs. The place was like a show home, not a thing out of place.

"We have a good life, don't we, wife?"

"Yes, Bri."

"Do we sit here wringing our hands and wailing, 'When are the children coming to visit?'"

"No, Bri."

"Because we have a life, and so do Ollie and Ellie. Let them get on with it and stop fussing."

Faye was silent for a moment, hanging her head. Then she said, "I'm ... I'm just so ... *bereft*."

"Adjust," he said.

"I'm not sure I can."

"You'll have to, because this is happening and there's nothing you can do to change it."

"Maybe if I asked them to – "

"No, Faye." He softened his voice. "We're going to have a great Christmas by ourselves."

"Are we?"

"We are."

"Okay, Bri."

"Good lass."

He went back to his ice frosted shed with his fingers crossed.

Faye cleaned for two whole days, wailing and howling at regular intervals. He heard her sniffing in bed at night and in the morning when she got up. Nothing he could do or say would comfort her; he hugged her and kissed her and tried to convince her that spending time on their own was a good thing, but that just made her start WAAAAHing again.

Then, on the third day, when the house gleamed like a new pin and Faye was heading into the garden with a pair of polished shears, Olivia rang.

Tel and Sophie

"*How* much longer?"

Tel hesitated, then took a deep breath and said, "Middle of January."

"What? *January*? But they said they'd have the bathroom installed by Christmas! They *promised* us, Tel!"

"I know, but there were … delays."

"Too many tea breaks?"

"They're still waiting for the arrival of the bespoke, freestanding, marble, double-ended, roll top slipper bathtub with brushed brass feet and in-built jacuzzi to arrive from Italy." He sucked in air.

"So, you're blaming me?"

"I wouldn't dare, although I will remind you that I did say it was too ostentatious, overpriced and overly optimistic to expect a fast delivery from Italy."

"I've always wanted one."

"Meanwhile, we've no bath."

"So, you *are* blaming me?"

"Not at all." Tel felt the sting of sweat on his forehead. Sophie was stoney-faced – quite apt under the circumstances, he thought. "I'm just explaining the delay."

"The delay that I apparently caused."

He sighed heavily. "We can either argue about this or we can just accept it."

"But they promised, Tel!"

"I know! I've called the bath company three times and each time they promise delivery by the following week – at least, I think that's what they said, their English was bad and their accents quite strong, and now we've run out of weeks."

"But there's still a few days left, they could still – "

"They're closed."

"Closed? The company or the country?"

"It's Italy, they're Catholics, they take Christmas very seriously, apparently."

Sophie thought for a moment, standing up and pacing up and down the living room, tapping her fingers on her lips. "Could the workmen get a cheap bath from B&Q or something, just to tide us over?"

"They've gone."

"Gone? Are they Catholic too?"

"No idea, but they've gone to finish another job."

"Another job? What about *our* job?"

"They said they can't cap the water pipe in the bathroom because it's wider than normal to accommodate the ridic-perfect tub, and there's nothing they can do until it arrives."

Sophie's finger tapping speeded up. Her eyes rolled around like loose marbles, searching for an answer. "What are we going to do? We can't stay here with no bath or shower." She paced up and down. Tel watched her. "At least we have the toilet and the sink, we could make do with – "

Tel coughed loudly.

"What?"

"Remember I said about the bathtub pipe being bigger than the average water pipe due to the all-singing, all-dancing tub?"

"Yes, and?"

"They couldn't cap it, so they had to turn the water off."

"They had to ... ?"

Sophie stared at him. He stared back, thinking there were two outcomes to this: she would either lose patience and start shouting or crying or both, or she'd shrug her shoulders, pour another glass of wine and say, "Ah well, these things happen." He didn't hold out much hope for the latter, it wasn't her style – arguing was more her forte, usually in court, but sometimes at home too. He rarely won.

"There's no water?" she asked.

"Not in the bathroom. The kitchen sink is up and running though."

"Oh, fantastic! I can wash and pee in the kitchen sink then."

"Look, Sophs, I'm just the messenger. We can either let it ruin Christmas or we can go with the flow."

"The flow that *isn't* in our bathroom, you mean, that flow, or lack of?"

Irritated now, Tel got to his feet, snatched the empty bottle of wine from the coffee table and marched into the kitchen, where he furiously tossed the bottle into the recycle bin and flung open the fridge door. "We could spend Christmas at my parents, if you prefer?" he snapped, taking out a new bottle and struggling with the cork.

"Spare me, *please*!"

"It's not that bad!"

"I love them to bits, you know I do, but your mother talks too much and your father hardly speaks at all, and aren't David and Travis staying there this Christmas? It's a three-bedroom house, we'll be squashed together like sardines, all of us draped in David's feather boas and suffering from tinnitus due to your mother's constant – "

"Your parents then!"

"I saw enough of my relatives at the wedding, thank you very much. Anyway, they've gone on a cruise to celebrate their 40th wedding anniversary."

"I didn't know they'd been married for 40 years."

"They haven't, mummy just wanted to make sure daddy didn't forget, so she booked an early celebration, no doubt one of many. She likes to get her money's worth."

"So, it's not their 40th anniversary then?"

"It's best not to try and follow mummy's tangled logic, it'll take you down a dark path, believe me."

Tel came back to the sofa and refilled his own glass.

"You're not pouring my wine now?" she asked. "You'll be telling me you haven't got me any presents next."

"I haven't got you any presents."

"What?"

He poured wine into her glass and said, "We agreed to not partake of the chaotic commercial Christmas and have a less materialistic celebration instead."

"Did we?" Sophie thought for a moment, then sighed. "So, no presents and no functional bathroom. Some first Christmas this is going to be as a married couple."

"Might have been a better idea to upgrade the kitchen."

"Why?" They both looked at the open-plan, little used kitchen off the dining/living room and laughed. "We only use it for storing wine, glasses, boxes of cereal and bowls."

"Is there any actual food in there?" Tel asked.

"Don't be ridiculous, we wouldn't know how to cook it if there was. Oh wait, there might be a couple of M&S ready meals in the fridge."

"How long have they been there."

Sophie gave it some thought. "A while. Last time I looked I remember thinking that chicken in white wine sauce didn't normally have huge clumps of broccoli on top."

"Ugh."

Sophie sighed. "I imagined us spending most of Christmas in the bathtub together."

"Really? I would have been firmer with the Italian company if I'd known that."

"It was going to be my Christmas present to you," she grinned.

"Damn."

"You've not got me anything at all?"

"We said we wouldn't indulge."

"Yes. Seemed like a good idea at the time, to cut down on all the interminable shopping, but … it's a bit boring, not having anything to open."

"It's not too late to change your mind. I could dash out tomorrow and – "

"No, no, I don't want a hastily bought present just for the sake of it. We'll put the money towards a holiday abroad next year instead."

He handed her her glass of wine and she coiled onto the sofa next to him. The tension between them fizzled out.

"I could order a commode and an industrial sized pack of baby wipes for pits, tits and bits from Amazon Prime?" he said.

"No." She sighed again. "We'll just go native and not wash at all, become like Morlocks and search the streets for food at night. Oh, it's going to be a terrible Christmas."

"It's certainly going to be a smelly one," he laughed. Relieved that the crisis was apparently over he started singing. "Have yourself a very smelly Christmas. O come all ye smellies. We wish you a smelly Christ– "

"Stop. What are we going to do, Tel?"

"We have each other, isn't that enough?"

"It is and … it isn't. Personal hygiene is kind of important to me. Obviously not high on your list of priorities."

"We could stay in a hotel?"

"Too sad for words."

"Escape it all and go abroad?"

"Too late to book anything."

"Spend Christmas in the caravan?"

She stopped twirling her hair between her fingers and looked at him. "You know, that's not a bad idea, husband of mine."

"It has a heater, cooking facilities, and – "

"A fully functional bathroom, of sorts."

Tel sat up, feeling a bit excited. "Where shall we go? Outskirts of London? The countryside?"

"The Cotswolds."

Tel laughed. "I think, between us, we may have come up with a plan."

She kissed him on the cheek and said, "I'll ring Olivia."

Jim and Beth

The washing machine was playing up again. Jim had already called the repairman out twice; both times he'd mostly leaned against said washing machine talking about how materialistic Christmas was, while accepting one mince pie and helping himself to another. He said he'd changed something, Jim couldn't remember what it was called, accepted his payment – cash only – and left. The washing machine still didn't spin.

He loaded the dripping laundry into the tumble dryer. Upstairs, Beth called out to him.

"What was that?" he yelled back, standing up to listen.

"Can you make me a cup of tea, babes?"

"Yeah, babes."

Jim slammed the dryer door shut, turned the knob, and watched the wet clothes thump from the top of the drum to the bottom. He put it on for two hours drying time, he thought that might be enough.

He put the kettle on, staring out of the kitchen window at the frozen garden and sighed heavily. He was knackered; a full day on the building site, followed by an entire evening looking after Beth and the house. He didn't mind, he loved her and it was his contribution to her pregnancy, but man, he was so tired.

Sighing again, he made tea and took it upstairs to Beth, lying resplendent in bed surrounded by magazines, laptop, phone, bags of sweets, packets of biscuits and a litre bottle of Lucozade.

"So," he said, squeezing the mug of tea onto the already cluttered bedside table, "How long did the doctor say you had to be on bedrest for?"

"Till the babies have finished cooking."

"And how long until the babies make an appearance?" he asked, throwing himself down next to her and scrunching up her magazines.

"Jim, I musta told ya a million times, mid January."

"That's weeks away!" he sighed.

"All good fings are worth waiting for, babes."

"I'm not sure I'll survive." He flopped back onto the pillows beside her. "I'm so tired I could ..."

"Could what, babes?" Beth flicked through a magazine. "Could what? Jim?" She turned her head and saw him fast asleep, one leg off the bed and an arm across his face.

"I think I'm killin' me 'usband," she told Olivia on the phone later. "Poor bloke."

"I'll try to come over more often," Olivia said.

"No, no, you've got a pub to run."

"What will you do for Christmas?"

"Well, the doctor said I can't travel down to family in London, but Jim says he's got it all taken care of." Beth bit her bottom lip. "Scary thought, isn't it. I've seen the turkey in the freezer, it's the size of an emu and will never fit in our oven. He also can't cook, so Christmas is going to be a carbon fest followed by food poisoning. Good job we got two loos," she laughed, ending with a sigh.

"Come here," Olivia said brightly. "Brian and Faye *and* Tel and Sophie are coming."

"Are they?"

"Yes. Come today and I'll take care of you, take the pressure off Jim a bit. I *love* taking care of people."

"Olivia, you are a star!"

Olivia and Mark

Mark finished putting the last of the baubles on the Christmas tree in the corner of their living room and stood back to admire it. It was a surprise for when Olivia came up from the bar. He threw himself onto the sofa, hands behind his head, and put his feet up on the coffee table. "I can't wait," he said.

"Can't wait for what?" Olivia asked, coming into the room and spotting the Christmas tree in the corner. "Ooh, that's lovely. Well done, you."

"Thanks very much."

She stared at it some more, then said, "Not a fan of fairy lights then?"

"Oh *damn*! I forgot about them!"

He started to get up but she put a hand on his shoulder to stop him. "We'll do it later. Now tell me, what can't you wait for?" She pushed his feet off the table before sitting down next to him.

"For Christmas Day," he sighed dreamily. "I feel like a kid all excited because Santa's coming."

"You know he's not real, don't you," she giggled.

Mark sat up straight. "What? Santa's not real? Why did no one tell me? Why are you telling me? I'm crushed, *crushed*."

Olivia laughed. "The tooth fairy's not real either."

"Oh I never believed in the tooth fairy," he said, falling back against the cushions. "I always thought if she was that desperate for teeth she'd find a graveyard, dig up the corpses and take their teeth for free."

"Ugh, gross."

"I can't wait until it's just us," he said, leaning sideways to nibble on her ear, making her giggle again. "No bar staff, no temperamental chef tossing knives across the kitchen, just you …" He pulled her closer and moved in for a kiss. "… and me."

Olivia pulled away. "About that."

"What?"

"It's nothing terrible. In fact, I think you're going to like it. At least, I hope you do."

"You're pregnant!" he gasped, sitting up straight with his eyes wide. "Oh Livs, I – "

"No! *No!*" She put her fingers to his lips. "Nothing like that."

"Oh. What then?"

She took a deep breath. "I had some phonecalls when I was downstairs."

"Not Richard again!"

"No. Well, yes, he called and texted, and texted again – "

"You need to be firm with him, Livs."

"I am! You know I am!"

"Alright, keep your eyebrows on."

She took a deep breath and said, "Brian and Faye are coming for Christmas."

He shrugged. "Okay."

"You don't mind?"

"They're practically family anyway."

"Oh good, I'm glad you're glad. I mean, I don't need your permission or anything, it's my pub after all and I can do what I like."

"Absolutely."

"Which is why Tel and Sophie are coming too."

Mark looked at her. She gave him her biggest, overbite smile. She didn't need his approval, but she'd quite like him to not be annoyed.

"That's fine," he said, smiling.

"Excellent. And Jim and Beth are coming too, isn't that lovely?" She glanced at her watch. "They'll be here in about an hour, Jim's just packing her things."

"Ah."

"Happy 'ah', or a 'what was she thinking?' kind of 'ah'?"

"It's a 'not sure how to respond' ah."

"Ah."

"So not quite the quiet Christmas I was envisaging then, just you and me, naked except for strategic placing of festive holly?"

"Ooh, bit painful, but no," she laughed, "We can do that after."

"I might not feel like it after." He lifted his eyebrows. "I might be too full."

"Oh, you'll feel like it."

She pushed him back onto the sofa and leaned over him, kissing him softly. "I'm sure we'll be able to fit in some special time somewhere."

CHAPTER 2

23rd December

The trip down had been quite nerve-wracking.

"I thought the weather forecast predicted a light sprinkling of snow?" Faye said, pulling the blanket around her on the passenger seat. "There was no mention of a snow bomb. Do you think it'll pass? Do you think we'll get there okay?"

Brian, who hated icy roads and hated towing a caravan on icy roads even more, leaned towards the windscreen as if that would help see through the thick snow that came at them like a mass of white Kamikaze flies. He could barely see forty feet ahead, the rest of the motorway was a white-out – and yet cars were still flying by him doing at least sixty, and nearly every one of them bibbed their horn.

"I'm not sure it was a good idea to fill the caravan with fairy lights," he said, "It's attracting a lot of attention."

"It'll make people feel Christmassy."

Another car beeped at the flashing caravan making its way down the motorway.

"Will we make it, Bri?"

"We will if you stop talking to me, I need to concentrate."

Faye briefly considered taking the humph at his tone, but decided it was probably best to just leave him alone.

"Would you like a blanket?" she offered instead.

"I'd like a bit of peace and quiet while I navigate through nothingness."

She huffed but didn't say anything else. He was the driver,

in bad driving conditions, she didn't want to irritate him – he'd been known to stop the car and get out if she yabbered too much.

She put the radio on. The Pogues *Fairytale of New York* played.

"Ah," said Brian, "Nothing says Christmas like people hurling abuse at each other."

* * *

"Tel."

"Hmm?"

"You okay?"

"Yes, I just didn't anticipate driving through Narnia."

"It was barely snowing in London when we left."

"I can hardly see anything." His windscreen wipers were batting left and right as if on steroids, but they did nothing to enhance his view of the motorway. Passing cars disappeared into the whiteness ahead. He didn't like driving in snow. Snow was unpredictable.

"Should we turn around and go back?" she asked.

He glanced at his sat-nav. "We're closer to the Cotswolds than London."

"Can I offer any words of encouragement?"

He grinned. "Such as?"

"Oh, I don't know. You're an excellent driver, Tel."

"Thanks."

"I know you won't kill us. Not intentionally anyway, so if we do die just know that I forgive you."

"That's your idea of encouragement, is it?"

"It's just a bit of snow, it'll be fine. How about some music to calm the protruding tendons in your neck?"

She turned on the radio. Chris Rea sang *Driving Home For Christmas*.

"Ah," said Tel, "*Now* it feels like Christmas."

* * *

At last, Brian turned left into the Woodsman car park and let out a sigh of relief. It was dark. The pub was decked in a myriad of fairy lights. Standing out front were a giant blow-up snowman and two reindeers, all wobbling in the wind. There were lights strung across the upstairs windows, as yet unlit.

"Oh my God," Faye gasped, "I didn't think we were going to make it."

"Neither did I. My buttocks were clenched the entire time."

"Well done, husband."

"Cheers, wife."

"I had every faith in you."

"Did you? What about the screaming?"

"Oh, that was just to vent some frustration at other drivers."

"You should audition for horror films."

"I might."

The car park was full, except for a large area to the left that had been cordoned off with orange cones, each building peaks of snow on the top.

"Go move the cones, lass," he said.

"What?"

"Go move the cones."

"Why?"

"So I can park up."

"But …" She looked outside her window. " … it's snowing."

"Is it? I hadn't noticed."

"It's bloody freezing out there, Bri!"

"Take your blanket, I'm sure you'll survive."

"I might not."

"Go move the cones, Faye."

"Why can't you do it?"

"Because a ninety-minute journey has just taken us three and a half hours of solid concentration, and my buttocks are not yet unclenched."

With a tut, she opened the car door and shivered as the brittle coldness tore through the heated air inside. She got out, wrapping the blanket tight around her, and bent her head to peer at Brian. "I may be some time," she snapped.

"The quicker you do it the better your chances," he hollered.

He watched his wife spend more time wrapping the blanket around herself than actually moving cones. She tiptoed up to them and delicately brushed away the layer of snow on top. Using finger and thumb, she gingerly carried one to the edge of the car park.

Inside the car, now reheated, Brian shook his head as Faye slowly headed towards a second cone, pausing on the way to adjust her blanket and kick the snow off her boots. She threw a brief glare of misery in his direction.

He wound his window down a couple of inches and yelled, "HURRY UP!"

Faye took a few moments to deepen her glare, her lips tight, before brushing the snow off another cone. When she tried to pick it up it slipped from her frozen fingers. She bent to pick it up, dropping it again.

"JUST KICK THE BLOODY THING!" Brian shouted.

Faye kicked at the cone. He knew, without a shadow of a doubt, that she was imaging it was him. She kicked again, with more ferocity this time, and slipped, falling flat onto her back.

"Oh, for crying out loud!" he groaned,

He got out stiffly, crinkling his eyes against the sting of the snow blasting into his face. He helped a furious Faye to her feet, where she muttered something about being freezing and now she was wet and on the verge of hyperthermia, and with one giant foot he kicked the cone to the side of the car park.

"Get in!" he shouted, striding back to the car.

"I can barely move from the cold!" she shouted back.

"Then stay there and freeze to death."

"You're not being very husbandly, Bri."

Brian had a suitable retort on the tip of his tongue, but jumped into the car instead. He watched through the snow sweeping across the windscreen as Faye struggled towards the car, where she plonked herself into the seat, slammed the door, and turn to glare at him like a melting snowman, her hair wet and the snow on her blanket rapidly melting. She growled, "I'm going to die of frostbite, thanks to you!"

Brian put the car into gear and pulled into the parking spot. "You only had to move a couple of cones."

"It was a near-death experience. I've seen it happen before?"

"Where?" He turned off the engine and savoured the brief silence.

"In horror films."

"A horror film set in a blizzard? Abominable snowman goes on a mad killing spree with an ice pick?"

"Shut up. It could happen. We're practically in the middle of nowhere. Our bodies may never be found."

"It's the Cotswolds, Faye, and we're sitting outside a busy pub."

She stared at the snow building up on the windscreen. "I wonder who would play me in the film?"

"We're not in a horror film, Faye."

"Aren't we?"

"No, we're not."

"People die in snowstorms, Bri. Remember Jack Nicholson in *The Shining*."

Brian gave up and turned in his seat. Faye followed his gaze and said, "Oh, isn't it pretty!"

The Woodsman looked so festive and inviting, with its twinkling lights and people milling around inside. As they looked, the front door flew open and what can only be described as a well-padded, bright yellow teddy bear teetered out. They saw a smiling face beneath the fur hood and recognised the cute overbite immediately. A hand raised and waved at them. They got out. The freezing temperatures cut through them like a knife.

"Oh, you're here!" Olivia squealed, beckoning them over, "I'm so excited!"

She suddenly threw out a hand to stop them in their tracks and shouted over her shoulder, "NOW, MARK!"

The unlit lights across the top floor lit up, spelling out MERRY CHRISTMAS in a myriad of colours. From unseen speakers came the sound of children singing *We Wish You a Merry Christmas*. Brian and Faye paused for a millisecond and went 'Oooh' really fast, before quickening their pace across the snow-covered car park. Olivia greeted them with a huge hug.

"How was your journey? I'm so glad you got here safely. Isn't the weather horrible! Come in, come in! We have hot toddies to warm you up, and a very convivial atmosphere to get you in the festive mood."

In the hallway Olivia took their coats as they stamped snow from their boots, and immediately burst out laughing.

Brian was wearing a skin-coloured jumper with chest hairs, nipples and a protruding bellybutton printed on it. The 'naked look' was covered in festive tattoos.

Faye's jumper had a picture of Noddy Holder on it, surrounded by tinsel. "Listen to this," she said, finding the button on the bottom hem. *'It's Chriiiiiistmas'* the jumper shrieked. "Isn't it funny!"

"Hysterical!"

Olivia pulled off her bright yellow jacket. Underneath she was wearing a bright yellow jumper which had 'Asda Just Essentials: Christmas Jumper' printed on it.

"Oh that's hilarious," Faye giggled.

Olivia put their coats on the stand by the front door. When Brian and Faye walked into the front lounge their senses were assailed; happy chatter from a throng of customers eating and drinking, laughter, the clinking of glasses. The smell of hot food, pine needles and spices from mulled wine wafted up Brian's nose. Faye could smell nothing, but she could hear the carols playing in the background and sense the buzz of festive cheer. A fire raged in the fireplace. A huge Christmas tree stood in a corner. Pots of poinsettias and draped tinsel were everywhere. It was warm and cosy and very, very Christmassy.

"This is *lovely*," Faye gasped.

"Good atmosphere," said Brian.

Mark was serving behind the crowded bar. His face broke into a huge smile when he saw them and he hurried round to hug them both; his jumper was a mass of multi-coloured tinsel.

"Glad you made it alright," he said. "How was the drive down?"

"Epic," Brian said. "Didn't help that our caravan looks like a Christmas tree on wheels, I have tinnitus from all the horn blowing appreciation and Faye's high-pitched screaming."

"I didn't scream, the skiddy bits irritated my vocal chords."

"Have faith in your husband, wife. The lanes were bad though," he said to Mark, "It's really building up in places."

"Yeah, it's always bad around here, they don't bother gritting."

"It's so lovely to have you here," Oliva screeched, breathless with excitement. "Come and say hello to Jim and Beth," She pointed over to a group of leather sofas and armchairs in the corner, upon which lay Beth, covered with a big faux fur blanket. Jim sat on a comfy chair next to her, his arm draped protectively over both leather arms, holding her hand.

"Oooh," said Faye, walking towards them, "It looks just like that café in *Friends*. I'll be Jennifer Anniston."

"In your dreams, woman."

"In your dreams, Bri."

"Central Pint," Beth laughed, as Faye bent to kiss her cheek.

"Good God, woman," Brian cried, "How many people have you got under that blanket with you?"

"Just two little ones," Beth said, accepting the kiss he strained to bend and plant on her other cheek.

"Let's see them then."

Beth threw back the blanket, and he and Faye both gasped at the size of her bump. It stuck out from her body like a man-made mountain – which, of course, it was. Jim grinned proudly.

"Are you sure it's only two?" Brian asked. "There's at least a football team in there."

"You're not saying I'm fat, are you, Bri?"

"Not fat," he winked, holding out his arms, "*Enormous*!"

"Says the giant," Mark laughed.

"You look well," Faye said, "Being pregnant obviously suits you."

"It don't. I 'ave to lug these two around with me everywhere, and they fight all the time."

"Bit like us," Jim laughed, standing up to shake Brian's hand and give Faye a hug.

"We don't fight, babes," Beth said, "I'm just loud when I tell you you're an idiot."

"Clever enough to marry you though, ain't I."

Beth smiled. She really did look healthy in a voluminous, about-to-explode kind of way.

"Can I touch it?" Faye said, sitting on the coffee table in front of her.

"Don't go near it!" Brian cried, making several people turn their heads, "She could blow at any minute!"

"Nah, it's alright, I got another four weeks left yet."

"Are you sure?" Faye said, gently running a hand over the bump and squealing when she felt movement beneath. "Twins usually come early, don't they?"

Jim leaned forward in his seat and whispered, "We're not mentioning the word 'early', Faye."

"Oh. Sorry."

"S'alright, babe, these twinnies are like their dad, slow as a sloth on tranquilisers." She gave a scream of laughter. "They ain't coming early, they'll probably be late."

"Let's hope so," Brian said, pulling a nervous face.

"Drink of choice?" Mark asked, heading back to the busy bar.

Brian followed as Faye and Beth began discussing swollen feet. "My good man," he bellowed, silencing a good portion of the bar, "What do you recommend in the beer department?"

23

"Beer," said Mark.

"Any particular one?"

Mark swept a hand over the shiny pump handles. "We have a plethora of brown and fizzy liquids, take your pick."

"Surprise me," Brian said.

"Lemonade?"

Sue, the blonde barmaid, came over, giving Brian a huge smile. "Hello, trouble," she said. "I remember you."

"Once seen, never forgotten," Mark said.

"Nice to see you again, lass."

Before he had finished his sentence, Faye was at his side. "Don't forget we have to pitch up the caravan, Bri."

"Yes, my love."

"You're perfectly welcome to stay here," Mark said. "We have five guest rooms upstairs."

"Thanks," said Faye, "But we want to experience a proper white Christmas in the comfort of our own caravan, you know, staring through the skylight at the fluffy snow and the stars, and snuggling up together, all warm and cosy."

"She makes it sound romantic, doesn't she," Brian said. "We'll probably freeze to death."

"We should pitch up now, Bri, before the snow gets too deep or you get too drunk?"

"I never get too drunk."

"I beg to differ."

"Name one instance where you've witnessed me 'too drunk'."

"How much time have you got?"

"All of Christmas, my love. Let me know when you have a viable example to share with the group."

Faye tutted, staring at Sue, who was busy serving other customers. "I don't want to wake up in the morning with the caravan at a funny angle, Bri."

"I'll do it when Tel and Sophie get here, it can be a group exercise, a re-bonding session."

"See who can pitch up the fastest before frostbite sets in,"

Mark laughed.

"I think we should do it now, Bri."

Brian turned to Faye, just as Mark tentatively placed a pint on the counter in front of him. "Woman," he said, "It's Christmas, and I – " He lifted up his pint and took a deep pull. " – am going to enjoy myself."

Faye glared at Brian, who supped again.

"Can I get you a drink, love?" Sue asked Faye.

"If ya can't beat 'em, join 'em," Mark grinned.

Faye hesitated, before breaking into a grin and saying, "I'll have a Prosecco, thanks."

"Good lass, get into the spirit of the thing."

"Christmas spirit?" Mark asked, "Would you like a double brandy with that, Bri?"

"He would not," Faye snapped, adjusting her face into a brief smile when Sue put a glass down in front of her.

"Faye," Brian said, staring straight ahead at the spirt bottles on the wall opposite.

"What?"

"Stop nagging."

"I don't nag," she hissed, "I'd just like to pitch up before – "

He lowered his eyes to her and raised a hairy eyebrow. Faye shut up, picked up her glass and stormed back to the sofas in the corner.

Mark's phone rang. "Okay," he said, and hung up. "LIV!" She looked over. "THEY'RE TWO MINUTES AWAY."

Olivia threw up a thumb and stood up. Mark stood next to a switch on the wall behind the bar that had a label reading LIGHTS: DO NOT TOUCH! Olivia rushed into the hallway and pulled on her giant padded coat with the fur hood. There was a sudden rush of cold air as she opened the door and went outside.

***

"Christ!" Tel gasped, as he pulled into the pub car park. "I didn't think we were going to make it."

"Me neither," Sophie said, her face still rigid in horror.

"More words of encouragement?"

"You did well. You didn't kill us."

They both turned to look at the pub.

"Wow, Liv's gone all out with the Christmas decorations."

"They look amazing!"

"There's Brian's caravan, I'll pull up next to it."

"Don't hit anything," Sophie said.

"I've driven all the way up from London in a snowstorm, I'm not likely to – "

There was a small crunching sound. Tel slammed on his brakes. His extended wing mirror had touched another wing mirror. Thankfully, they weren't broken.

"You were saying?" Sophie laughed.

"Shut up."

She laughed again.

"I think it's Liv's Mini."

"No!"

"I didn't see it."

"Because it's so tiny?"

"Because it's so dark."

He wound down his window, letting the cold air steal away the heat inside, and reached out towards the bent mirror. He pulled it back and it clunked into place.

They parked and got out.

"Gorgeous people!" screamed a high-pitched voice.

Olivia stood bouncing on the doorstep wearing what looked like a bright yellow duvet with fur around her face. "I'm so glad you made it!"

* * *

They greeted and hugged each other in the busy lounge. Brian held Sophie at arm's length and said, "You're wearing white from head to foot."

"I wasn't aware that you'd become a fashion guru, Bri," she grinned. "I went all out festive." She pursed her bright red lips and blew him a kiss.

"Let's hope we never have to find you in a snowstorm," Brian said. "Don't fall over in the snow or you'll be lost forever."

"Let me take your coats," Olivia said.

Sophie let the white jacket slip from her shoulders, revealing her Christmas jumper; a glittering wine glass topped with a Santa hat, 'A Very Cheery Crimbo' was printed underneath. Tel handed his jacket over and thrust out his chest; 'On the Naughty List and Proud of It' was emblazoned across his bright red jumper.

"Beth!" Sophie cried, spotting her resplendent on a sofa in the corner. "You look ... *huge!*"

"Ta very much. Do you want to see it?" she asked, grabbing a corner of her blanket.

Sophie threw up a hand. "Absolutely not. No offence."

"None taken. I wouldn't look at it either if it wasn't attached to me. Right now, it's *all* I can see."

"Does it ... hurt?" Sophie asked, trying to keep her expression of horror down to a minimum.

"Only when they move."

"Sit down," Tel whispered, as Sophie wavered slightly on her feet. "I'll get you a brandy."

"Make it a double," she whispered back.

While the men went back to the bar, a young girl with a tray of steaming cups came over to their table. "These are for you," she squeaked, "Mulled wine, courtesy of the management." She glanced at Olivia, sitting on the arm of a sofa, and said, "Did I do that right, miss?"

"Lovely," Olivia said, and the girl scuttled back behind the bar with a beaming smile. "New girl," she told them, "Rachel's covering for ..." She glanced at Beth.

"It's alright, babes," Beth said, "You can say the wench's name."

"She's covering for Melissa, who's off on ... sick leave."

"Off on 'she'd better not get anywhere near my man again' leave," Beth cackled, glaring at Jim, who lowered his head. "I'm a changed man," he muttered.

Beth shifted on the sofa, trying to find a comfortable position. Jim was on his feet in a millisecond, asking if she was alright, if she needed anything, was there anything he could get her.

"Scaffolding," Beth muttered.

The blanket slipped off her, and Sophie caught sight of the enormous bulge beneath. The breath caught in her throat. The thing was enormous.

"Oh look," Beth cried, and Sophie found she couldn't tear her eyes away from it, "They're moving."

Sophie sucked in air and held it. The bump was indeed moving beneath Beth's voluminous red top with SANTA BABIES printed on it. She quickly picked a cup up off the tray and frantically sipped it – blow, sip, blow, sip.

"You okay, Sophs?" Olivia asked. "You look a bit funny."

Sophie forced a smile as she blew and sipped, and briefly nodded her head.

"Wait till it's your turn," Beth laughed.

It was then, at that very moment, that Sophie decided she was *never* having babies and was definitely *never* having sex again to *ensure* there were never any babies. She would inform Tel at the earliest possible opportunity.

"BARKIN' SERVICE!" came a holler from the kitchen just off the bar.

The women looked at each other. Nobody else around them seemed much bothered by the sudden bawling that cut through the jovial chatter like a knife.

"That's our chef, Tony," Mark laughed, coming back to the sofas with the others. "He's a character."

"Culinary genius," Olivia added, "But a bit highly strung."

"I blame Gordon Ramsay, and you," Mark said, tipping his drink towards Olivia.

"Yes, well, I may have over-encouraged him a little, told him this pub wouldn't survive without him, and it kind of went to his head a bit."

"In the summer he was watching Jamie Oliver cookery

programmes."

"He was lovely then," Olivia sighed.

"There were a few complaints about the skin being left on the garlic in some dishes, and the kitchen always looked like a bomb had gone off in there because he lobbed ingredients together."

"Started speaking cockney," Olivia giggled.

"Cheers to cockneys," Beth said, raising her red-filled glass.

"Then he moved on to Gordon Ramsay." Olivia pulled a face. "He doesn't actually swear, said his mother would be so disappointed in him if he did, so he improvises."

As if on cue, a voice from the kitchen cried, "WHERE'S MY FLUFFIN' BEEF ORDER? BRING ME MY BARKIN' ORDERS! WHAT'S THE MATTER WITH YOU PEOPLE!"

And then there came a thump and a metallic twang.

"Then," Mark said ominously, "He moved on to *Hell's Kitchen*, and the knives came out."

"He has a dartboard in there, and when he gets stressed he throws knives at it."

"I bet the kitchen staff are terrified, aren't they?" Faye gasped.

Mark and Olivia shook their heads.

"They take it in their stride," Olivia said. "He's a lovely man when he's not acting like a mad chef."

"We leave a lot of Nigel Slater books and DVDs lying around."

"Oh, that would be so much nicer."

"And we pray every night he doesn't discover Heston Blumenthal and blow the place up."

"But he's a jolly good chef," Olivia finished, just as Tony bawled, "WHO MADE THIS FLUFFIN' CARBONARA?"

"Smells delicious," Brian said, smacking his lips.

Olivia took her phone out of her pocket. "We're ready," she said, and almost instantly three bar staff – Rachel and two young men – moved away from the busy bar and hurried into the kitchen.

"THERE!" screamed Tony, "THEY'RE RIGHT THERE! SERVE THEM BEFORE IT GOES BARKIN'COLD! COME ON PEOPLE, KEEP UP!"

Rachel and the two young men came out of the kitchen, giggling together, clearly not the least perturbed by Tony's outburst. They carried a large casserole dish on a wooden board, a smaller casserole dish, and several bowls, which they laid out on the coffee table between them all; rice, mashed potatoes, roast potatoes and chips. Another girl in a white uniform hurried towards them with hot plates, cutlery, napkins and serving spoons, and hurried off again.

"This is Dane," Olivia said, pointing at the first handsome man, "He's been with us for a few weeks now."

Dane, staggeringly good looking, with floppy hair reminiscent of Hugh Grant in his heyday, smiled and nodded his head, before dramatically flicking back his hair.

"Broken many local hearts in that time?" Sophie asked mischievously.

Dane didn't answer, he just pierced her with a steady look from his ice blue eyes, and winked.

"Yes," she drawled, "I guess you have."

Tel reached over and took hold of her hand, just to remind her that he was there.

Faye cried, "Oooh, hello, Dane."

Dane kept his eyes firmly on Sophie.

Faye huffed.

"And this is Jay-Zee," Olivia said.

"Jay *dash* Zee," he said, fluttering his mascaraed eyelashes at them. He wore pale blue eyeshadow and pink lipstick. His blond hair was dyed to within an inch of its life, and his drawn-in eyebrows would make Nike think about litigation.

"Just do it," Sophie whispered, avoiding Dane's constant stare and the tight grip Tel had on her hand.

"Your mother called you Jay dash Zee?" Brian asked.

Jay-Zee threw out a hand as he rolled his eyeballs. "No,"

he sighed, "She named me *Paul*, but only my mum calls me that." He tapped the name badge on his waistcoat. "I identify as nonbinary and my pronouns are – "

"What?" said Brian. "Your pro-whats?"

"Pronouns, how you refer to me, are zie, zim, zir and – "

"How do I grab your attention at the bar?" Brian asked.

"Server," Jay-Zee said with a flourish of his hands.

"Well," said Brian, "I identify as a hungry man who'd quite like to eat now."

Mark sat up in his chair and said, "That's enough of your personal profile now, Jay-Zee, you have customers waiting at the bar. You too, Dane."

Jay-Zee minced back behind the counter. Dane stood still for a second, staring at Sophie. "If there's anything you need," he said, in voice deeper than his years, "You know where to find me."

"But only until five o'clock, when we close," Mark laughed.

"I think," Tel said, pulling Sophie's ring hand towards him, "If my *wife* needs anything she'll be coming to me."

Dane gave his hair a final run through with his fingers and sauntered back to the bar.

"Eyes straight ahead, lass," Brian said to Faye.

"I'm trying."

"Try harder."

Rachel, after giving Olivia a nervous look, said, "Born appetite," pronouncing 'appetite' in English without the French inflection.

"I'm saying it like that from now on," Brian laughed.

"Did I do it wrong, miss?"

"It's fine, Rachel, and please, call me Liv."

"Okay, miss."

Mark handed out plates as Olivia lifted the lid on the casserole and said, "Ta da!"

"Beef bourguignon," Tel grinned, picking up the serving spoon just as Brian was reaching for it, "With dumplings. Fantastic."

"Has it got red wine in?" Beth asked.

Olivia reached over to the tiny casserole dish and lifted the lid with a squeaky "Ta da! Sans wine."

"White wine?" Beth enquired.

"No wine."

"What kind of wine?"

"It's alcohol free."

"Oh good."

"Born appetite," Brian cried, and they all dived in.

* * *

The snowstorm outside got heavier and louder, the wind howling and the snow pitter-patting endlessly against the windows.

The men stood at the bar, Mark helping to serve, Brian and Tel interrogating Jay-Zee about nonbinary pronouns. Brian simply didn't get it.

"Zie instead of he or she," Jay-Zee told him, for the umpteenth time, "Zim instead of him or – "

"So I just add a 'Z' to the beginning of everything?"

Tel, slightly sloshed, couldn't stop laughing.

"No, you don't just add – "

"Brian!" Faye shouted from the *Friends* corner. "BRIAN!"

Brian slowly turned around. "Yes, my love?"

"The snow's getting worse. We should go and park up the caravan."

Brian looked at Tel. "You sleeping here or in the caravan."

"In the caravan," Tel winked, "Sophie's brought candles and smelly things."

"Serious then."

"Seems so."

Back at the table, Sophie hoped Tel wouldn't leave her alone with the heavily pregnant woman who kept clutching her bump and making strange noises. Eager to escape the endless tension, she jumped to her feet and grabbed her white padded jacket from the stand by the door, briefly wondering how Tel would take the news that they were never having sex again.

Brian sighed. "Better get it over with before the wife expires from nagginess."

"I heard that, Bri!"

"Get yer coat, love," he yelled back, "You've pulled."

* * *

Outside it was freezing cold, pitch black and still snowing heavily. The snow on the ground was two inches deeper than when they'd arrived, even the tyre tracks had almost disappeared. The gentle breeze that had stirred up the falling flakes into ultimate prettiness was now getting stronger, the flakes bigger. Brian and Faye, Tel and Sophie, trudged to their cars and started up their engines. Brian led the way through the entrance gate to the campsite beyond, marvelling at how different everything looked covered in a thick blanket of snow.

"Are you alright, Bri? You're not drunk, are you?"

"I'm fine, lass."

"Are you sure, Bri?"

"It's private land, I can drive on it even if I was as pissed as a newt."

"But you're okay to pitch up?"

"Of course!"

The first caravan area was, unsurprisingly, empty. He drove through the fencing around the second and spotted Liv's RV and Mark's shabby caravan at the bottom. Brian pulled onto the pitch Tel and Sophie would soon inhabit and put the car into reverse. He was just noting that the snow was falling faster and the wind was gusting them sideways across the windscreen, when he heard a heavy, metallic crunch.

"*Brian!*"

For a moment he was confused; he'd had a pint of beer and a mulled wine in a dainty teacup, but he didn't feel drunk, just warm and cosy inside. Oh, and there was the cherry brandy he'd tried, which was disgustingly but he finished it off because he hated waste. He might have had a second mulled wine. And perhaps another beer, he wasn't sure.

He dared to glance over his shoulder. His car had reversed, but he'd completely forgotten about the attached caravan, which was now jack-knifed at a sickeningly acute angle to the car.

Tel appeared at his driver's window, tapping it quickly. Brian wound it down. Snow and freezing wind gusted in.

"You alright, Bri? Only you seem to have forgotten how to reverse."

"Thought he was parking up at Asda," Faye called over, "Caravan? What caravan? Do you want me to do it, Bri?"

Brian was so amazed by her offer – this from the woman who couldn't park her tiny car in a space big enough for an articulated lorry – he burst out laughing. Faye pinched her lips, folding her arms as best she could across her padded chest.

Leaning on the open window, Tel glanced back and said, "I could park mine at a jaunty angle on the other side so our caravans could meet together in the middle and they won't feel lonely any more."

Brian looked up at him. "Drunk, Tel?"

"Think so, Bri."

"I'll give it another go."

"Try and hit the spot this time," Faye said.

"Later, my little minx."

Faye was so surprised by this she burst out laughing, feeling an unexpected rush of excitement. Then the icy cold settled in again.

Brian got it right the second time. Tel flawlessly reversed his caravan onto the opposite pitch. Neither of them unhitched the cars from the caravans. In the gusting snow they put the stabilisers down and plugged it into the electricity hookup.

Faye jumped out of the car and began running for the caravan door.

"OH!" she screamed as she ran, "IT'S SO BLOODY – "

She slipped, fell straight onto her back, and lay there, spreadeagled, watching the flakes gusting down from a grey sky onto her face – each one a little pin prick of pain.

"Getting up or staying there?" Brian asked.

"Give us a hand."

He stretched one out for her. She pulled on it and tried getting up, but her feet kept slipping. After three failed attempts she started laughing and couldn't get up at all. Brian grabbed both her arms and hauled her up, then fell back into the snow himself. Faye could barely catch her breath from giggling as Brian rolled and struggled to get up – he looked like a great big grizzly bear, growling in frustration. Giddy from the mulled wine and three, or was it four, Proseccos, she bent, scooped up snow, patted it into a ball, and threw it at Brian just as he winning his fight against gravity – straight in his face.

Brian loomed up, his face a mask of fake fury. A growl erupted from deep inside him, and Faye laughed so hard she almost threw up.

"How *dare* you!" he boomed, and Faye, giggling, turned and started running away into the blizzard.

Half way to the fence that ran around the caravan area, a solid ball of snow hit her on the back of her head and she face-planted into the snow with her arms outstretched. Behind her she could hear Brian yelling, "Faye! I didn't mean to throw it that hard! I don't know my own strength! Are you okay?"

With her face buried up to her ears in snow, she continued laughing, choking on the ice crystals that filled her mouth. She thought maybe the mulled wine and Prosecco had gone to her head, or maybe she was just giddy with Christmas. When she felt Brian fall to his knees beside her, she grabbed a handful of snow, quickly rolled onto her side, and mushed it into his face.

"Now that's not fair," said the giant snowman.

"Neither is ... knocking your wife out ... with an ice ball." She could hardly draw breath. "You've got snow in your beard! You look like Father Christmas!"

"This," Brian growled, as amusement sparkled in his eyes, "means war!"

He jumped to his feet and did an impromptu salsa dance before regaining his balance. He bent down to gather snow and, before Faye could get to her feet, lobbed it at her. She collapsed in a heap, now so hysterical she was no longer laughing but squeaking.

"Is this your idea of foreplay or can anyone join in?" Sophie asked languidly, trudging through the snow and still looking impossibly elegant.

In response, Brian thew a snowball at her. She stood stock still. Behind her, Tel cried, "How dare you assault my wife with a fist full of snowflakes!" and retaliated with a snowball of his own, which was meant for Brian but which hit Sophie in the back of the head instead. She stood there, nonplussed, looking into the distance and sighing.

"These men are brutes," she calmly told Faye, who was still sprawled on the ground squeaking. "Let's go and make snow angels instead, much more civilised." And she sauntered towards the pristine snow on the camping field like a supermodel, her white outfit disappearing into the snowstorm.

***

"Brian, I'm cold. No, 'cold' doesn't come anywhere near how I'm feeling, I'm frozen to the core of my soul."

"Making 150 snow angels in a foot of snow will do that to a person."

"Is this heater actually on?"

Brian held a giant hand in front of it and slowly pulled it back. "It gets to … about here," he said, hand six inches from the heater, "and then the cold air eats up the hot air."

"Hot?" Faye huffed, "There's nothing hot about this heater. Look!" She blew air out of her mouth. It hung between them like a tiny little cloud. "It's *Baltic* in here!"

They had changed out of their wet clothes and were now sitting on the edge of the pull-out bed wearing almost everything they'd brought with them.

"Brian," Faye sniggered, "Do these three jumpers, pair of

jeans over a pair of leggings, two pairs of thick socks, woollen scarf, gloves, dressing gown and pom-pom hat make me look fat?"

Brian laughed and pulled her back onto the bed with him. Faye immediately pulled the winter duvet and several blankets on top of them.

"Snuggle up," Brian said, "Share body heat."

"I have no body heat, only ice running through my veins."

He pulled her close. "Now, about this 'spot' you claimed I couldn't hit earlier."

"Not now, Bri."

"It could mean the difference between life and death."

"I choose death." They laughed again. Brian made a move and Faye cried, "Stop moving the blankets! You're letting a draft in."

Outside, above the sound of the wind whipping up, Sophie's tiny voice cried, "Could you keep the noise down please, the grown-ups are concentrating on trying to stay alive in sub-zero temperatures!"

"Have you got any extra blankets, Faye?" Tel yelled.

"We're using them all, Tel." Faye drew another breath and Brian covered her mouth with his hand, knowing, without a shadow of a doubt, that she was about to offer up *their* blankets, right off their bed.

"Goodnight both," Faye yelled instead.

"Good luck," Tel called back.

CHAPTER 3

24th December – Christmas Eve

Brian looked at his phone. It was 3.15am. The wind was furiously buffeting the caravan, and the snow now fell so thick and so fast it pattered constantly against the windows and covered over the skylight. Also, it was absolutely freezing.

"Brian?" Faye mumbled, "Am I dead? I feel dead. I can't feel anything. Might be warmer if we crawled into the fridge."

Brian's teeth chattered. Next to him, under the crumpled layers of blankets and an Antarctic duvet, he could feel Faye shivering.

It was cold, *really* cold. He couldn't remember the last time he felt this cold – probably as a kid, staying out too long having snowball fights with his mates. He couldn't feel his feet at all. He wondered if frostbite had set in. He wondered what the temperature was and glanced at his phone again.

"Christ!" he gasped.

"What is it, Bri?"

"It's minus five!"

As he held it, the phone rang and he brought it up to his ear.

"You okay, Tel?"

"N-no, not r-really." Brian could hear his teeth chattering, and yet he still managed to add, "We've b-been trying to get in t-touch with you about your c-car insurance."

Brian gave a cold laugh.

"We're not going to make it, Bri. We're too afraid to go to

sleep in case we don't wake up."

Sophie's voice cut in. "I've n-never been ... so c-cold ... in my l-life."

"We're cutting our losses and making a run for it," Tel said. "You in?"

"We're in!" Faye screamed, already sitting up and shuffling to the edge of the bed, dragging the duvet and blankets with her.

"What's the plan?" Brian asked, following her, mostly because she'd taken all the blankets.

"On my count, open the caravan doors and run for the pub. We stand a better chance if we stick together. Don't stop for anything."

Brian held the phone to his head as he slipped his feet into his boots. He heard Sophie cry, "Look at my hands! They're blue! *Blue*!"

"We're ready," came Tel's voice. "Just get to the pub."

"Okay."

"Three. Two. One. *Go!*"

Brian threw open his caravan door, which was immediately snatched by the wind and banged hard against the side of the caravan. He was assaulted by a howling gust and an incessant blast of snow. It blew into the caravan, catching Faye off guard. She gasped at the cold as she clutched the duvet around her. Brian grabbed her hand and jumped down the steps. The snow was half way up his calves. When Faye jumped down, she squealed as the snow reached her knees.

"Don't let go!" Brian shouted, gripping her hand tightly as he struggled to shut the caravan door.

Tel and Sophie trudged by with their heads down, Sophie making a mewling sound and Tel looking grim and determined. Brian followed them – until first Sophie, all in white, and then Tel vanished into the snowstorm ahead.

"TEL! I'VE LOST YOU!"

"Follow the leg tracks!" came Tel's distant, wind-ravaged voice.

Just walk in a straight line, Brian thought to himself, then realised that, in a white-out snowstorm, there was no reference to go straight. They should be going slightly right, towards the pub, but were they? He'd read once that a man in the middle of a desert, walking straight with no surrounding landmarks, would always favour his right foot, ultimately walking in a full circle. Brian thought they should compensate by steering slightly left. Or was it the left foot and he should be going right?

He couldn't see anything but snow, not even shadows of trees or bushes, or a great big building covered in fairy lights.

He realised Faye's hand had gone heavy. Without stopping, he glanced over his shoulder and saw that she'd fallen at some point and was now being dragged along like a sledge behind him. She was still clutching the duvet, which was dragging across the snow. He raised his arm until she found her feet again. She was at arm's length and he could barely see her, she was entirely covered in snow, with just a gaping hole for a mouth.

"TEL!" he boomed, and from far, far away a faint voice cried, "THIS WAY! FOLLOW THE SOUND OF MY VOICE!"

The sudden appearance of a snow-covered hedge almost tripped him up – the bushes around the second caravan area. Making his way through, he felt Faye's hand go heavy again. He yanked as hard as he could and suddenly she and the duvet were flying through the snow towards him. He grabbed her and flopped her over his shoulder, the duvet hanging down his back and blowing against his legs.

"Aaaaah-uh-aaaaaah!" Faye screamed, as Brian plodded through the snow, his hands gripping her lower legs in a vice-like grip.

"I CAN'T SEE THE PUB!" Tel cried, his voice a little closer this time. "CAN YOU SEE IT?"

"I THINK IT'S THIS WAY," Brian guessed.

"WHICH WAY?"

"STAND STILL UNTIL I REACH YOU."

"WE'RE OVER HERE. OVER HERE!"

Suddenly, out of the blinding whiteness, the faint shadow of Tel appeared. Next to it, as if in hovering next to his head, was a bright red pair of lips. Faye crawled up Brian's back to raise her head. "Hi," she said with a beaming, slightly manic smile, "I think we're all going to die."

"Think positive," Sophie shouted, "We're going to make it, I'm sure of it."

"We shouldn't have split up!" Tel yelled.

"Stay together!" Brian boomed.

"I think it's over there," Sophie cried, raising a red glove on the end of an invisible white arm.

"What makes you think that?"

"There's a light."

"Over at the Frankenstein place," Tel sang.

"Could be aliens," Faye yelled, "Lost, frozen, and now about to be abducted by – "

"I can see a faint twinkling of fairy lights!" Sophie shouted.

They looked. They saw.

They went that way.

* * *

The dark shadow of the pub gradually appeared through the whiteout. They had never felt so relieved to see anything in their lives.

Faye scrambled down from Brian's back and ran to the door, tapping on it with her gloved knuckles. Tel began pounding on it with a fist. Brian brushed them both away and walloped his giant hands against it. The door shuddered.

"LET US IN!" he hollered.

They stood and waited. Nothing. No sound of running footsteps from inside, no lights being turned on.

Faye bent to make a snowball. "You want to play at a time like this?" Brian gasped.

Faye gave him an evil look and tossed the snowball towards one of the upstairs windows. The wind took it away before it had a chance to hit the glass, disintegrating it.

Brian bent to make a snowball. It was a big one and he packed it tight before lobbing it up upwards. It exploded against the window above them with a small *pfff* sound. No light came on.

Faye resumed tapping on the door. Tel pounding on it, shouting to be let in. Brian balled his hands into fists and hammered them against the wood until it seemed that the whole building was shuddering.

Behind them, Sophie gave a little cough, wriggled her way through them, stretched out a hand and brushed the snow off the rectangular Ring door camera. She pressed the button. Brian glanced awkwardly at Tel. Tel sucked his frozen lips in.

"Hello?" came a sleep-drenched voice, "Who is it?"

"Who do you think?" Brian boomed.

"Well, it looks like four snowmen of the apocalypse at my door."

"Frozen, weary, defeated – "

"And death!" Faye yelled, "Or we soon will be if you don't open this bloody door!"

"Calm yourself, woman."

"Frustration is the only thing keeping me alive!"

"We seek refuge!" Sophie bawled at the doorbell.

"Let us in!" Tel bellowed.

Sounding more awake now, Mark laughed and said, "There's no room at the inn."

Another voice cackled, "That's what he said when we arrived."

"JIM!" Mark screamed, "What are you doing in our room?"

"I was looking for the loo."

"You've been here a week and you don't know where the loo is?"

"The light was on in here and I thought I'd take a – "

"If I could just intrude on the banter, amusing as it is," Sophie said dryly. "Can you let us in?"

"Yes, yes," said Mark, "I'll come down."

They waited. And waited.

"I'm freezing my knackers off!" Tel hissed.

"Oh," Brian said, raising his hairy eyebrows, "You still have yours?"

"Is he taking a shower and getting dressed first?" Sophie complained, wrapping her arms around herself.

"You know," said Brian, staring at her, "All I can see of you is your lipstick."

"Made sure to put it on before we started trudging," she replied. "Survival instinct kicked in. I'd blow you a kiss, but I'm afraid my lips might drop off." She could no longer feel her face. Or her feet. Or any extremity, including her nose.

Faye was bent double, hugging her knees and crying, "I'm so cold! I'll never be warm again!"

Tel was banging his arms around himself, puffing out clouds of frosted steam.

Brian, his massive beard and eyebrows now completely white, with icicles hanging from them, stared at the ornate door handle, willing it to turn and open before he lost all feeling in his body.

Finally, the door clunked a couple of times, clicked and *phdunked*, and flew open. The four of them rushed in, moaning and groaning and dragging snow in with them.

Olivia was running down the stairs. "Oh, you poor things!" she cried. "Get in. Shut the door, Mark. Get those wet coats off. Go into the lounge, it'll still be warm in there. I'll get you some brandies to thaw you out."

Brian raised an eyebrow. Not all bad, after all, he thought. "No ice!"

Olivia bustled them into the lounge, rushing behind the bar to pour brandy into glasses and placing them on the counter in front of them. They used two hands to pick them up, shivering and gasping. Mark threw a couple of logs on the fire in the corner and herded them towards it.

"So," he said, surveying their frozen, dripping forms, "What was you saying about wanting to spend some romantic time in your caravans?"

* * *

It was still snowing the following morning when they came down for breakfast. Olivia was in the kitchen, plating up and looking happy. Mark stood at the huge table in the back lounge. The patio windows gave a panoramic view of the white wilderness outside. Snow was slowly creeping up the glass.

"How are you all feeling?" he asked.

"Better."

"Warmer."

"As if we might actually live."

"Hungry," said Brian.

"On the menu today we have full, hearty fry-ups," Mark announced. "Help yourself to tea, coffee and orange juice." He leaned down next to Brian and whispered, "Extra for you, of course, big man."

Brian grinned broadly. From across the table Tel hissed, "Favouritism!"

Olivia was just bringing out laden plates when there was a slow, heavy plodding coming down the stairs. Jim's voice filtered through to them: "Take it easy, babes. Another step. That's it, nice and slow. Careful now."

Beth appeared in the far doorway on the other side of the bar and, leaning heavily on Jim, made her way towards them. "Smelt the bacon," she said. "Morning, all."

"Morning, Beth. How you feeling today?"

"Pregnant. Very, very pregnant."

Sophie stared at the bump as Jim helped Beth into a chair. How could anyone even move when they were carrying such a heavy load, she wondered. She'd have to have that talk with Tel about celibacy soon ... or maybe after Christmas, no point spoiling anything yet. Definitely no fun stuff between now and then though.

"Everyone okay?" Beth asked, as Olivia placed a full plate in front of her. On a separate plate was a pile of fried tomatoes, which Beth started on right away.

They nodded, except for Brian, who was staring at her plate, which definitely contained more than his did. He looked at Mark. "I thought you said extra for me?"

"Favouritism," Tel spat.

"She's feeding two other people, Bri? Are you feeding two other people?"

"I sometimes wonder," Faye muttered.

"Do you want more?" Olivia asked, jumping to her feet.

"No, no, it's fine, lass." Under his breath he muttered, "It's been noted though."

"If it's fine, why are you complaining?" Tel asked.

Brian pulled a face and, in a child's voice, whimpered, "She's got more than me."

"Grow up, Bri," Faye snapped.

"Don't want to, don't have to."

"Did you sleep well?" Olivia asked.

"Those beds are so comfy," Sophie said, "I slept like a Christmas log."

"Best sleep I've had in ages," said Tel, briefly wondering why Sophie pushed him away last night – was the honeymoon period over already?

"So warm," Faye said through a mouthful of toast.

"Will you be going back to your caravans tonight?" Mark laughed.

"No!" they all said in unison.

"Happy to have you under our roof," Olivia grinned brightly. "I love looking after people. Jim and Beth have been here a week already, haven't you."

"We've been totally spoiled," Beth laughed, as Brian side-eyed her plate again. "I've barely had to lift a finger. The woman is a superstar."

"We've always thought so," said Tel.

Olivia blushed and waved a hand. "Stop!"

"She's my little treasure," Mark said, draping an arm across her shoulders and planting a kiss on her cheek.

"Couldn't your mum come up and help you?" Faye asked.

Beth laughed. "You think I'm loud? My mum is louder, and she don't go anywhere without her dogs, and they're loud an' all, bark all the time. She don't cook or clean, bless 'er little cotton socks, and it would 'ave just been 'orrible, so I told her not to come. I think she was secretly pleased, she ain't very domestic, my mum."

"I hired a cleaner from the village," Jim said, "But Beth would clean the house before she got there."

"Didn't want her thinking we were dirty, babes."

"Hired a woman to do the ironing, Beth didn't think she was good enough."

"Didn't do it properly," Beth told them.

"I even thought about handcuffing her to the bed to stop her getting up," he laughed. "Did you?" Beth grinned, "I don't remember talkin' about that, babes."

Sophie's eyes were constantly drawn towards Beth's bump, which was keeping Beth a good foot away from the table and making her lean forward to eat her breakfast. "Do you know what you're having?" she asked.

"Babies," Jim said, "Definitely two babies."

"We want it to be a surprise," Beth said. "We don't know yet."

"It'll certainly be a surprise when a football team emerges from your – " Brian struggled to think of a suitable word to use in public.

"Flange," said Faye.

"Pardon?" said Sophie, thinking this probably wasn't an appropriate conversation to be having over breakfast and wishing they'd change the subject – it was putting her off her eggs.

Faye looked up. "You know, a woman's ..." She waved a hand in the air. "... flappy bits."

Beth burst out laughing. "I'm so using that at the hospital. 'Hey, nurse, can you get these babies out of my flange when you've a minute?'"

PITCHING UP AT CHRISTMAS!

"Flush the flange," Jim howled, as Sophie winced.

When the laughter around the table faded, Tel asked, ""Have you decided on any names?"

"Well." Beth sat back on her chair, cricking her back. "We thought maybe Thing One and Thing Two."

The table was an uproar of nodding, approving heads. Beth held a serious face for a good few seconds, silencing them. "Kidding!" she screamed. "You should see your faces! No, for girls names we were thinking Dotty, after my mum, Sophie or Olivia."

Sophie and Olivia both ahhed. Tears sprouted in Olivia's eyes. It was such a privilege, she was so touched. She quickly brushed the tears away as Mark patted her hand.

Sophie held a hand to her chest, fighting with her emotions – a child, named after her. It was the closest she was going to get to having a baby. She could spoil it and hand it back when it made a noise … or filled its nappy.

"For boys …" Beth ran her hands over the vast expanse of her tummy. "… we haven't decided between Stephen, after my dad, Tel or Brian."

Brian looked at Tel. Tel was wide-eyed. "Blimey," he said, "Didn't expect that."

"Or we might shorten it to Bry, with a Y, and maybe an E," Jim said.

"But not lengthen Tel?" Tel quickly asked.

"To *Terence*, you mean?" Brian laughed.

Tel threw a bread roll at him. "I told you never to call me that!"

Beth asked, "You don't mind, do ya, if we steal your names?"

They fervently shook their heads. Brian felt a blooming warmth inside him. Tel and Sophie were both smiling broadly.

"Haven't considered Faye as an option then?" Faye asked. "No worries, I'm used to being in Brian's gigantic shadow, nobody ever notices me, boring old Faye."

"You're joking," Brian gasped. "Nobody notices you?

47

You're like a human dervish, frantically running around giving away all our possessions!"

"The bringer of blankets and cushions!" Sophie laughed.

"The mummy of the group," Olivia said.

"Makes me sound old," Faye grumbled.

"Take it, woman."

"You're our Bonny to Brian's Clyde." Tel's face crinkled up before he'd finished the sentence. "Not a very good example, is it."

"You're our Eve to Brian's Adam," Sophie said, leaning across the table to touch her hand.

"Ooh," Beth cut in, turning to look at Jim, "Adam and Eve?"

"Our Josephine to Brian's Napoleon," said Olivia.

"Our Judy to Brian's Punch," Mark said.

"That's the way to do it," Brian screeched in a high-pitched voice.

"We love you, Faye," Jim said, earnestly cutting into a sausage. "Your name, not so much."

"JIM!" Beth gasped.

"What?"

To Faye she said, "Your name was on the list."

"I made the list?"

"Course you did, we wanted to name our kids after people who've inspired us. That's right, ain't it, Tel, *inspired*?"

Tel nodded.

"But we didn't like the name Faye," Jim said, and Beth gently whacked the back of his head, making the sausage fall out of his mouth and onto the plate.

"You were in the top five," Beth said.

"Happy now?" Brian asked his wife.

Faye nodded and, with a pacified smile, carried on eating.

They chatted, mostly about the weather, the babies, then more about the weather. Beth suddenly cried, "Ow!" and leaned back in her chair with her hands over her bump. "OW!" Her eyes were wide and her mouth was open.

"S'up, babes?" Jim asked, reaching for her hand.

Sophie threw herself back in her chair, her heart racing in her chest. "You're not having them now, are you?" she screamed. Her hands were at her face, her eyes bulging. Was she imaging it or was the bump actually *moving*, like something from a horror film? "Are they coming?" she gasped. "Oh my God, not now, not here, not – "

Tel leaned into her, whispering, "Calm down, Sophs."

"Are they? Are they coming? Oh my God, what should we do? Call an ambulance? Towels, in films there's always lots of towels, and hot water, I don't know why. Should I boil a kettle?"

"Braxton Hicks," Beth eventually said, relaxing again.

"Who's that?" Sophie asked quickly. "Is that the name of your doctor? Gynaecologist? We should call him, get him here. Or is it some kind of medication?" She looked at Olivia. "Do you have any Braxton Hicks?"

"I don't," Olivia said with the glimmer of a smile, "But I think Beth might have."

"Calm down," Tel urged.

Sophie took a deep breath and forced a smile. She allowed her shoulders to slip down from her jawline.

"OW!" Beth cried.

Sophie stopped breathing. Faye leaned into her and said, "They're practice contractions."

"What are?"

"Braxton Hicks." She nodded towards Beth, holding her bump again and breathing slow and deep. "Her body's just flexing its muscles, you know, practising for the real thing."

"So they're not coming now?"

"No, I don't think so."

"You don't *think* so? You've had babies, haven't you?"

"Not twins."

"But ... you know when they're coming, don't you?"

"Not really, you just sort of hope for the best and pray the hysterical husband can get you to hospital in one piece."

"Oh my God," Sophie cried. "We should get her to

hospital."

"Nah," said Beth, as a contraction died away and she nonchalantly resumed eating her breakfast, "Got another four weeks yet."

Sophie stood up. "I might ... might go and lie down for a bit."

"Want me to come with you?" Tel asked, and Sophie quickly snapped, "No!"

Tel frowned. Sophie forced a smile and a wink, and went upstairs to their room.

Olivia's phone rang. She glanced at her screen and sighed. Mark glanced at her screen and said, "Don't answer it."

"I'll do what I want, Mark."

"Yes, yes, of course."

She pressed the red button and the ringing stopped ... for ten seconds.

Olivia smiled wearily at the group as she pressed the red button again. "It's ... Richard," she explained.

"Dick," Mark snarled.

"He's ... he's taken to drinking."

"Raging alcoholic," Mark said.

"He calls me."

"A lot," Mark said, tightening his lips. "I don't know why you don't just block him or turn your phone off, Liv."

"I can't! We're short staffed as it is and I'm praying no one else calls in to say they can't make it. We've already lost two of our kitchen staff and the cleaner." She bit her bottom lip.

"Where's Chelsea, the manager?" Sophie thought to ask. "I liked her."

"She's gone to her daughter's for Christmas." She started chewing on a nail. "I hope Tony's in today, the lunch and early dinner diary is full. Roll on five o'clock when we close."

"And start drinking," Brian laughed, raising his glass of orange juice.

"Brian!"

"Faye!"

Mark huffed loudly as the phone started ringing again. Olivia pressed the red button.

"How often does he call?" Faye asked.

"Up to a dozen times a day," Mark growled. "More in the last few days, in the run up to Christmas."

"He's got nowhere to go," Olivia said.

"You're too soft with him, Liv."

"I am not, you know I'm not!"

Mark shrugged.

"Show a little empathy, darling."

"I did. It ran out when he started calling you in the early hours of the morning."

"Poor you," Sophie said.

"It's fine," Olivia sighed. "He just needs somebody to talk to."

"Doesn't have to be you though, does it?"

"He's got nobody else."

"Because he's a complete – "

Beth coughed loudly. "Not in front of the children, babes."

"No. Of course. Sorry."

The phone kept ringing. Eventually, Olivia picked it up, stood up, and walked off into the kitchen.

"Is it a problem?" Brian asked Mark.

Mark shuffled awkwardly in his seat. "It's causing a few ... squabbles. He lost his job, then his flat. He says he's been sleeping on park benches and in shop doorways."

"Oh," Faye gasped, "That's so sad."

"Bit of a comedown," said Tel, "Considering what he used to have."

"His loss, my gain," Mark grinned harshly. "He's probably making it all up to get sympathy from Liv. Seems to have enough money to buy booze."

They all went quiet. Inside the kitchen they heard Olivia saying, "No, Richard, you can't come here. I'm sorry, I have a full house, there's no room for you, and ... I don't want you here. Well, go to your parents! I'll transfer some money into your bank for a taxi." At the table, Mark rolled his eyes. "What do you mean, you don't want to go to your parents? That's what they're there for, to help you in time of ... Richard, can you please just stop calling me!"

The kitchen door burst open and Olivia stomped into the room, tossing her phone down on the table. "He wants to come here," she said.

"Not a chance!" Mark snapped.

"It's *my* pub and *I* get to decide who can and can't stay!"

"You can't be serious! Here? You don't think Dick and I might clash if you bring him in from the cold?"

"How can I let him spend Christmas on a park bench?"

"Easy, just say no!"

"Uh-oh," Brian breathed at Faye, "Trouble at mill."

"You're letting him spoil what you two have," Beth said softly. "Just ignore him."

"Easier said than done."

"I know, babes, but he's giving you hassle, probably on purpose. Don't let him."

"Be firm," Faye added. "Don't let him tell you all his problems, they're of his own making. Just hang up."

Olivia exhaled slowly. The phone rang again. Mark snapped it up. "Listen, Dick, you're not welcome here and I don't appreciate – Oh, hi, Jay-Zee, everything okay?" He listened, nodding. "I'll be down in a sec." He looked at Olivia. "Jay-Zee's struggling to change a barrel, says he, I mean, zee, has already broken a nail. I'll just go down and give zim a hand."

"Thanks, Mark."

He put a hand on her shoulder as he left.

"It's very difficult," she told the group. "Richard's in such a bad way, I can't ignore another human being in need, even if he is my ex-husband."

"He's taking advantage of your good nature," Tel said.

"He's still trying to manipulate you," said Sophie.

"I doubt he's sleeping on park benches," Beth said, "Not in this weather."

Olivia took a deep breath and said, "Let's not allow him to spoil Christmas." She said this even as her phone started ringing again and, from somewhere below, Mark's voice yelled, "Turn the bloody thing off!"

She looked at her screen and answered it. "Hi, Sue, everything alright? Oh, you can't make it in today? I know, isn't it terrible out there. No, no, we'll cope, don't worry. Stay warm, and Merry Christmas."

She sighed as she hung up, then brightened and said, "Does anyone want anything more to eat? Drink?"

They shook their heads as they leaned back in their chairs and rubbed their full stomachs. Except for Brian, who said, "Is there any more bacon?" And Beth, who said, "More tomatoes?"

CHAPTER 4

Tony, the chef, who didn't live far away, came in around midday, making his way through the lunchtime crowds to check the bookings diary, smiling at the people who greeted him. He looked about twelve, but Olivia told them he had a wife and two children.

He went through the bar and into the kitchen. The yelling started almost immediately. "WHO THE FLUFFIN' HELL LEFT THIS COOKER LIKE THIS? IT'S A BARKIN' DISGRACE. GET IT CLEANED UP *IMMEDIATELY*!"

No one, not the bar staff or the many customers, paid it any attention.

Everyone except Olivia were seated in the *Friends* corner, with Beth languishing on the sofa propped up by several pillows and sipping on a tomato juice. On the coffee table next to her was a plate of neatly sliced tomatoes with a drizzle of what looked like salad cream.

"I have this mad craving for tomatoes," she said, pushing one into her mouth.

"We should call the babies after tomatoes," Jim laughed.

"Cherry," Sophie suggested, "And … I can't think of another type."

"Beef," Faye said.

Beth leaned her head back and stared at the ceiling. "Cherry and Beef," she mumbled.

"No," said Jim.

"Cherry and Rainbow?" said Faye.

Beth lowered her head to look at her. "Cherry and –"

"No," Jim said again.

Tony's voice hollered from the kitchen, "THIS ISN'T COOKED! WHO DID THIS? JUST FLUFFIN' LOOK AT ..." There was a beat of silence, and then his lowered voice said, "Oh, it hasn't been prepared yet? My bad?"

"Honestly," Beth said, spearing the last slice with a fork, "I just can't get enough tomatoes inside me. RACHEL!" she suddenly screamed, and the whole pub went silent, "CAN YOU ASK TONY TO DO ME SOME MORE TOMATOES, BABES?"

Rachel raised a thumb and hurried through the kitchen doors.

"Did you have any cravings when you were pregnant, Faye?" Beth asked.

Brian burst out laughing. "Go on, lass, tell them."

"I had a mad hankering for Marmite and strawberry jam sandwiches with my son, Ollie."

There was a beat of silence as everyone took this in and pulled faces.

"And?" said Brian.

"Pickled beetroot and cherry flavoured jelly in a bowl together with Ellie, my daughter."

"Pregnant women are odd, aren't they," Jim said.

"They don't have to be pregnant, lad, they're just odd."

"Can you believe it's Christmas Eve already?" Sophie said, desperate to change the subject; it was making her feel a bit ill.

"Wah," cried Faye, "Christmas Eve and no family."

"We're your family."

"Though I'd never admit it in public," Mark laughed, "Especially you, Bri."

Brian peered at Mark, then at Tel. "Do you know this man?"

"Never seen him before in my life," said Tel.

"I'm your *host*," Mark grinned, "So you'd better be nice to me or I'll throw you out."

Olivia came back to the corner and threw herself into the squashy armchair. "You're the landlady's *fiancé*," she told Mark with a wink, "You have no power in my establishment."

"Powerless," Tel cried, throwing a fist in the air.

Olivia frowned. "That's the fifth dining cancellation we've had today. People are worried about the weather, they're predicting heavy snow this afternoon and all through the night. Should we be worried about it?"

They all turned to look out of the windows. Everything outside was smothered in a thick white blanket. The flakes looked bigger, and there was a lot more of them. It piled up on the windowsills and was slowly creeping up the glass.

Mark was looking at his phone. "All the weather forecasts are predicting heavy snowfall late afternoon and throughout the night."

"Oh, a white Christmas!" Faye cried, "That'll be nice, won't it, Bri."

"It will, unless we get snowed in and can't move again until March."

Faye looked thoughtful. "Would that be a bad thing?"

"Only if you want to keep your job, and the house, and not eat for long periods of time."

Faye was still considering it, so Brian said, "You'd have to sell your cushions and blankets in exchange for food."

Faye stopped considering, just as Olivia's phone began to ring. "I bet that's another … oh."

"Dick?" said Mark.

Olivia rolled her eyes and brought the phone up to her ear. "Look, Richard, I've already told … we don't have the … No, my friends are here. Yes, the big, hairy one."

Brian ran a finger over his eyebrow.

"You can't! I'll call the police if you do."

Sophie held out her hand and said, "May I? Purely in a professional capacity?"

Olivia handed her the phone.

"Mr Harrison," she began. "I'm a lawyer acting on behalf of our client, Ms Harrison. It's my understanding that you're barred from the premises and if you set foot on said premises we shall be forced to take out another restraining order to keep you away from our client. Hello?"

Sophie handed the phone back. "I think he hung up on me, rude man."

Olivia lifted it briefly to her ear and heard Richard saying, "… dare you set a lawyer on me, on Christmas Eve! Don't you realise I have *nothing* and *nowhere* to go? How can you be so heartless after everything I – "

Olivia hung up. "Gets a bit tedious after a while," she sighed, "He does love to wallow in his own misfortune."

"Don't let him suck you into his whirlpool of misery," Mark said softly.

"I won't, darling."

The phone rang again. Olivia glanced at it and jumped up, hurrying to the bar and saying, "1 o'clock booking? Yes, I'll cancel that for you."

A group of four at the next table were eating quickly and glancing at the weather swirling outside the windows. A couple approached the bar to cancel their food order, as did a group of six. Olivia made a decision and dashed into the kitchen.

"Tony, stop cooking."

"Stop cooking?"

"Customers are leaving."

"Because of my cooking?"

"No, because of the weather."

"The weather has ruined their appetites?"

"No, it's made them want to go home while they still can."

"Oh, okay. STOP COOKING, MINIONS! I REPEAT, STOP BARKIN' COOKING!"

Panic suddenly wafted around the pub and people began getting up and putting on their coats, calling out 'Merry Christmas' as they hurried out the door. Big snowflakes battered against the windows. The sky darkened and the wind started howling in earnest.

Mark hurried to the bar with his phone in his hand. "Forecast is red, Liv. A big storm is coming in."

She bit her lower lip, thinking for a moment, then took a deep breath and shouted, "Can I have your attention please?" The room fell silent. "We have a red weather warning. Please finish your meals if you have one, if you don't you can either take it away with you or receive a full refund, but I do urge you to get make your way home as soon as possible."

Chairs scraped across the floor. Some customers approached the bar for refunds or polystyrene boxes. Hearty festive greetings abounded as they hurried out to the car park.

Olivia opened up the diary and started dialling everyone who had booked a table, explaining that the pub was closing due to bad weather.

The excited chatter died down as the pub emptied.

"Can we go too, miss?" Rachel asked.

"Yes, of course. Just collect the glasses and tidy the bar first."

Olivia thought she had never seen her employees move so fast. Rachel rushed around with a tray, clearing and cleaning tables. Jay-Zee collected plates, picking them up delicately with his painted fingertips. Dane stayed behind the bar, mostly brushing his floppy hair back with one hand and clearing the counter with the other, occasionally stopping to glance at himself in the mirror behind the optics.

"Mark," Olivia whispered, "Can you help me with the presents?"

They both left.

Beth sighed. "RACHEL, TOMATOES?"

"Coming right up, miss," the girl shouted, as she loaded up the glass washer under the counter. Milliseconds later she'd forgotten all about the tomatoes and was hurrying to pull on her coat and scarf.

Jim got up and sauntered behind the bar and into the kitchen, colliding with the kitchen staff stampeding through the door. Tony was wiping down counter tops.

"Tomatoes?" Jim shouted over to him.

"Fridge."

Jim opened the fridge and drew in air. "There's ... there's only one in here."

"Not much call for fresh tomatoes in winter so I didn't order many, and Beth's eaten most of those. I couldn't even put tomatoes on the lasagne last night."

"What shall I feed my tomato-craving, hormone-raging wife?"

Tony reached into a cupboard and took down two tins of tomatoes. "This is all we've got."

"Two tins?"

"We were closing at five o'clock today, and then the pub's shut for two days, so – "

"I'm dead," said Jim.

In the lounge, the staff were gathering to leave, all excited and nervously staring through the windows.

Mark and Olivia came down the stairs carrying wrapped packages. As the staff made their way to the front door they handed them out, saying, "Your bonuses are inside. Thank you for all your help and have a lovely Christmas."

When everyone had gone, they came back and threw themselves onto a sofa. Olivia immediately jumped up again as Tony and Jim came out of the kitchen; Tony looking happy, Jim, carrying a tea plate, looking a bit panicked.

"All tidy in there, Olivia."

"Thank you, Tony." She hugged him.

Mark stood up and shook his hand. "Cheers, mate, couldn't do this without you."

"That's my line," Olivia frowned. She handed him his parcel. "There's a bonus for you in there, too. Have a lovely Christmas."

"Your family's very lucky to have a chef to cook their Christmas dinner," Faye said.

"Oh, my mum cooks the dinner, she doesn't let me anywhere near the kitchen."

"Really?"

"Who do you think taught me to cook?"

"Ah."

"Have a good one," Tony said to them all as he made his way out.

"And a barkin' Merry Christmas to you, too," Tel laughed.

Mark followed him out and locked the front door. When he came back he threw two arms into the air and cried, "It's Chriiiistmaaas!"

Faye pressed the button on her jumper.

"Mine's a pint," Brian said, and Faye elbowed him. "It's Christmas!" he told her.

Olivia sauntered up to the bar. She turned with a big smile, stretched out her arms, and said, "I know we weren't doing presents, but – "

"Aren't we?" said Faye and Beth together.

"I sent you a WhatsApp group message," Tel said.

"Did you?"

"Yeah, saying not to bother with presents, Christmas is way too materialistic and we should just enjoy each other's company instead."

"I didn't get that," Faye said, picking her phone out of her bag.

"Me neither," said Beth, nudging Jim to pass her phone off the table.

Tel took his out. "I sent it on … " He laughed briefly. "Oh, I forgot to press SEND."

Their phones pinged with a WhatsApp message.

"It's a bit late now, Tel!"

"So you've all brought presents?" Sophie asked.

Everyone nodded.

"Well that's awkward. Well done, Tel."

"I forgot!"

"Stealing my thunder," Olivia said, her arms still spreadeagled along the bar counter.

They all turned to her and said, "Did you get the message?"

"No. Sophie told me. I thought you all knew."

"No."

"Oh. Well, I know we *almost* said not to bring presents, but my gift to you, which isn't really a gift, it's something to acknowledge the *spirit* of Christmas." She gave a little giggle. "Consider my pub as your pub, and help yourselves to anything."

"Anything?" Brian asked, his eyes lighting up.

Olivia nodded and wafted both hands towards the shiny beer taps and optics at the back of the bar. "Open bar," she beamed.

Brian started to get up, but Faye pulled him down and hissed, "It's only just gone midday!"

"It's Christmas!"

"It's a holiday!" Faye said, mimicking his deep voice, "It's Friday! It's the third Thursday in the month! Use some self-control, Bri."

"I am. I'm waiting until you turn your head so I can sneak up to the bar without you noticing."

"Not notice a huge bear of a man 'sneaking' behind the bar?" Tel cackled.

"I'll be like a ninja," Brian said, jutting out his hairy chin. "You won't see me, you won't hear me – "

"We'll hear the chugging of lager though," Mark laughed. "Like water down a drain."

"You'll be like a man mountain, dragging and pounding your way across the room," Tel said.

"The walls will shudder," Mark gasped, tears slipping from his eyes as he gripped onto Tel's arm, "The ground will vibrate beneath our feet."

"Pictures will fall from the wall." Tel slapped his thighs, struggling to draw breath.

"Glasses will shiver from the shelves," Mark wheezed.

Brian glared at them both. "Have you quite finished?"

Tel nodded. Mark mouthed, 'Can't breathe!'

"I'll show you," Brian said, and then he suddenly let out a huge bellow of a scream, widened his eyes, pointed at the window and howled, "WHAT'S THAT?"

They all turned their heads. There was a heavy thumping sound, and when they looked back Brian was standing proudly behind the bar. "Didn't see that, did ya?"

They all fell about, except for Faye, who glared at him with pinched lips.

"Get you a drink, lass?"

Her pinched lips relaxed enough to tut and say, "Prosecco, please."

"Ooh," Olivia said, lifting herself onto a bar stool, "I'll have a gin and tonic."

"Me too," Sophie cried, raising her arm.

Olivia said, "It's so lovely to be served for a change."

"I serve you when the pub closes," Mark said.

Jim and Beth snickered.

"A drink," he threw at them.

"Yes, darling, you're almost a barman."

"Almost? I'll remember that the next time a coach pulls in and you ask me to help out."

"Okay, darling. Can I have a slice of lemon with mine, Bri?"

Brian picked a lemon from a bowl of lemons and stared at it. He looked under the counter and found a small wooden board with a knife on it. He sliced the lemon in half and cut a sliver off. It sat, almost translucent, on the board. "Pith off?" he said.

"Don't talk to my fiancé like that," Mark sniggered.

"Pith off?" queried Olivia.

"Do I leave the pith on or off?"

"Off if you're making a citrus salad," Tel laughed.

"How would you know?" Sophie asked.

He wobbled his head and said, "Saw it on a cookery programme once."

"You've been watching cookery programmes?"

"I was waiting for the football to start."

"Ah."

Brian seemed undecided as he stared down at the lemon.

"Have you never made a gin and tonic before, Bri?"

"Faye drinks Prosecco."

"Which I'm still waiting for," she said.

"Patience, woman, can't you see I'm busy?"

"Busy staring at a slice of lemon, while your wife sits here shrivelling from dehydration."

Olivia went behind the bar and made herself and Sophie a gin and tonic, cutting another slice off the lemon and throwing one into each glass, adding ice from a bucket. "You're fired," she told Brian.

"But I have children to feed!" he wailed.

"Can you manage to pour me a tomato juice?" Beth asked.

Brian glanced at the shiny beer taps.

"It comes in a bottle," she giggled.

Brian turned and glanced at the optic bottles.

"If you think me and my babies can drink any of those you need your 'ead looking at, mate."

"Fridge," Olivia laughed.

"Under the optics counter," Mark added.

"Left a bit. A bit more."

"Ah-ha!" Brian cried. "Fridge located. There's only three bottles in here, just so you know."

Beth and Jim both inhaled sharply. Olivia said, "Panic not, there's more boxes in the basement.

"Basement?" said Faye.

"Yes, the basement."

"You have a basement?"

"All pubs have basements," Brian said, struggling with the bottle opener and sending the cap flying over the counter. He poured the contents into a pint glass. Jim wandered over and said, "Might as well put the other two bottles in there, there's enough room and it'll save my legs."

"I didn't know that," Faye gasped again.

"Where do you think they keep all the beer and alcohol, lass?"

"Under the counter."

"Don't you like basements, Faye?"

"It's …" She licked her lips nervously. "It's where all the monsters live."

"Faye," cried Brian, "Give up the horror films."

"I won't."

"Then learn to live with basements."

"I … I can't."

"Bit of a Catch 22 situation then," Sophie grinned.

Tel started singing, "Do I stay or do I go."

Jim came back to the table with a pint of tomato juice and a pint of beer. Brian brought Faye her Prosecco, also in a pint glass, and a beer for himself.

Mark said, "Other glasses are available, you know, Bri."

"These were all I could find."

They all turned to look at the shiny collection of glasses hanging above the bar, right in front of his face. "I thought those were for decoration."

"Brian," said Olivia, "Never work in a pub."

"I much prefer this side anyway."

Jim stood up, giving a sideways glance to the last slice of tomato on the plate. "I'm just nipping out for … "

"For?" Beth asked.

"For … a bit of fresh air."

"It's zero degrees outside, babes."

"I'm going for a fag, alright?"

"Does Jay-Zee know about this?" Tel laughed.

"I thought you'd given up," Beth said.

"Given up the *fags*, eh, Jim?"

"I have given up. Sort of."

"Sort of not, then?"

Jim grabbed his padded jacket from the coat stand by the bar and strode towards the patio windows in the back lounge, taking a cigarette out of the packet as he went. When he pulled one door open, snow fell inside and a gust of wind raced around the room, making them realise how warm and cosy they'd previously been.

Olivia suddenly sat up straight. "Oh," she cried, "I forgot

to buy cinnamon sticks for the Christmas pudding."

"We'll survive," Mark said, trying to pull her back into him again, but she resisted.

"No, it won't be right without cinnamon infused brandy." She started getting up. "I'll just nip down to the village shop, they might have some left."

Mark pulled her down again. "I'll go, I'll have more chance of making it there and back in my van than you in your Mini."

She gave him a huge, cute smile. "My hero."

"No problem," he said, puffing out his chest.

"Shut the patio doors while you're up," Sophie said, "Jim hasn't closed them properly and there's a terrible draft."

Mark made his way over to the back lounge. He kicked the pile of snow out of the way and was about to close the doors when something caught and held his eye.

He couldn't believe what he was seeing.

CHAPTER 5

Mark stepped out onto the snow-covered patio, glancing quickly behind him as he shut the door.

"Jim!" he hissed, "What the bloody hell do you think you're doing?"

Jim was standing inside the smoker's hut with his padded arms in the air, one hand holding an unlit cigarette.

He wasn't alone.

Another padded body was wrapped around him like a boa constrictor. Jim looked like he was being mugged and hugged at the same time. The other person also wore a padded jacket with the hood up. Mark couldn't see who it was, but it was an intimate pose: like two fat teddy bears embracing.

"Help!" Jim squeaked.

The smaller teddy bear turned its hooded head.

"Hello, Mark," said Julie.

"Oh, you need help alright, mate," Mark growled. "You've got a pregnant wife in there who loves the bones of you, for some inexplicable reason, and you're out here playing with fire, *again*? You need your head looking at."

"I ain't touched her. She was out here waiting for me. I was ambushed!"

"Beth will be devastated! What are you thinking, messing around with Jools again?"

"It's not how it looks, Mark."

"How is it then, Jim?" Mark crossed his arms over his chest, really bloody annoyed. A leopard never changed its spots, Jim was living proof of that. How could he be so stupid and risk everything for a *fling*? Poor Beth.

"Get her off me," Jim spat, "She latched on as soon as I stepped through the door and won't let go!"

"Get off him, Jools."

"He's the love of my life." She wrapped a leg around his and Jim struggled to keep his balance.

"Your life's barely started," Mark sighed.

"I thought you had a boyfriend anyway?" Jim said, looking down at her.

Jools pulled a face. "Mick? It's over with him, he didn't treat me like you did, Jim."

Mark stepped towards them and half-heartedly pulled on one of her arms, but she pulled it out of his grasp and wrapped it around Jim's neck again.

"Mark," Jim whined, "You gotta help me."

"Let him go, Jools, before somebody sees you." He glanced back at the patio doors again. Someone could walk by at any minute.

"I can't," she said.

"Why not?"

"I ain't got nowhere else to go."

"I thought you were staying with your mum?"

"She threw me out, Mick kept coming round to the house causing trouble after I dumped him. Kept coming to the pub where I worked, too, so they sacked me." She started crying, lifting her face up to his and letting huge tears slip down her young face. "I got no money and nowhere to go. I'm all alone, Jim. I don't like being alone. You're all I've got. Remember the good times we had?"

"No. I'm sure your mum will have you back, especially at Christmas."

"I don't want to go back, I want to be with you."

"Jools, this ain't gonna work, it was never gonna work." He lifted pleading eyes to Mark.

Mark tutted and tried once more to prise an arm away. Julie wriggled it free and gripped Jim's neck so tightly that he choked. Mark inserted his arm between their two bodies and squeezed himself between them, facing Jim, whilst keeping one eye on the patio door the whole time.

"We must stop meeting like this," Jim grinned, nose to nose.

"It's Jools you should stop meeting, you idiot."

"I didn't meet her, I told you, she was lying in wait."

Jools gasped and whined as Mark prised her away.

"Your breath stinks," he said.

"It's the fags."

"Jim!" Julie cried out pitifully.

"Shush!"

"JIM!"

Mark spun round to face her, his back pressed up against Jim to keep her from latching onto him again. "Ooh, Mark, I didn't think you were like that," Jim laughed.

"This is no time for joking," Mark spat. To Julie he said, "He's got a heavily pregnant wife in there. You don't need *him*, you need a proper man."

"Oh, thanks Mark!"

"You want help or not?"

"Yes please."

"Go home, Jools."

"I want to stay here with Jim," she pouted.

"And what do you think Beth will say about that?"

"As long as I'm near him, I don't care."

"I don't want you, Jools," Jim said, from over Mark's shoulder.

"You do, I know you do."

"I bloody don't!"

"You're so cruel, and it's Christmas!"

"Jools," Mark said calmly, "You *have* to go home. You can't stay here, you must see that."

"I've got nowhere to go. No job, no money, no home."

"Your mum will – "

"She won't, she's got a bloke staying with her, she never

wants me when she has a bloke."

"Jools, it's not my problem. You *have* to go."

"Go where? You'd send me away on a night like this?"

Jim glanced at his watch. "It's only lunchtime."

"Oh Jim, we were meant to be together!"

"We weren't, Jools. It was just a bit of fun."

"It was more than that," she sobbed.

"Not for me, it wasn't."

"You don't mean that."

"I do."

"Jools," Mark said, glancing at the patio doors again, "You *have* to go."

"I'll freeze to death, and then you'll both be sorry."

Mark raised his eyes to the white heavens and let out a heavy sigh.

"Mark?" came Olivia's voice from inside.

Instinctively, both men pushed Julia to the side, against the pub wall, where hopefully nobody would see her. Mark reached into his pocket and pulled out a bunch of keys. As he struggled to pull one off he said, "You can stay in the utility shed with the big windows just inside the camping field. There's blow up beds and sleeping bags in there. I'll bring food when I can. You *can't* come up to the pub, you *have* to stay away, do you understand?"

"What about Jim?" she asked, taking the key from him.

"Oh, I'll be alright," Jim said, "Pub's nice and warm."

"Jim!" Mark hissed.

"What?"

"Will you come and see me, Jim?"

"No, Jools, I won't. I love my wife, I ain't hurting her again."

"But –"

"But nothing, Jools, it's over. It never really started, but it's definitely over."

"How can you say that?"

"Because I'm gonna be a dad, and that means more to me

than anything else. And I love my wife."

Tears poured from her eyes. Her bottom lip trembled.

"Go, quick!" Mark said. "Make sure nobody sees you or you really will be homeless."

"Jim?"

"Bye, Jools."

Mark stepped back to peer through the patio windows. They were all in the front lounge, talking and laughing in the *Friends* corner. The back lounge was clear.

"Go!" he hissed, "Quick!"

Julie sniffed, bent low, and dragged herself through the snow to the side of the pub, where she turned and gave a sad little wave to Jim before disappearing.

"Get in!" Mark snapped.

Jim lit his cigarette and said, "I'll just have this first, calm me nerves a bit."

Huffing, Mark turned and headed to the side of the pub, following Julie's deep footsteps.

"Where you going?" Jim called after him.

"The shop in the village."

"Get us some tomatoes, would you?"

Mark huffed.

* * *

As he reached the end of the alleyway at the side of the pub, Mark saw Julie scampering awkwardly through the camping field gates, falling over in the snow every third or fourth step, but he saw her reach the shed. There was heating inside, she'd be okay, purely as a temporary measure. Jim really needed to sort this mess out.

He shook his head as he stepped onto the front patio. There was someone standing there, huddling from the snow and the wind under the overhang of the front door. For a second he thought it might be Dick, but Dick would never wear a neon pink puffer jacket with a giant, fur trimmed hood, complete with a matching handbag over his shoulder.

"Jay-Zee?"

The kid turned and frowned.

"What are you still doing here?"

"Dad said his car was packed away in the garage, but he said he'd try and pick me up in the tractor, which will be *uber* embarrassing!"

"But you only live down the road, can't you walk?"

Jay-Zee lifted a pink, high-heeled boot. "In these?"

"Boots not made for walking, eh?"

"They'll get wet and be ruined, just like my makeup." He delicately brushed flakes off his cheeks.

"Want a lift? I'm headed to the village."

"Nah, you're alright, I'll wait for my dad, he should be here in a minute."

"Have a good one."

"You too."

Mark got into his van. As he was pulling out of the car park he saw a tractor coming up the lane on the right. Inside the raised bucket was a blanket. Mark laughed as he turned left, imaging Jay-Zee's face as he was driven home on farm equipment.

He didn't see the figure clinging precariously onto the back of the tractor.

* * *

Mark quietly muttered to himself as he entered the shop and picked up a basket. "Cinamon sticks, tomatoes, bouquet garnet, whatever the hell that is."

He waved at James, the young man behind the counter, and began scouring shelves.

He'd found a bag of fresh tomatoes, and was just loading the basket with tinned one, when a sultry voice behind him said, "Hello, Mark."

His heart jumped into his throat as he spun round, instantly recognising the voice.

"Janis! What are you doing here?"

She stood in front of him, her hair longer and a different shade of blonde, her makeup a little thicker, but it was definitely her, his ex-wife. She was wrapped in a long, camel-coloured and expensive-looking coat. The scarf beneath made her look decidedly top-heavy.

"I was just passing through," she shrugged, "And I saw your van."

"Just passing through?" He pulled a face. She was lying. He wondered if she'd taken it up full time now.

He didn't trust her, and he didn't like her being here.

"You look … well," he said, conversationally, thinking he'd forget about the bouquet garnet and make a quick escape.

To his horror, she stepped closer to him until their bodies were almost touching. He couldn't step back, a shelf of baked beans was like a wall behind him. He felt trapped. He knew now how Jim had felt, finding Julie in the smoker's hut.

"I'm heartbroken," she said, frowning.

"Lost another boyfriend?"

"Lost my husband."

"You married again? That was quick."

"You, Mark, you're my husband – "

"We're divorced."

"I miss you."

Mark felt a familiar rage ignite inside him. Politeness skitted away like a wounded dog. He went to step around her, but she blocked his escape. He considered shouldering her aside, but thought better of it – the last thing he needed at Christmas was his ex-wife screaming assault, and she was more than capable of it.

"Let me by, Janis."

"Are you so keen to get away from me?" she simpered.

"Yes."

"How rude of you."

"You're trouble, Janis, you've always been trouble and you always will be."

"Have you missed me?"

"Missed you?" He was genuinely surprised. He hadn't seen her in almost two years, and here she was, like a bad penny, trying to step back into his life? "What do you want, Janis?"

"I want my husband back – "

"I'm not your husband."

" – or I want my fair share of the house, *our* house."

"*My* house, the divorce settlement was finalised ages ago."

"It wasn't enough."

"Probably should have mentioned it at the time." He tried to brush by her, but she side-stepped in front of him again.

"I'm broke," she said.

"Ask your latest bloke for money."

"He doesn't have any, that's why I dumped him."

Mark shrugged. "Not my problem."

"It will be your problem if you don't give me what I want."

Her painted smile vanished, her painted mask slipped.

"There she is," Mark grinned coldly, "There's the real Janis."

"I need twenty grand."

Mark burst out laughing. "I need a bigger van for my nursery but I'm not getting that either. We don't always get what we want, Janis, no matter how much foot stamping you do."

"I want to start a new life in a different country, I haven't decided which one yet, and I need – "

"I don't care what you need or what you expect, you're not getting a single penny out of me."

A sly grin spread across her face as she stepped forward and pinned him with her quite expansive chest against the baked beans. Mark turned his head sideways, away from her mouth.

"I hear you've taken up with the local landlady," she said, sliding her hands up to his shoulders, making him shudder. "Bit desperate, hitching up with some tart in a pub, but I understand you had a gap to fill. How would she feel if she found out we'd been seeing each other again?"

Mark turned his head to face her. "Blackmail, Janis? Really?"

"Whatever it takes."

"My fiancée knows how I feel about you."

"Ooh, *fiancée* is it? Does she know how you *really* feel about me, Mark?"

"She does, she really does."

"You never really got over me, did you."

"I was the happiest man on the planet the day our divorce came through."

He pushed her away with his body. Several tins of beans fell to the floor.

"You okay back there?" James shouted from the counter. "Do you need help with anything?"

"Do you have any garlic and a wooden stake?" Mark yelled back. To Janis he said, "You're not getting anything from me, so you might as well sling your hook."

Janis grinned. "I think I might stick around, the Cotswolds looks quite pretty in the snow. Do you know of any local B&Bs? A pub, perhaps?"

He put his face as close to hers as he could stand. "Not a single penny," he hissed.

"You know how annoyed I am when I don't get what I want."

"I still have nightmares about it, and about being married to you."

"You old charmer. You love me really, I know you do."

His patience at an end, he turned, ignored her stepping into his path, and barged his way passed. Janis staggered, but, sadly, he thought, she didn't fall and break her neck against the soup tins on the other side of the aisle.

He marched quickly to the top of the shop and tipped the tomatoes onto the counter. He could hear the clack of her heels hurrying up behind him and felt his heartbeat increase.

"Everything okay?" James asked.

"Yeah, just need to get home quick before the storm hits."

He wasn't talking about the snow.

"Yeah, I'm shutting up shop in a – "

"How much do I owe you, mate?"

James started telling him but, as the heels came to a stop behind him, he slapped a note down on the counter.

He didn't see or feel something being slipped into his jacket pocket as he raced from the shop.

* * *

Mark hurried across the car park, jumped into his van and started it up, hoping to get away before she came out, but she came staggering towards him through the snow in high heels. He found himself imaging her slipping and hitting her head against a rock, and hated himself for it even though he hoped for it.

She didn't.

"MARK!" she called out, as he slammed the van into gear. "MARK, WAIT!"

He smashed his foot on the accelerator and the van jerked forward. He missed her by inches, and skidded onto the lane.

He wanted to get back to Olivia and his lovely, Janis-free life.

Home had never seemed more like a warm, inviting sanctuary.

* * *

He thought at first she wouldn't follow him, wouldn't dare or couldn't keep up with his pretty reckless driving down the narrow country lanes. The snow fell thicker and the wind blew it into drifts at the side of the road. He kept glancing in his rear-view mirror and saw nothing but his own tyre tracks in the snow. He'd lost her.

He smiled. Catastrophe averted.

He should have known better.

Next time he looked in the mirror it was getting dark and he saw two headlights behind him. *Could be anyone*, he thought, *someone from the village, or maybe the local bus was still running,* anything but Janis, following him.

As he turned with some relief into the car park of the Woodsman Pub, a car turned in with him. Janis sat behind the wheel. She stopped, turned off the engine, and stared at him through the windscreen. She didn't get out.

Mark was surprised how fast his heart was beating. He ran from the van to the pub door, grabbing the keys from his pocket and struggling to find the right one. He was running, actually running, from his ex-wife.

But still she didn't get out of the car.

He fumbled to get the key in the lock, and then it was opened from inside and he was falling through it, bringing snow in with him. He lifted his head to see red slippered feet next to him.

"Mark?" Olivia gasped, falling to her knees.

"Shut the door!" Mark cried. "Shut it and lock it!"

"Why, what's wrong?"

"Shut the door, Liv! Shut it *quick*!"

Olivia stood up and moved towards the door.

Mark scrambled to his feet, turning.

Just as Janis appeared on the doorstep.

* * *

"I'm sorry," Olivia said, "I'm afraid we're closed."

Janis put on her innocent face and held out her fingers. "Hello. We've not been introduced. I'm Janis, Mark's wife."

"*Ex*-wife," Mark snapped.

Olivia took the proffered hand looking confused. "Mark?"

"She followed me from the village shop."

"Where we just happened to bump into each other," Janis giggled. "Isn't that an amazing coincidence!"

"No," Mark snapped again.

"I was just passing –"

"Through the Cotswolds?"

" – and I wanted to wish you both a Merry Christmas."

"Thanks," Mark snapped. "You too. Bye."

PITCHING UP AT CHRISTMAS!

"Mark!" Olivia gasped. "Don't be so rude!"

"Liv!"

To Janis she said, "Please, come in, you must be frozen."

"From the heart outwards," Mark muttered.

"Can I offer you a warming drink? A mulled wine or a brandy?"

"Oh, that's so kind of you, thank you."

Janis stepped across the threshold in red high heels and Olivia slowly closed the door behind her. Janis made a big drama of sweeping off her long, camel coat, leaning forward to pull down the mid-thigh hem on her very stretchy, very tight red dress. She pushed the coat at Olivia and unwrapped the chucky woollen scarf from around her neck.

They both sucked in air when they saw the swooping neckline and the two mounds of blancmange protruding from it. Mark's eyes bulged. Olivia had to tap his arm to get his attention back.

"Those are new," he gulped.

"Had them especially for you, Mark."

"Why? I don't want them."

"You wanted them before," she grinned.

"We were *married* before and I didn't know what a nasty little – "

"Mark!" Olivia hissed.

Janis thrust the scarf at her and took another step forward. "Through here?" she tinkled, tapping her way towards the lounge door.

Mark hissed, "She's not stopping!" at Olivia, before chasing after Janis, saying, "One drink and you're out."

"We'll see," she grinned.

Olivia put the coat and the scarf on the stand by the door, and took a deep breath.

* * *

"Hey, everybody," Mark said to everyone chattering and laughing in the *Friends* corner, "This is Janis."

"Hi, Janis," they said, immediately staring at the vast acreage of exposed flesh protruding from her chest.

"Mark's ex-wife," Olivia said, coming into the room.

"Oh," said Brian. "Bit awkward."

"Just a bit," Mark flustered.

Janis threw out her arms and cried, "Hi, everyone, I was just passing."

"They're like a couple of risen bread rolls, aren't they," Sophie couldn't help whispering, or looking.

"Cobs," Faye breathed.

"Teacakes," Brian said, wide-eyed.

"I think I can see the raisins," said Tel, sitting on the chair beneath them.

"How do you keep them in?" Julie asked out loud.

Janis seemed pleased with all the attention. "What, these?" she said, cupping one in each hand and leaning forward to expose them fully, making Tel flinch and slightly raise a protective arm. "Very carefully," she winked.

There was a brief breath of awkward laughter from the group.

"I'm sure I've seen that dress on Shein," Faye whispered to Beth, "They always come up a size too small."

Tel moved over to the sofa, next to Sophie.

"Life flashed before my eyes," he whispered.

"Nearly took an eye out," she laughed.

Mark stood awkwardly, praying Janis wouldn't sit down amongst them.

She sat down amongst them, on the armchair Tel had vacated. "Oh!" she cried, looking around, "Isn't it lovely and festive in here, and so warm!"

"Don't get comfortable," Mark hissed, "You're not staying."

Janis wriggled into the chair. "I don't know," she said, "I think I could get used to this, despite the kitschy decor."

She spotted Beth, lounging on the sofa under a faux fur blanket. "Are you ill?" she asked, thinking the woman looked extraordinarily large.

"She's pregnant," Jim said proudly.

"It's okay, babes," Beth said, "I can talk for meself."

"Just wanted to save you some energy, babes."

"By talking?" she laughed. "Talking's all I got left, babes."

"You're very large," Janis said, reaching forward to grab a mini pork pie from the table laden with nibbles, holding her bent pose for a second longer than necessary.

"We've seen your expansive attributes," Sophie tutted, "You don't need to keep pushing them in our faces."

Janis swivelled her head round to Brian, catching him off guard. "I bet you'd like them pushed in your face, wouldn't you, big boy."

Faye threw both arms across Brian's chest as a gaping hole appeared in his beard. "Oi!" she snapped, "He's with me."

"Nothing for you to worry about," she said, biting into the pork pie. "He's not my type."

In a strangled voice Brian said, "Oh, thank God for that!"

"He's broke," Mark said, "Not your type at all."

"I don't do too badly," Brian said, slightly peeved. "Had a bit of a glitch before we went to America but – "

"No offence, mate, I'm just protecting you from the praying mantis."

"That's my job," said Faye, holding his hand in both of hers.

Janis continued, "I always think pregnant women are like human grow bags, you know, the ones you buy for the garden? You look just like one, lying on the sofa like that, a very large grow bag, growing another one, like *Invasion of the Body Snatchers*." She gave a high-pitched tinkle of amusement.

There was a millisecond of silence as Beth furrowed her brow.

"And so it begins," Mark breathed, "And so soon."

"Mark," said Olivia, "Fetch Janis a mulled wine, would you? Or would you prefer something else, Janis?"

"No, a mulled wine sounds perfect."

Mark pulled a face, huffed, and walked off behind the bar. Brian quickly followed.

"I thought you two didn't speak?" he said.

"We don't, and I much prefer it that way." He picked up a ceramic jug and poured the steaming contents into a tiny mug. He briefly wondered if they had any poison lying around, strychnine maybe, or perhaps there was rat poison in the kitchen.

"What's she doing here?" Brian whispered.

"She said she was 'just passing'." He did air quotes. "She's come for money."

"What money?"

"For the house."

"I thought all that had been sorted ages ago."

"It was. She's run out. Probably spent it on those boobs."

"Go big or go large," Brian breathed, staring over at them bouncing up and down in the armchair as Janis gave a high-pitched shriek of laughter.

"Supersized," said Mark.

"They're like two balloons struggling to escape."

"She's here for more."

"What are you, a cash machine?"

Mark glared over at her, chatting animatedly with his friends. "She seems to think so."

Brian thought she was a nice enough woman, if a little exhibitionist, but exes were exes for a reason and he knew Mark had no warm, fuzzy feelings towards her. "Just give her a drink and send her on her way."

"Yeah, sounds easy, doesn't it, except we're dealing with a full-blown narcissist of the worst kind. She wants to stir things up."

Brian sighed. "First Richard begging to come, now Janis. Hope none of my exes turn up or Faye will have a fit." He was silent for a moment. "Especially Vicki, she was a stun–"

"Have you got Janis's drink, darling?" Olivia called over.

Janis laughed. "Yes, *darling*, have you got my drink,

darling?"

Mark was about to move, but Brian grabbed his arm. Looking down at the mulled wine in the mug he said, "Have you put anything in it?"

"No."

"Okay, just checking."

"Thought about it though," Mark said, striding back to the throng.

He thumped the ceramic mug on the coffee table in front of Janis, and turned to Olivia. "Can we have a word?"

"Yes, darling."

"Darling, darling, darling," Janis sang.

They went into the back lounge and sat at a table.

"I want her gone," he said.

"She's just having a quick drink. I'm sure she'll leave afterwards."

"She won't."

"It's Christmas, she'll have somewhere to go."

"She hasn't."

"How do you know?"

"Because I know Janis, she's a drifter and a grifter. She's also a money grabbing little – "

"Mark! Where's your festive spirit, good will to all men and all that?"

He grabbed hold of her hands. "With you," he said. "With them." He glanced back at their friends. "Not with *her*."

"Look, I think you're panicking over nothing. She'll have her drink and go. She doesn't want to be here at Christmas with strangers."

"Doesn't she? You don't know what she's like, Liv. She's dangerous."

"Oh Mark, don't be so – "

He gripped her hands tighter. "You don't know her like I do. She wants to cause trouble, it's what she does best. Even her own sister won't speak to her any more."

Olivia thought for a moment, looking between Mark and

the well-endowed woman over on the leather armchair. "I must say," she said, "She's prettier than I imagined."

"It's a mask, Liv, she paints it on. Underneath she's a monster."

"We all think that about our exes. Look at me and Richard."

Mark sighed. "We certainly know how to pick them."

"We do now," she grinned, kissing him on the cheek.

"How sweet," said Janis, sidling over and sitting down next to them. "I was just saying to ... Bernard, is it?"

"Brian," said Brian, who had appeared on this side of the bar pretending to search for something.

"Do you need anything, Bri?" Olivia asked.

"No, no, I'll find it, you carry on."

"I was just saying to Brian," Janis continued, "I can't possibly drive in this weather, it's very dangerous out there."

They looked through the patio windows. The snow was certainly deeper and was growing heavier by the minute. It was also starting to get dark.

"No," Mark snapped, "You can't stay for Christmas."

Janis leaned back in her chair. "Oh, so you'd send me out in this, would you?"

"Yes."

"But – " Olivia began, and Mark shook his head. She saw the look of determination in his eyes and decided not to finish the sentence. She stood up, slightly annoyed, and said, "I'll let you two deal with this," and stomped off.

Great, thought Mark, *she'd only been here five minutes and she'd already upset Liv.*

He turned to Janis and said, very slowly, "Finish your drink and leave. I don't care if you end up in a ditch, I don't want you here."

"I'm sure Olivia wouldn't mind, she practically – "

"*I* would mind. I would mind very much."

"Frightened I might say too much, Mark?"

"There's nothing for you to say."

"Oh," she grinned, "I could make up a thing or two, set the cat amongst the pigeons."

"You won't, because you're *not* staying."

"Then give me my money!"

Mark furiously patted his jumper and trousers. "Well, do you know what? I don't seem to have twenty grand on me."

Janis leaned forward, her breasts resting on the table, and snarled, "How much do you have?"

Mark fished out his wallet and opened it. "About a hundred."

"A hundred?"

"Yeah, I'm not bloody Rockefeller, I don't walk round with thousands of pounds in my pockets."

"How much does your girlfriend have?" She languidly leaned back to glance back at Olivia, adding, "I must say, Mark, you've certainly let your standards slip. Had I known you'd set the bar so low I'd have given it another go myself."

"Liv is the nicest, kindest – "

"Nice enough and kind enough to make up for those teeth? Don't they have dentists round here?"

Mark pounded his fist down on the table.

Behind the bar, Brian coughed and said, "No brawling, please."

Mark clamped his mouth shut. Brian started polishing a glass with the hem of his Christmas jumper, quietly humming.

"Leave Liv out of it," Mark said. "She has nothing to do with this."

"I *want* my money!"

"You're not getting any!"

"I'd better, or – "

"Or what? You'll cause trouble? Me and Liv are on solid ground, there's *nothing* you can do to – "

"Can't I? *Watch me.*"

He stared, almost mesmerised, as Janis's face morphed from hard and determined into that of a woman about to burst into tears. She sniffed. She caught her breath. Her eyes filled with tears. She wailed, "No, Mark, don't send me out there, *please*!"

Mark shook his head. She was such a drama queen.

"Please, Mark! Don't throw me out. It's Christmas Eve, I don't want to die on Christmas Eve!"

"And the award for worst actress goes to – "

Olivia came hurrying over, followed by the others. Beth shouted, "I'm there with you in spirit. Jim, keep me posted."

"Will do, babes."

"What's going on?" Olivia asked.

Jim shouted back at Beth, "Liv wants to know what's going on."

"It's an act," Mark snapped.

"Mark says it's an act."

"Shut up, Jim," said Tel.

"He said ... " Janis sobbed, her voluptuous chest heaving with emotion, "He said ... I had to leave and he ... he hoped I ..." She hitched and wiped her eyes. "... I ended up in a ditch!"

"No," said Faye, as Jim hurried off to tell Beth and came hurrying back again.

"Really?" Sophie said, raising a sceptical eyebrow. "Mark said that? This Mark? *Our* Mark? Sounds very out of character to me."

"She's putting it on!" Mark said. "There's not even any real tears. There's nothing real about her except her desperate need for money!"

Sophie turned to Brian, still polishing a glass with his jumper behind the bar. "Did you hear him say that, that he hoped she ended up in a ditch?"

Brian gave a single nod of his head. "He said he didn't care, not that he hoped, there's a difference."

"I *don't* care!" Mark cried, jumping up and throwing his arms up in frustration. "I don't care if she ends up in a ditch, I just want her out of here. She's *poisonous*!"

Mark watched in horror as Olivia sat down next to a still hitching Janis and put her arm around her shoulders, whispering soothing words.

"She has to go!"

"I'll decide that," Olivia said.

"See, she's got between us already! It's what she does!"

"I'm not even a very good driver," Janis whimpered, whilst turning her head slightly to grin at Mark.

"I don't want her here, she has to leave!"

"Mark, calm down."

"I won't be calm until this woman is *gone*!"

"I didn't know you could be so heartless," Olivia said.

"Only when I'm around *her*, for this very reason!"

"I think she should stay."

Mark glared at Olivia. She held his gaze. He felt as if he'd been punched in the stomach.

"Of course you can stay," she whispered to Janis, giving her a cute, overbite smile. "You can't possibly drive in this weather, nobody could." She looked up at Sophie. "Could you get her a glass of brandy?"

Sophie raised an eyebrow, biting on the inside of her mouth. She didn't move.

"Faye?"

Faye looked at Sophie, then at Brian, still behind the bar. He picked up a bottle and glugged the contents into the tumbler he'd been polishing. He held it out to Sophie, who was the nearest. She still didn't move. Faye came over and got it.

Janis took a trembling sip, peering over the glass at Mark. He saw the tiniest of smiles playing on her painted lips.

Growling in frustration, he jumped up and stormed from the room.

Brian and Tel glanced at each other before following him.

Jim, exhausted from all the running backwards and forwards, stood still with his hands on his hips, trying to catch his breath.

* * *

They raced up the stairs after Mark. He stormed through

to their flat, slamming the door hard behind him.

Tel tapped first. "Mark, you okay?"

"Go away."

"What can we do to make it better?"

"Get rid of that bloody woman."

"Can we come in?" Brian asked.

"No. Leave me alone."

"We can talk about this, get it out of your system."

"Let's not ruin Christmas, eh?" Tel said.

"It's not me, it's *her*."

"We know, but … there's not a lot you can do about it."

"Liv is so gullible!" There was a pause of silence. "And so lovely."

"Let us in, Mark."

Silence, and then the door clicked and opened. Mark stormed back down the hallway into the living room, turned, and started pacing. And huffing. And ranting.

Brian and Tel sat and listened.

***

Downstairs, Janis was back in the fold of the *Friends* corner, surrounded by the women, and Jim. Footsteps pounded to and fro across the ceiling above them, and there was some distant shouting.

"He's always had a temper," Janis sniffed.

"Has he?" Olivia frowned.

"Yes. He's very good at hiding it."

"He must be."

"Or maybe Livs doesn't wind him up quite like you do," Sophie said, slowly sipping on her gin and tonic.

"No, he knows I know what he's really like and that's why he's so angry that I'm here, he doesn't want me to tell Libya."

Olivia looked at Sophie, who firmly shook her head.

"Brian loses his temper sometimes," Faye said. "He'll suddenly go 'AAARGH!', usually when my sister, Flo, comes round, and then goes into his shed, makes something, and comes back with a bird box or a – "

"Lovely," Janis said, deadpan.

"Some people just don't fit well together," Beth suggested.

"We fit together, don't we, babes."

"Yeah, Jim." She smiled benevolently at him, then turned back to Beth. "Maybe you and Mark just clash, like opposite ends of a magnet."

"He's certainly never lost his temper with me," Olivia added.

"Not yet, but you'll see."

"How long were you married?" Sophie asked.

"A year."

"Wow, a whole year?"

"Yeah, I couldn't take it after that, I had to get out."

"Didn't you flirt with your sister's husband?" Olivia said.

"No, he got that all wrong. He's *so* jealous."

Olivia pulled a face. Were they even talking about the same man?

"You mark my words, Lib," Janis warned, "You'll find out what he's like soon enough."

"I don't believe you," Olivia said.

"Me neither," said Sophie.

Beth raised an arm, and Jim did the same.

"You'll see." Janis finished her glass of brandy. "Can I have another? I'm still a little shocked from Mark's brutal attack."

"Help yourself," Sophie said, nodding towards the bar.

"Oh, I'll never find the right bottle. Could you get me one, Libya?"

"It's *Olivia*," Sophie said.

"Oh. Right, Drink?"

Olivia stood up and went to the bar with a confused look on her face.

Sophie followed her. "She's lying," she breathed.

"How do you know?"

"You think I'm not familiar with people lying? I'm a lawyer," Sophie said, rolling her eyes, "I see it all the time.

Everyone has a 'tell', something they do when they're being deceitful, like touch their ear or rub their nose."

"What's Janis's 'tell'?"

"Her mouth moves."

Olivia quietly laughed.

"Massive sense of superiority for no apparent reason," Sophie said, watching her and shaking her head. "She definitely has MCS."

"Oh no! Is that serious?"

"It is for us. Main Character Syndrome, totally believes she should be the centre of attention at all times. She's a hero in her own head. She's up here," Sophie said, raising her hand and drawing an invisible line in the air, "And we're down here. Just take no notice, Liv, she's just a cartoon villain. She wants to stir things up for you and Mark. Best thing to do is just stay happy and smiling. You're good at smiling."

Olivia smiled as she poured brandy into a glass.

Sophie poured herself a very weak gin and tonic, and whispered, "I have your back, Livs. I can be a mean girl when I put my mind to it; I am Sophie, fear my roar!"

"Thanks, Sophs."

"More than welcome, Liv. Let the games begin."

* * *

They let him rant for a while, until he seemed to calm and eventually sit down.

"Well," Tel puffed, raising his eyebrows, "That was certainly a concise rundown of your ex-wife."

"Please don't call her that," Mark said. "I wish I'd never met her, let alone marry her."

"I've seen this type of behaviour before," Brian said, and they both stared at him.

"Faye?" Tel gasped.

Brian laughed. "No, not Faye. Women in the office, nasty types, will say and do anything to get a response and some attention. The secret," he whispered, "is to not react."

"Difficult," Mark said.

"But not impossible."

"I keep imagining my hands around her neck."

"Whatever she says, don't react, think happy thoughts."

"Like my hands around her neck."

"And deflect," said Tel. "Change the subject. Take the attention away from her."

"She'll soon get bored."

Mark took a deep breath. "Nothing but a strait jacket and a gag can stop her, but," he sighed, "We'll give it a go." He stood up. "Best go and save Olivia."

"Once more into the fray, dear chaps," Tel cried, as they headed back downstairs.

* * *

"Were you fat before you got pregnant?" Janis was asking Beth, as the men came back into the room.

"Bloody rude," Sophie said.

"I was just curious."

Beth narrowed her eyes and forced a smile. "Yes, actually. Big and proud."

"And gorgeous," Jim grinned.

"I seem to be able to eat anything and not get fat at all," Janis giggled.

"Oh, poor you," said Faye.

"Everything alright?" Brian asked.

Faye was wearing her 'couldn't be more bored' face. "Yes," she sighed. "Janis was just telling us about how successful she is in business and that she's an independent, self-made woman."

Mark laughed out loud. "Is that the Avon business or the transcription company you started before you got bored of typing? How long did that last now, a week, was it?"

Brian glared at him and slowly drew a flattened hand over his head. Mark snapped his mouth shut and nodded.

"Soph," said Tel, as casually as he could manage, "Could we have a word?"

"Yes. Actually, I wanted a word too."

They walked over to the back lounge.

"Faye?" Brian queried lightly, "Can I borrow you for a minute?"

"What for?"

Brian put on his serious face and Faye stood up.

They also walked into the back lounge.

"Liv," said Mark.

Olivia immediately stood up and followed the others.

Beth nudged Jim and said, "Follow them and report back."

Jim did as he was told.

Beth smiled at Janis. Janis smiled back and said, "Is it something I said?" There was a sparkle in her eye as she said it. She turned in her armchair and shouted, "Can someone get me a drink?"

"Get it yourself!" Mark yelled.

"Charming." She flopped back into her chair. "Service here is terrible, isn't it, Brenda?"

"Nah, it's brilliant. Mark and Olivia are the salt of the earth. I guess it's all down to expectations, Judith"

Janis huffed.

CHAPTER 6

They were all in agreement. A plan had been made.

Sophie didn't have a chance to talk to Tel before they dispersed back to the *Friends* corner, where Jim quickly whispered in Beth's ear.

"Sorry, darling" Olivia whispered to Mark as they walked back.

He reached out and squeezed her hand. "We can do this."

"Teamwork."

Janis, pleased to have her audience back, immediately picked up her empty glass. "Any takers?" she asked, waving it around.

"Ooh," Faye cried, "I like your shoes."

Janis lifted a foot above the coffee table to show them off. "They're Jimmy Choo's."

"Does Jimmy mind?" Faye asked.

"Does he mind what?"

"You wearing his shoes?"

Beth snorted.

"It's a brand," Janis sneered. "You're probably not familiar with it."

"I mostly favour Louis Vuitton or Manolo Blahnik myself," Beth said.

Janis cracked a fake smile.

"I shop at Gee-or-gee," said Faye.

"Oh?" Janis said, "I'm not familiar with them."

"George at Asda," Faye laughed. "Oh, except I saw some lovely boots in Selfridges the other week, lovely they were. I took a photo and sent it to Brian."

Brian grinned smugly.

"Hoping to get them for Christmas," she grinned.

"You'll have to wait and see, lass."

Janis, bored now, held her empty glass in the air and wobbled it a bit. "Drink?"

"Let's see the other shoe," Faye said.

"It's the same, it's a *pair* of shoes."

"Just show me."

Huffing, Janis lifted her other foot.

"So your legs *do* move," Faye laughed. "I'll have another Prosecco while you're up."

Beth grinned over at Faye, who winked back at her.

Janis did a big huff and got to her feet, lifting her chin as she turned and sashayed up to the bar in her tight, red dress. When she turned and saw no one was watching her, she slammed the glass down on the counter, which drew no attention at all.

"What's going on?" Beth whispered to them.

"We have a battle plan to stop Janis causing trouble," Brian whispered back.

"Deflect and distract," Tel said.

Beth pulled a face and shrugged.

"Whatever she says, change the subject and don't react."

"That'll be easy," Beth said, "Woman's as boring as a cardboard box, me this and me that, and oh, aren't I so wonderful and perfect and – "

"Shh, she's coming."

Janis returned with a single glass.

"Prosecco?" Faye asked.

"Oh, sorry, I forgot."

"I'll get you one, lass."

"Ta, Bri."

"So what's the plan?" Janis asked.

Jim sucked in air and gasped, "You know about the plan?"

Beth flicked his ear.

"Ow, babes! What was that for?"

"Loose lips."

Jim touched his mouth and frowned.

"Plan for what, Jennifer?" Beth asked.

"The plan for Christmas Eve," Janis elaborated. "Any entertainment? Male strippers, Santa turning up and whipping all his clothes off, a mad splurge of Christmas presents?"

"Bugger," Brian said, staring out of the window at the snow falling outside, "All the presents we weren't supposed to get are in the caravan." He turned to Tel. "We might have to take a trek out there before it gets too dark."

"Not me," said Tel, "I didn't get anyone anything, as per my WhatsApp message."

"That nobody got," said Faye.

"I need some clothes," Sophie said, and Tel groaned.

"It's okay if you haven't got me anything," Janis said magnanimously, "I know you weren't expecting me."

"No," Mark growled, "We weren't."

Brian moved his hand over his head. Janis noticed. Brian scratched the back of his head.

"Do you have headlice?" she asked.

Brian was momentarily dumbfounded.

"You don't have pubic ones, do you?" Mark snapped.

Janis's mouth fell open.

"Don't give it if you can't take it," he added.

"So," Olivia said brightly, "We could play cards?"

"Dull," Janis sighed.

"Listen to music and have a dance?"

"Spare me, *pur-lease*."

"See who can stand outside in the snow the longest without dying," Mark said. "You first, Janis."

"Anyone would think you didn't like me," she grinned.

"I don't, I absolutely – "

Brian's hand flew over his head again.

" – think nothing of you at all," Mark said instead. "Not ever. Completely indifferent. Drink, Bri?"

"I won't say no."

"Try," said Faye.

"Do you have a problem with your arm?" Janis asked. "You keep throwing it over your head. Do you have Tourette tics as well as headlice?"

"Tourette's!" Mark suddenly cried, slapping his leg and grimacing. "Why didn't I think of that! Janis, I have Tourette's and you're a – "

"Mark!"

"Yes, darling?"

"Can I get you another drink?"

"Well, I was just getting up, but that would be lovely, darling."

"No problem, darling."

"Darling, darling, darling," Janis sang.

Mark drew in breath to sing an altogether different word, when he caught Brian's warning face and Tel's tiny shake of the head. "I'll help you, darling," he said, getting up. "Anyone else?"

Brian glanced at his watch and cried, "Whey-hey!" He hurried over to the bar and reached for the bell, ringing it with great enthusiasm. "I know we've all been casually sipping diluted drinks all afternoon," he boomed, "Except for Janis, who's had a spiced wine and two brandies since she arrived."

Janis raised her glass in response.

"It gives me great pleasure to announce that it's *almost* five o'clock and we can officially start drinking in earnest."

They cheered.

Janis said, "I simply must tell you about the time that Mark and I – "

"Got anything new for the caravan this year, Tel?" Brian shouted over, as he attempted to pour a pint.

"We got one of those folding washing-up bowls," Sophie laughed. "Honestly, it's a *life-changer*."

"Oh, we've got one of those," Faye said. "First time Brian used it he said, 'There's not much room for water in here'. He hadn't unfolded it!"

They laughed, except for Janis, who said, "As I was saying –"

"Had the car mapped," Tel said.

"Really?" Brian looked at his pint. Three-quarters foam. He frowned. Olivia picked up another glass and pushed him out of the way. "Notice any difference in performance, Tel?"

"Goes like a bullet and uses less petrol. You should have yours done."

"I might."

"If you touch anything on that car it'll fall to pieces," Faye said. "It's only the muck and the rust holding it together."

"Bit like our old caravan," Brian laughed.

"When Mark and I got into a fight in the middle of Birmingham –"

"My home town," Faye cried.

"Yes, I gathered from the accent," Janis sneered.

"Innit," said Faye.

"The Bullring was packed and Mark was being a complete –"

"I love the Bullring," Faye sighed. "There's so much choice, and it's all indoors, and there's so many places to eat, and," she added, glancing over at Brian, "they do really nice boots."

"Fascinating," said Janis, rolling her eyes.

"I've been to the Bullring," Beth said. "Back when I was young and unburdened." She gave a heavy sigh.

"You okay, babes?"

"Yeah, babes, just reminiscing about the time I could walk unaided and see my own feet."

Janis, bored, huffed and stood up. "I'm just popping to the loo, don't talk about me while I'm gone."

"We barely know you," Sophie drawled, "What on earth would we talk about?"

Janis sashayed out of the room, pausing and turning provocatively in the doorway. Nobody was watching her. The red smile slipped from her face.

"Where's she going?" Mark asked, bringing over the drinks. Then his eyes lit up with hope and happiness. "Is she leaving? Tell me she's leaving."

"She's gone to the loo."

Mark's face fell, then he looked alarmed. "Did I lock the door to the flat?" he gasped, racing from the room. "Oh God, she'll be into everything; private mail, tax returns, everything."

He caught her halfway up the stairs.

"You've literally just walked past the door that says Toilets on it," he said.

"Have I?" It was hard for Janis to look innocent, but she gave it a good go. "Are there no toilets upstairs?"

"Only in the guest rooms."

"I'm a guest."

"An unwanted one."

"You don't have to be so mean, Mark."

He pointed at the door at the bottom of the stairs, and Janis stomped down, pushed by him and went inside. Mark stood in the hallway with his arms across his chest, waiting. He wondered if maybe a baby gate would be a good idea to stop people – primarily his snoopy ex-wife – from going upstairs, though they'd not really had a problem with it before. Then he started to think about a wire stretched across the top step. He shook his head and took a deep, calming breath. He'd just have to keep a close eye on her.

She came out and was startled to find him still standing there. Then a smile spread across her face. She glanced at the door to the lounge and took a step towards him.

"Don't even bother, Janis."

She took a step closer until they were face to face at the bottom of the stairs, too close for comfort, her breasts like a marshmallow-filling in a human sandwich. Mark stepped back, but she followed him, pushing her mounds of flesh against him. "You're wasting your time, Janis?"

"Am I?" she breathed, running her hands up his chest. "Seems to me you might be a little … excited?"

"That's my phone."

There was a cough, and Brian bounded towards them with some haste.

"Need the loo," he boomed, pushing between them and winking at Mark. "Liv wants you."

"Cheers, Bri."

Mark took the opportunity to extricate himself and hurry back into the lounge. Janis tottered along behind him, her chest bouncing like semi-set jelly in front of her.

Someone had changed the music from Christmas Carols to disco music. Faye and Sophie were stood up, dancing on the spot and singing along – neither of them could hold a note.

"Oh my God," Janis sighed, "Kill me now."

"With pleasure," Mark said, catching a firm look from Tel. "If you don't like it you can always leave."

"In this?" she snapped, turning to look through the window at the snowstorm raging outside.

She screamed.

Everyone turned to look at Janis, and then followed her wide-eyed gaze to the window.

There was a face outside in the dark, peering in at them.

A horribly familiar face, wearing a woolly hat and covered in snow.

"You have *got* to be barkin' kidding me!" Mark gasped.

"Is that – ?"

"It is!"

"Or it could be a very lifelike snowman?"

The lifelike snowman brought something up to the side of his head. Olivia's phone rang. Without looking, without tearing her eyes away from the face at the window, she picked it up off the coffee table and answered it.

"Can I come in?" Richard whined. "It's freezing and I'm so cold."

"What are you doing here?"

"I had nowhere else to go." Outside, he pulled a sad face. "Oh, and there's someone else out here as well."

"It's not daddy, is it?"

The sad face frowned. "No, I never thought to ask him. Do you want me to call – ?"

"No!"

Richard turned his head sideways. "I'm not sure who it is. They seem to be wrapped up in some sort of padding. Maybe they're a Christmas present for someone."

Jim gulped.

"Can I come in?" Richard pleaded. "I'm cold and hungry and very, very sad."

Olivia stared at Mark. "We can't leave him out there."

"We can. He got here, he can get himself back."

"Well, *yours* is here," she snapped, glaring at Janis, "Might as well let Richard in and have a full deck. Has anyone else invited an ex for Christmas and not told me?"

Jim sucked his lips in.

Mark huffed.

Olivia went to the front door, just as Brian came back from the toilet.

"S'up?" he asked all the startled faces.

"You'll never believe it," Faye said.

"Believe what?"

"You'll see."

Brian sat down.

There was a blast of cold air, followed by the thud of a door being slammed shut.

Richard stepped into the room wearing a long black coat, buttoned up to his neck. It was dirty and, they soon realised, as the cold air wafted through, that it absolutely stank. He pulled the grungy hat off his head, revealing unruly, greasy hair, and said, "Hello, everyone."

There was a mumbled reply as they all wafted their hands in front of their faces.

Olivia came into the room, followed by someone shuffling along inside a sleeping bag.

A young girl pulled a hand out and shyly waved at them

all. "Hi," she squeaked. "Sorry about this, I didn't know where else to go."

"Jools?" Sophie gasped.

"No," Faye breathed, instantly looking at Beth.

Mark's mouth fell open and he, too, looked at Beth.

Brian said, "Blimey."

"Sorry, Jim," Julie said, "It was too cold in the shed."

"You have to let the heating run for – " Mark snapped his mouth shut.

Olivia glared at him.

Everyone else continued to stare at Beth.

Beth stared at Julie. Her eyes turned slowly to Jim. "What the bleedin' hell is *she* doing here?"

"She had nowhere to go," he cried. "I didn't know she was coming. I didn't know what to do. It was Mark who said she could stay in the shed."

"Throw me under the bus, why don't you?"

"You knew she was out there?" Olivia gasped. "And you didn't tell me?"

Beth took a deep breath and yelled, "WHAT THE HELL ARE YOU PLAYING AT, JIM? WHY IS SHE HERE?"

"I … I … I … "

"I'm so sorry," Julie kept saying.

"Now *this* is my kind of Christmas," Janis howled, picking up another pork pie.

"I need a word with me 'usband," Beth yelled.

"Go right ahead," Janis said, "Don't let us stop you."

"You'll 'ave to leave the room on account of …" She waved her hands over her baby bulge.

"Of course," Mark said, jumping up. "We'll just be in the other room if you need us."

"For body disposal or evidence cleanup," Janis cackled.

They hurried towards the back lounge, except for Janis, who remained sitting with a smile on her face, merrily chomping on her pie. Brian went back and said, "Come on, give them some space."

"No, I want to watch."

Brian leaned down to her ear and growled, "You can either get up and walk, or I'm going to pick you up throw you over my shoulder."

Janis turned wide eyes up towards him and, with a huff, stood up.

Richard and Julie, not knowing what else to do, followed everyone else, Julie shuffling along in her sleeping bag. Richard got distracted by the bar full of bottles and staggered behind the counter with a big smile.

Jim started to scramble to his feet.

"Not you, Jim," Beth hissed, and Jim gave a little whimper.

CHAPTER 7

The argument started and quickly escalated from angry hissing to full-on yelling.

"Rhubarb," Faye said, as they sat around the big table in the back lounge. "Rhubarb, rhubarb, rhubarb."

"Are you hungry?" Olivia asked.

"It's what they do in films to pretend everyone's talking. Rhubarb, rhubarb."

In the other room, Beth was doing most of the shouting and Jim just made squeaky noises. At one point she yelled, "GIVE ME SOMETHING TO THROW AT YOU! NO, NOT A BLOODY CUSHION, SOMETHING HEAVY WITH SPIKES ON IT!"

"Rhubarb, rhubarb," Olivia said. "Oh, this is terrible. She shouldn't be stressed in her condition."

"She could explode," said Janis.

Sophie gripped Tel's arm. He soothingly shook his head.

"It's hot in here," said Julie, leaning against the bar.

"Unzip yourself from the cocoon then," said Brian.

"Oh yeah." Julie wriggled a little and let the bag slip down to her feet. She kicked it to the side. Olivia tutted and retrieved it from the floor, hanging it over a chair to dry. Julie unzipped her padded jacket.

"Is that a crop top?" Sophie asked in amazement.

"Yeah, I got it from the market last week."

"You're fully prepared for Arctic temperatures then."

Tel glanced down at Julie's shredded jeans. "Were you attacked by a dog on the way here?"

"No," she laughed. "All jeans come like this."

"From the recycle bins outside Tesco's?" Janis laughed.

"No." She frowned, then beamed again. "Can I have a drink? I'm a bit thirsty."

Mark raised an arm towards the kitchen door at the end of the bar and said, "Tea, coffee, water, help yourself, just don't leave a mess or our chef will hunt you down and inflict pain."

Julie squelched away in her soggy trainers.

An increased wave of yelling came from the other room. They winced at some of the words being used.

"I hope she doesn't kill him," Faye said.

Brian suddenly gasped, "There's a sharp knife on the counter!"

"Oh my God," Olivia cried.

"Oh dear," said Janis, looking down at her glass, "It appears I've run out of drink. Could you get me one, Mark?"

Mark threw both arms towards the front lounge. "Not right this minute!"

"I'll get it myself then, shall I?"

They all started chanting, "Rhubarb, rhubarb."

"Not together," Brian hissed, "We're not cheering on a football game."

Janis stood up, huffing, and wriggled over to the back bar. She heard a clink of glass from the front bar and poked her head round the partition. Richard, oblivious to the war of words going on in front of him, was pouring himself another drink. She stepped up next to him, wincing at the smell that hung around him like a sour cloud, and watched him sip from the glass, pull a face, and lift the bottle to read the label.

"I don't recommend the cherry brandy," he said, as she reached for the Courvoisier.

He grabbed a yellow bottle from the collection on the shelf and poured it into the same glass as the cherry brandy. He sipped the orange liquid, gagged, read the label, and said, "Advocaat is terrible."

"Do you intend to try them all?" Janis asked.

"As many as I can before Olivia stops me, or I slip into an

alcoholic coma, whichever comes first."

Beth was still shouting from her prone position on the sofa. Jim was trying to both soothe her and avoid all the missiles she was lobbing at him; coasters, Christmas ornaments, a glittery garland, her slippers.

"Who are you anyway?" Janis asked, filling her glass almost to the top.

"I'm Richard, Olivia's husband. Well, reluctant *ex*-husband."

"How interesting." She held out her fingers. "I'm Janis, Mark's reluctant *ex*-wife."

Richard briefly shook her painted talons, just as Beth started lobbing the contents of her handbag at Jim one by one.

"Why are you here?" Richard asked Janis, neatly ducking a mascara tube, which twanged against a bottle of whisky and landed in Janis's blonde, coiffured hair.

"I was bored," she shrugged, picking it out. "Thought I'd find myself a little Christmas entertainment."

Richard smiled, pouring the contents of another bottle into the same glass as the cherry brandy and the advocaat. "Me too," he said.

They raised their glasses in a toast. Janis sipped, a glint in her eye. Richard gagged, tears in his.

* * *

The yelling continued unabated.

"Let's go upstairs," Mark said. "We shouldn't be listening to this."

They hurried into the front lounge, smiling awkwardly as they raced by the arguing couple and into the hallway. Mark, spotting Richard and Janis behind the bar, said, "Come on!"

"We were just getting acquainted," Janis said, stroking the top of Richard's arm. Richard blindly slapped her hand away. Janis squeaked in alarm. Richard said, "Sorry, I thought the rat had come back to chew on my coat."

"You got the rat bit right," Mark said, urging them out.

Richard grabbed a bottle of wine and a fresh glass as he went.

"Mark!" Beth growled, and he froze to the spot. "Do you have a gun so I can shoot my philandering, can't-keep-it-in-his-trousers, lowlife, soon-to-be ex-husband?"

Mark quickly patted his body. "Not on me, no."

"A knife then?" she screamed, "So I can cut the bloody thing off!"

Mark quickly snatched the knife off the wooden cutting board on the counter.

Janis had come to a standstill in front of him, loitering and listening. "All men are the same," she tutted at Beth.

Mark rolled the knife in his hand. With great effort, he used his free hand to push her into the hallway. He started pulling the door closed behind him and, in the decreasing gap, he said, "In his defence, Beth, he didn't know Julie was going to turn up like that, she said she had nowhere to go."

"All men are the same," Janis cried from the hallway. "Don't trust them, they're savages!"

Mark quickly slammed the door shut and herded Janis and a swaying Richard up the stairs.

* * *

"Look at nothing, touch nothing," Mark snapped at Janis as they entered their private living quarters.

Janis dragged a painted talon over some letters on the hallway table. Mark nudged her forward.

"The star of the show has arrived," Sophie sighed, from her vantage point in the living room, "

"The Janis Show," Brian chuckled over his pint of beer, "Staaaaaring Janis, as Janis."

"Janis World, the Musical," Tel laughed, swigging back the remains of his whisky.

"Careful," Sophie told him, "You get very loose-lipped when you're drunk."

Tel raised a finger to his mouth and strummed his full

lips.

Sophie leaned into Olivia as Janis slowly made her way down the hallway towards them. "You see how she walks?" she whispered, "Like she's sashaying up to the podium to collect her Oscar? In her head she imagines cameras following her every move, and the world is perched on the edge of their seats waiting to see what she does next, hanging on every word she speaks." Olivia giggled. "See her turning her head, looking at herself in the mirror? She can barely tear her eyes away from her gorgeousness. We're so lucky to have her," Sophie said, cracking up. "And now, turning her head the other way, acknowledging the imaginary crowds all around her, clamouring for photographs."

"Stop it," Olivia giggled.

"See her arm twitch there? She's desperate to give a royal wave to her make-believe fans. No one has ever been more amazing than her. She is ... *magnificent*."

They fell against each other, laughing.

Richard staggered down the hallway and threw himself down into an armchair, grinning at the bottle and glass in his hands. His face fell when he noticed there was a cork standing between him and the lovely liquid.

As Mark walked past him he caught a whiff. "You want to take your coat off, Dick?" he said, "It bloody pongs."

"No, no, I'm fine."

"But you're sweating."

"I ... I've caught a chill."

Richard shuffled in his seat and Brian cried, "Ah, the rancid aroma of distant farts."

"I'd have said dirty feet," said Tel.

"Rotten eggs," said Sophie.

"Cooked cabbage that's gone off," Olivia said, holding her nose.

Faye, who had no sense of smell, threw her arms out and cried, "Fresh air!"

"You sit next to him then," Sophie said.

"No, I'm alright here," she laughed, snuggling up to Brian.

Olivia liberally sprayed air freshener over Richard, who coughed as he struggled to take the cork out of the bottle with his teeth.

"I'll dig out the VapoRub to put under our noses," Mark said. "Top up, Tel?"

Everyone raised their glasses, except for Janis, who had a full glass and was busy wandering around the room running a finger over shelves and surfaces.

Olivia got to her knees beside a sideboard and said, "I'm afraid we don't have much alcohol up here."

"Why would you, when you have a whole pub downstairs," Brian laughed.

"Do you have a corkscrew?" Richard asked.

From her position on the floor, Olivia handed Mark a corkscrew. He stood looking at it for a moment before tossing it to Richard. In his head he saw it plunging into Richard's chest and Richard, mad from the pain, jumped up and pulled Janis's head off. The bloody scene disappeared when Olivia handed up a bottle of whisky and a tall bottle of flavoured vodka. "There's sherry if anyone wants it?"

"Why, are we characters in an Agatha Christie novel," Tel laughed.

Olivia scrambled to her feet. She glanced around the room, at Faye and Brian and Tel packed tightly together on the sofa, Sophie in one armchair and Richard in another, and Janis, who was lifting a finger from the TV set in the corner and tutting.

"Our cleaner couldn't make it in today," Olivia said.

"Just today?" drawled Janis, heading towards a bookcase.

"Shush, I think they've stopped," Faye suddenly said, and everyone held their breath and listened, except for Richard, who popped the cork on his wine bottle and cried, "Yay!"

"They've probably wore themselves out," Sophie said.

"Or they're making up," said Faye.

"Or she's killed him," Tel said.

Wide-eyed, Faye said, "Should we go down and check on them? Make sure they're okay?"

They listened again. Silence. They nervously looked at each other.

"Where's Julie?" Olivia suddenly asked.

* * *

They raced down the stairs. Richard stayed in the flat, drinking, and Janis was diligently running a finger over surfaces and pulling an array of faces. In a rugby scrum they surged down the hallway towards the kitchen. Faye let out a scream as they hurried by the Door Under the Stairs that led down to the basement, and pressed herself against the far wall, fully expecting the door to fly open and Something Horrible to drag her away.

They hurtled into the kitchen and found Julie standing at a cluttered counter drinking tea and chomping on toast and peanut butter. She jumped as they burst through the door and stood there, surveying the mess.

"Has there been an explosion?" Mark gasped, noting the wet teabags, spilled sugar, pools of milk, the open peanut butter, the catering tub of margarine, spoons, knives and, oddly, a carving knife.

Julie grinned proudly. "I get things done quick. You should hire me."

"I'm a bit peckish myself," Brian said, holding his beer and staring inside the open fridge.

"We're ordering takeaways tonight," Olivia beamed. "Nobody wants to cook on Christmas – "

"Takeaways won't deliver this far out in this weather," said Mark.

"Oh." She thought for a minute. "There's pizzas in the freezer."

"Your chef uses frozen pizzas?" Tel laughed.

"For the kids who won't eat unfamiliar food. He jazzes them up a bit. I guess we could – "

"This freezer?" Julie said, rushing over to the big one at the far end of the kitchen and throwing it open. "Wow, you've got a lot of stuff in here!" She pulled out a whole, frozen lobster. "Can you cook this in the microwave?"

"No," Mark said. "Now clean up after yourself."

Olivia turned and hurried back down the hallway to the lounge door, where she put her ear against the wood.

Faye joined her, as did Brian and Tel, their four heads fighting for space. Sophie stood at the bottom of the stairs, gripping onto the banister rail. "She hasn't gone into labour, has she? Tel, we really need to talk, I have something – "

"Shhh," hissed Tel. "Can you hear anything, Bri?"

"I don't know why he's got his ear against the door," Faye said, "He can't hear me half the time."

"Selective hearing," Brian breathed, and Tel stifled a laugh.

"I can't hear anything," Olivia said.

"Me neither," said Brian.

"Maybe it's just women's voices you can't hear," Tel said.

Brian gave a heavy sigh. "I can hear Flo well enough."

"Fair point."

Mark prised Brian away and thudded the side of his head against the door.

"You can come in if you want," Beth called from the other side.

Gingerly, they turned the handle and entered the lounge. It was a wreck of Christmas decorations, personal items from a handbag, scattered cushions and tossed beer mats. Two chairs had been toppled, and a curtain pole sat at a jaunty angle above a window

Beth was straightening the faux fur blanket around her legs, her hair in disarray. There was mascara around her red eyes, but she seemed calm.

Jim was sitting in the armchair next to her, his face in his hands.

Beth said, "We've thrashed it out."

"I'm such an idiot!" Jim wailed.

"Yes, you are," Beth told him, "But I still love you, for my sins. So do the babies, who will come out with quite an extensive vobacularly ... vobacularly?" She looked at Tel, who said, "Vocabulary."

"Yeah, that. Anyway, it's sorted now."

Jim, his head hanging low, reached out a hand to grasp one of hers. Beth squeezed it and looked over at Olivia. "It's okay, Liv, the girl can stay, if that's alright with you?"

"Of course!" Olivia said, throwing her hands in the air, "The more the merrier. Come one, come all! In fact, Mark, nip outside and see if you can grab people in off the street. We've only five guest rooms but that doesn't matter, we can get at least three to a bed, more if they're small or particularly thin."

Mark put his hands on her shoulders and guided her to an armchair. Brian rushed to behind the bar to pour gin into a glass. He glanced briefly at the lemon on the chopping board and, seeing no knife, decided against unnecessary accoutrements. He rushed back to Olivia, saying, "Knock this back, lass."

Olivia did, and gasped, holding her throat while her eyes bulged. "No tonic," she wheezed.

"Ooh, sorry." Brian ran to the bar for a bottle of tonic, opening it as he ran back and sloshing some into Olivia's glass.

"Do you know how much planning went into making Christmas perfect for everyone?" she croaked.

"We do," Faye said softly, sitting on the arm of her chair and reaching down for her hand.

"Sorry," said Tel. "We really appreciate your efforts, the pub looks lovely."

"We didn't mean to spoil things," Beth said.

"Not you," Olivia said, reaching forward to pat Beth's hand. "Not any of you. It's *them*."

Mark looked around and said, "Where are *them*." He stiffened, then jumped up and ran into the hallway, his feet thudding quickly up the stairs.

He found Richard still in the armchair, hugging his half

empty bottle of wine to his chest and smiling.

Janis was on her knees in front of the sideboard, surrounded by folders and papers, *their* folders and papers. "Olivia's maiden name is Olgivy?" she gasped. "The Olgivys of Bath, who made a fortune from limestone quarries?"

Mark bent down and snatched the papers out of her hand. "Get downstairs!" he snarled. "And you!" he threw at Richard, who stirred in the armchair and struggled to stand up.

"She must be *minted*!" Janis laughed, as Mark herded them both down the hallway. "And you begrudge me a lousy twenty grand?"

"It's Liv's money, not mine."

"Just ask her for twenty grand."

"For you? No chance."

"She's got *loads* in her bank account, I saw the statements. She won't even *notice* twenty grand."

They reached the top of the stairs. Mark suddenly stood stock still, not daring to take another step, as a thought blew up in his mind: *One good push and it will all be over*. It shook him. He forced himself to take a deep, calming breath. He wasn't that man.

Janis started down the stairs, muttering, "The Olgivys, the bloody Olgivys! No wonder you latched onto her."

"Shut up, Janis." He wasn't that man.

"It all makes sense now. The buck-toothed woman has *money*."

"Don't judge by your own standards, Janis, we're not all money-grabbing little – "

Richard slipped his footing on a step and gripped onto the banister rail. The bottle he was clutching fell through the rails and smashed onto the floor below. One of his feet booted Janis in the posterior and she also slipped. It was only Brian, who had come rushing out of the lounge at the sound of breaking glass, the others close behind him, who stopped her toppling down the last three steps.

Mark groaned in disappointment.

A step below him, still hanging onto the banister and kicking his feet for leverage, Richard cried, "Has*h* anyone *s*heen my wine?"

* * *

Julie, like a robot vacuum cleaner, came rushing out of the kitchen and quickly cleared up the smashed wine bottle in the hallway, after which she busied herself in the kitchen, throwing several pizzas into the two industrial ovens and chopping salad from the fridge.

"I need a wee," Beth said, and Jim and the three women helped her to her feet and hovered around her with their arms outstretched as she slowly shuffled to the toilet.

The men sat down. Janis sat on the arm of Richard's armchair, until Brian pulled at the arm of his stinky coat and made him get up. Brian sat down with a sigh of relief. Richard crumbled to the floor in front of Janis, now seated on the sofa.

"Good Christmas so far," Tel grinned, to break the ice.

"Yes," said Mark, "We put a lot of effort into it."

"So Olivia said," Janis drawled. "Can't see it myself."

"That'll be the dark veil of evil over your eyes," said Mark.

"Shut up."

"I will, the minute you've gone."

She tutted.

"It's like *The Nightmare Before Christmas*, isn't it," said Tel.

"I'd have said *Krampus*, myself," Brian said. "What's next on the agenda, Mark? Murdering snowmen? A giant Santa Claus intent on killing us all?"

"That's tomorrow," Tel sniggered.

Brian sighed. "I suppose all we have left to do today is … eat and drink."

"I'll drink to that!" Richard cried. He drummed both palms on the coffee table. "Jus*h*t line them up here and I'll … ooh, went a little dizzy there."

"Are you okay, Roger?" Janis asked in a syrupy voice. "Is there anything I can do for you?"

"Seriously?" Mark asked. "Does he look like he has money?"

"Rich people, especially the aristocracy, are often bonkers," Janis said. "Howard Huges was a recluse. Elon Musk has Asperger's. Roger could just lack any …" She waved her red taloned hands over him. "… fashion sense."

"He stinks!"

"Rich people have a very relaxed attitude to personal hygiene. He's got all the markers."

"You're so wrong," Mark laughed. "He literally has nothing."

Janis went back to looking bored as she sipped on her brandy. Richard's head thudded down onto the coffee table.

Tel leaned forward in his seat. "Actually, Bri, there is something we need to do."

"Oh yeah? What's that?"

"We need some clothes and, in the interest of festive cheer and the continuation of your marriage to the delightful Faye, might I suggest that you fetch her Christmas presents from the caravan?"

Brian's eyes widened. "Blimey, I'd forgotten all about that!"

"It's just that a sobbing woman on Christmas morning might upset the status quo."

"Status Quo are coming?" Janis said, her interest piqued. "That's impressive."

"Yeah, Francis Rossi and his mates are popping in for a pint and a gig later."

Janis sat up straight. "Really?"

"No."

"Oh. *Swine.*"

Grinning, Mark turned to Tel. "What did you get Sophie for Christmas?"

"Nothing."

A pause. A shriek of laughter from Janis.

"What, nothing at all?"

"We agreed not to indulge in the excesses of Christmas and to put half each towards a holiday abroad next year instead."

Brian laughed. "And you believed her?"

"Of course."

"Fool," said Mark, and Janis laughed even louder.

Tel's eyes grew big. "You mean – ?"

"They *say* not to get them anything," Brian said. "What they *really* mean is, if you don't get them something fabulous they'll make your life a misery for the next six months."

"You're kidding."

"Does this marriage-worn face look like it's kidding?"

"Well, I can't see most of it for hair."

Brian sighed heavily. "It was a hard lesson to learn, I can tell you."

"Christ, what am I going to do? Its Christmas Eve and all the shops are shut!"

Brian and Mark sombrely shook their heads.

Janis sighed, "I'm so bored."

Richard remained face down on the coffee table.

The women came back and eased Beth onto the sofa next to Janis, who moved to the far end. Jim sat between them, holding Beth's hand. The others huddled together on the opposite sofa.

Brian stood up. "Right, I'm just nipping outside. I may be some time."

"Where are you going?" Faye asked.

"Just for ... a stroll."

"A stroll? Have you lost your marbles? Tel, take that beer off him, he's obviously had enough."

"Beer?" Richard said, lifting his head. "I don't mind if I do."

"I just need to check ..." Brian's mind went completely blank.

"The caravan," Tel said, also standing up. "We just need to go and check the caravans."

"What for?" asked Faye.

"See if they're still there," Brian said, "See if they've caved in under the weight of snow, if they're leaking, if there's any more exes hiding in there."

"God forbid," Mark gasped.

"I'll second that," Olivia said, taking a gulp from her glass.

"Don't forget that list of things I need bringing back, Tel," Sophie said.

He tapped his jeans pocket. "Got it here."

"Oh," Faye cried, "Clothes! Can you bring some back for me, Brian?"

"What do you want?"

"Everything."

He stopped zipping up his jacket from the coat stand by the bar. "I can't bring everything back, Faye."

"Why not?"

"Everything out of the wardrobes and cupboards?"

"And the stuff in the middle drawers. Oh, and my slippers, and my toiletry bag."

"Christ, woman, I might as well tow the caravan up to the car park."

"Ooh, could you do that?"

"Yeah, as soon as I've dug it out of the snowdrift and attached the huskies."

"Thanks, Bri."

He eyeballed her. "What, *specifically*, do you want, Faye?"

"Just some clothes and toiletries. Actually," she pondered, "forget the toiletries, Liv stocks a good guest bathroom, but bring my slippers, and my hair dryer, and – "

"Let's go!" Brian cried, slapping Tel on his padded shoulder.

"I'm not feeling very welcome," Janis suddenly said.

"That'll be because of your cold, dead heart," Mark said.

"Shut up."

"Won't."

"Stop bickering," Sophie said, "I think we've had enough domestic disputes for one day, don't you?"

"Sorry," said Beth, fidgeting to find a comfortable position for her bump.

"It's okay," Olivia said. "It's fine, honestly."

"Only bit of fun we've had so far," Janis said.

"Fun?" Faye gasped.

Janis continued, "Entertainment here is unacceptably poor."

"Then leave!" Mark snapped.

Janis tipped her almost empty glass towards the snow splattering against the window and screeched, "I can't, can I!"

"You'd end up like Jack Nicholson at the end of *The Shining*," said Faye.

"Don't give me ideas," Mark growled.

"Deep breaths, darling, deep breaths."

Tel and Brian started wrapping scarves around their necks and pulling on woolly hats and gloves, Mark went over. "A kid left his sledge in the back garden yesterday, you could use that."

Tel looked at Brian, who shrugged. "We hadn't planned to do any sledding while we're out there, in the howling wind, zero temperatures and blinding sheets of snow."

Mark raised an eyebrow. "To bring the presents back," he hissed, "Unless you're planning to use a big red sack to drag them through the drifts."

"Good thinking, Batman."

"I have my moments." He stepped closer to Tel and whispered, "I'll talk to Liv while you're gone, she's bound to have gone overboard on gifts, despite Tel's unsent message, I'll see if she has anything suitable for you to give Sophie."

"Cheers, Mark, appreciate it."

"Go out the back for the sledge before you head off to the caravans." He looked solemn as he shook their gloved hands. "Good luck, chaps."

The three of them moved towards the back patio windows, which opened outwards. It took all of them to push one of the doors open against the howling wind and build-up of snow. The wind and snow raced inside, making everyone in the *Friends* corner shout about the cold.

Brian and Tel forced their way outside and pushed against the door as Mark pulled from inside, finally closing it. A gust of wind hit their backs and pressed them both against the glass. The eyeballs on their smooshed faces peered at Mark, and at Faye, Sophie, Olivia and Janis standing behind him.

Faye waved sadly. "Bye, Bri," she mouthed.

"Maybe you should have gone with them," Sophie said to Mark.

"Why?"

"To drag their frozen bodies back," Janis cackled. "Ooh, empty glass, time for a top-up methinks."

The eyeballs on the other side of the doors looked at each other, then their gloved hands prised them away from the glass. Another gust of wind blew them, skidding and arm waving, across the patio.

"SLEDGE IS OVER THERE!" Mark yelled, pointing.

They couldn't hear him, but Brian spotted a length of orange rope sticking out from underneath a table, picked it up and pulled it. A plastic orange sledge appeared from beneath the snow.

They started trudging through the snow.

CHAPTER 8

Outside

"Follow my tracks," Brian yelled through the howling gale.

"What?"

Brian pointed down at his feet as he dragged them through deep snow. Tel put up a thumb and stepped into his grooves. Brian turned and dragged out another step. Something caught under his foot and he fell like a padded log, face first in the snow.

Tel crunched to his side. "You okay, Bri?"

Brian lifted his frosted face. "What?"

Tel bent to help him to his feet, but it was like trying to lift an immovable object. Brian struggled up on his own.

"I'll lead the way," Tel shouted.

"What?"

Tel waved an arm. "Herd 'em up and move 'em out."

"*What*?"

Tel started walking ahead. Brian got his feet caught in the orange rope and fell backwards. Tel turned, wondering what the heavy thump was, and slipped, landing on his back next to Brian.

Brian lifted his head. "Having fun yet?"

Tel, partially immersed in the snow drift up the side of the pub, shook his head.

They carried on.

The light from the pub was quickly lost as snow surged around them. It was pitch black, except for the pin-pricks of white that attacked their exposed faces.

Their noses were frozen before they'd even crossed the car park. Their feet lost all feeling just inside the gate to the camping field, and their fingers tingled in their gloves as they trudged, slowly and with great effort, through the blizzard.

The wind blasted off the open field, forcing them to walk at an angle with a hand at the side of their faces. The snow engulfed them, they could only just make out the shapes of the hedges around the nearest caravan area.

"Do you come here often?" Tel shouted as they plodded on, trying to keep his sense of panic to a minimum.

"No," Brian yelled back, "But I'm thinking of incorporating it into my annual exercise routine, assuming we survive."

"Positive thinking, Bri."

"All thinking stopped a while back, Tel."

They walked by the entrance to the first caravan area. Up ahead, they could just make out the shadow of the hedges around the second.

"Can't see the caravans," Tel yelled.

"They're white," yelled Brian.

"Can't see the cars either."

"I doubt anyone would steal them. They're out there somewhere, keep your eyes peeled."

"Eyes are frozen open. Should have brought walking sticks to counteract the wind, my back's killing me."

"You still have feeling in your back?"

"Yes, don't you?"

"Only thing I can feel are my teeth."

They trudged on.

"You've got icicles in your beard and eyebrows, Bri."

"It's my cool new image, do you think Faye will like it?"

"Only if she's into abominable snowmen. I think I can see the entrance."

Brian splatted face down into the snow again. Tel, knowing he couldn't help, stood waiting for him to get up, shivering in the wind, his teeth chattering. When Brian got up, Tel said, "D-d-did you i-i-imagine your C-C-Christmas to b-b-be like t-t-this?"

"Oh yeah."

Tel laughed. His lips cracked.

"Come on."

They entered the caravan area and their cars and caravans, covered in white blankets, loomed into view. They split up and made their way to their own. Snow had drifted up the sides of the caravans, blocking the doors. They had to kick it away before the doors would open.

Brian heaved himself inside and struggled to pull the door closed behind him. It was dark. He turned on a light. He turned on the heater and stood in front of it for a moment, hoping to thaw out. His jeans were soaked and he was colder than he'd ever been in his life. The heater did nothing. He gathered the wrapped presents together, including a big box for Faye, and piled them on top of a red blanket before tying the four corners together, making it look like Santa's sack.

He opened the wardrobe doors in the bathroom. It was full, with just a couple of hangers for his shirts on the end of the rail. He pulled a sports bag from the bottom shelf and plucked out his shirts, underpants and socks. He stared at the multicoloured array of garments Faye had brought, randomly took a handful of hangers and pushed them into the sports bag, followed by hastily picked underwear and socks.

He couldn't remember what else Faye had wanted, but the sports bag was full.

Tel tapped on his door. "Collection for Brian," he yelled.

Brian opened the door. The wind caught it and slammed it against the side of the caravan. There was a sports bag on the sledge outside. Brian handed out his bag and the red Santa sack. Looking at the snow landing on them, he stepped back into the bathroom and, with a faint sense of satisfaction, pulled the shower curtain from the rail and handed it out to Tel, who wrapped it over everything, pushing the edges under the bags to secure it.

Brian slipped down the steps and sat at the bottom.

"You okay?" Tel asked, when he didn't move.

"Yeah, yeah, just admiring t'view."

He got up and struggled to close the door. They turned and followed their leg lines in the snow, Tel leading the way and Brian dragging the laden sledge behind him..

The wind was blowing snow into the troughs they'd left, smoothing over the edges and turning them invisible. Just after the first caravan area they disappeared altogether, as did any visible signs of anything.

"JUST GO STRAIGHT!" Brian boomed.

"BUT THE PUB'S ON THE RIGHT."

"STRAIGHT, WITH A SLIGHT INCLINATION TO THE RIGHT."

They trudged on, blind and frozen to the core of their souls. Gale force winds blasted off the camping field, repeatedly blowing the hoods off their heads. Surrounded by swirling snow, it felt as if they were plodding in nothingness.

Inside

Faye and Sophie watched from the window as Tel and Brian traipsed through the snow. They lost sight of them when they were only half way across the car park, swallowed up in the snowstorm.

"Do you think they'll be alright?" Faye asked nervously.

"I'm sure they'll be fine," said Sophie.

Janis said, "I'm really quite bored."

"Shall I fetch your coat?" Mark asked.

"We could play a game?" Olivia suggested.

Janis sat up straight in her armchair. "What kind of game?"

"Charades, cards, name that carol; you'd be good at that, Beth."

"What?"

"You could hum some carols and we'll try to guess which one it is."

"I'm not much in the mood for humming, to be honest."

"No, of course."

"Key party?" Janis laughed, winking at Mark, who put a finger in his mouth and pretended to gag, but, due to his sensitive gag reflex, started gagging for real.

"You okay, darling?"

Mark dry heaved and nodded his head.

"Faye, any suggestions?" Olivia asked.

Faye, still standing at the window with Sophie, despite not being able to see anything outside, said, "Maybe when Brian and Tel get back."

Janis groaned. "Uber boring party, Bolivia."

"It's *Olivia*," Mark snapped.

"Oooh, sorry, I'm sure."

"Can you see anything?" Jim asked Sophie.

"Just snow, lots and lots of snow."

"Maybe they shouldn't have gone," Faye breathed.

"They'll be okay, they're tough, they'll make it."

"It's coming down so fast."

Janis said, "Mark, do you remember that time – ?"

"No, I don't, and if I did, I wouldn't want to relive it."

"Way to make someone feel welcome," she huffed.

"Janis, you're *not* welcome. You just turned up and ingratiated yourself – "

Beth started humming notes, her voice pure and clear.

"*O Come All Ye Faithful*?" Mark said, glad of the distraction.

"La la la la."

"*In Dulci Jubilo*?" said Sophie, coming away from the window.

"Ooh," said Faye, following her, "I don't think I know that one."

"You'd know it if you heard it."

A slightly higher note, "La la la la."

Even Richard lifted his head off the table. "*Good King Wenceshlash?*"

"*We Three Kings?*" said Olivia.

Beth took a deep breath and began singing in earnest. Sophie and Faye slowly sat down, instantly mesmerised. Mark closed his eyes. Jim stared at her in awe. Olivia was already dabbing at her eyes. Janis looked both surprised and enthralled, and slightly agitated that someone had stolen the spotlight.

Julie popped her head out of the kitchen door behind the bar, her mouth open, listening and watching the lovely woman on the sofa sing like she'd never heard anyone sing before. It was beautiful, so beautiful.

A ping sounded behind her and she dashed back into the kitchen again.

"*Carol of the Bells,*" Sophie breathed softly, as Beth held the last note.

"Ooh," Beth laughed when she'd finished, "That got the old vocal chords going."

"Oh Beth," Olivia breathed, "That was *beautiful*."

"Amazing."

"Easy enough to sing without putting strain on the flange," Beth cackled.

Sophie winced.

Faye broke out of her trance and hurried back to the window. She peered at the whiteout, trying to see through it, trying to *sense* Brian out there somewhere.

"There's still no sign of them," she said, as Sophie came to stand next to her.

"Do you think they're okay?" Olivia asked Mark. "They've been an awfully long time."

Mark stood. "I'll have a look from the upstairs windows."

Outside

"Brian," Tel yelled over his shoulder, "I've lost all sense of direction."

"I've lost all feeling in my … everything."

"Which way?"

Brian peered into the swirling sheets of snow. There were no visible landmarks. He looked behind him and saw only the troughs they'd left in the snow.

They stood there, shivering, their teeth chattering, the pricks of snow incessant against their cold faces. The wind howled around them. The falling snow was impenetrable.

"I think we're lost, Bri."

"Just keep walking."

"We could be walking across the camping field."

"Then we'll hit a boundary at some point and follow that."

"Assuming we don't freeze to death first."

They dragged their legs through the snowdrifts a couple of times, and stopped again.

"I don't see anything, Bri, do you?"

"Just snow."

"What should we do?"

"Keep walking."

"We don't know where we're going."

"Moving is better than freezing to the spot."

"Is it?"

"You have a better idea?"

"I'm too cold to think."

"We can do this, Tel. Nobody gets lost in the snow in this country, especially not in the Cotswolds."

"You have the statistics to prove that?"

"Not on me."

They trudged forward another three steps, four, and stopped again.

"Shouldn't we have seen the pub by now? Unless we're heading away from it. Do you think we're heading away from it? Brian?"

Tel turned and was horrified to find that Brian wasn't right behind him, nothing was.

"BRIAN! BRIAN!"

Brian's huge form broke through the whiteout and slowly came towards him. The front of him was entirely white.

"Thought I'd lost you there, Bri."

"You can't get rid of me that easily."

Tel laughed, mostly in relief. "It's like wading through treacle."

"Keep wading, I'm right behind you."

They dragged one foot in front of the other, their heads bent, their hoods flapping on and off their heads.

Inside

They were in Sophie and Tel's room, all leaning over the chest of drawers and peering out at the snowstorm, struggling to see any sign of the men.

"They're lost," Faye sniffed, "I just know it."

"Fancy going out in this weather," Janis huffed, "All for some silly Christmas presents."

"And clothes," Sophie snapped.

"Yeah, clothes are worth dying for."

"Shut up, Janis," Mark hissed.

"I think they're lost," Faye said again, tears filling her eyes. "I don't think they can find their way home."

Mark extricated himself from the huddle and dashed downstairs, hauled open the springed door to the cellar, and reached in for the giant torch they kept at the top of the stairs. He ran back, turning it on.

They moved away from the window as he brought it in. He shone it outside, a huge beam of light. It strobed across the car park and moved towards the gate to the camping area. It didn't go any further. Beyond the gate was just white, nothing else.

Faye struggled to move closer to the window. As she did, something on the floor next to the chest of drawers caught her eye. She reached out for it and held it in front of her face.

A megaphone.

"Oh," Olivia said, "I forgot about that. It's what Chelsea uses to scare the kids back to their parents at night."

Faye threw open the window, braced herself against the blasting coldness, and screamed through the megaphone. "BRIAN! COME BACK TO ME, BRIAN!" She wasn't sure if it pierced the howling wind, if Brian could hear her. *"BRIAN!"*

Sophie pulled the mouthpiece towards her. "TEL!" she yelled, *"TEL!"*

"BRIAN! *BRI-I-I-AN!*"

Suddenly they were all grabbing the megaphone and taking it in turns to yell.

"THIS WAY!"

"FOLLOW THE SOUND OF OUR VOICES!"

"OVER HERE!"

Mark waved the beam of light from left to right.

They all peered into the dark, snow-blasting, wind-howling storm, shivering and shouting from the window, trying to bring the men home.

Outside

"What's that?" Tel yelled.

"What's what?"

"I thought I heard something, saw something."

"Heard and saw what?"

"I don't know, a noise, like distant shouting maybe, and a beam of light." He raised a snow-covered arm and pointed to their right. "I'm sure it came from over there."

Brian looked. Stared. Saw nothing. Listened. Heard nothing. "Could be a car headlight."

"Who'd be driving in this weather?"

"Who'd be walking in it? Idiots, that's who."

He dropped his head to take another laborious step forward.

"Look, there! Did you see it? A light, and is that ...

shouting?"

"Could be the howling of the wind." Brian turned his head. Again, he saw nothing.

And then ... something. A dull shaft of light cut through the storm, there for a moment and then gone again.

"It's the pub!" Tel shouted. "It has to be, there's nothing else around here!"

Together, they made their way towards the gloomy beam that was swinging left and right.

Far away voices called out their names.

Inside

"I think I can see them!" Faye cried.

"Where?"

"Out there."

"I can't see anything."

"BRIAN!" Faye yelled into the megaphone. *"BRI-I-IAN!"*

"There!" Mark cried, and the shouting intensified as two distant, barely visible shapes appeared and disappeared in the snowstorm.

"BRI-I-I-AN!"

"TE-E-E-EL!"

"OVER HERE!"

"THIS WAY!"

"It's them!" Faye cried, beaming.

"Who else could it be?" Janis tutted.

The grey silhouettes solidified near the gate at the end of the car park and staggered through it with the sledge, buffeted by the wind and the snow.

They all thundered down the stairs and threw open the front door, letting the icy cold and wafts of snow inside and not caring.

"Are they here?" Beth shouted from the lounge.

Jim rushed out to stand with them at the open door.

"Brian!" Faye sobbed. "Oh Brian!"

She ran out to greet him at the bottom of the steps leading up to the patio, despite having no coat. She threw her arms around his snow-covered neck and leapt up to kiss his frozen, icicle-streaked beard.

Mark ran out to grab the sledge and Jim helped haul it up the steps. Sophie threw Tel's arm across her shoulders and helped him through the door. Olivia slammed the door shut, and they all helped to take off the men's hats, coats, scarves and gloves.

Brian and Tel panted with exhaustion. Their frozen faces turned red from the sudden heat. Tel hugged Sophie and said, "I didn't think we were going to make it!"

Janis, sitting on the stairs with an empty glass, tutted, rolled her eyes and said, "Such a drama queen."

"Says the drama queen," Mark snapped.

"B-b-brandy," Brian shivered.

"Of course," Olivia cried, waving her hands. "Mark, help him into the lounge."

Mark and Faye helped him stagger through from the hallway and into an armchair. Faye immediately fell to her knees and started taking off his frozen trainers.

"You shouldn't have gone!" she cried.

"I d-did it f-for you."

"Me?"

"For your p-p-presents."

"Oh Brian."

Sophie and Jim helped Tel to hobble to the other armchair. Jim rubbed his shoulders while Sophie pulled off his shoes. "Should have worn boots," she muttered, rolling off his sodden socks.

"B-b-boots were in the c-c-caravan."

"Did you get them?"

"F-f-forgot."

"What about my blue jumper, and my hairdryer? Did you get the hairdryer, and the – "

"Y-y-yes, g-g-got it a-a-all."

"My hero." She kissed his flushed but freezing cheek.

Richard remained kneeling on the floor, his head on the end of the coffee table, fast asleep and oblivious to it all.

Janis wandered over to the bar and put her glass on the counter as Olivia poured out brandies. "I'll have one while you're there."

Olivia picked up the two glasses she'd poured and snapped, "Get it yourself, I'm not your servant!"

"Ooh, do I detect a bit of sass from the nicer-than-nice girlfriend?" She sniggered as she moved around the bar, jumping when the young girl who'd arrived in a sleeping bag poked her head through the kitchen door.

"Are they back?" the girl asked.

Janis waited until she'd poured her brandy before looking up and saying, "Yes."

The girl disappeared again.

"Place is full of degenerates," Janis said, sipping on her fresh drink.

In the back lounge, Julie started bringing out plates. "Food's up!" she cried.

Everyone turned and looked at the table laid out in the middle of the room. On the tablecloth was cutlery, wine glasses, some bottles of wine, red and white, uncorked, large bowls of salad and garlic bread, and smaller bowls of chilli flakes and parmesan cheese.

"Jools!" Olivia gasped, as Julie put the first two plates of pizza in the middle of the table. "When did you do all this?"

Julie straightened up, saw them all looking at her and laughed nervously. "While you were all talking, and then running upstairs, and then running back down again. I heard Brian saying he was hungry before they went out."

"He's always hungry," Mark laughed, walking over and giving Julie a hug. "You clever little thing."

Julie went puce. "They taught me how to present pizza at the other pub, before they fired me," she squirmed. "I've put real tomatoes and mushrooms and some of that wet cheese in a bag on top, and a sprinkling of fresh oregano."

"You're very ..." Mark turned to Olivia, struggling for the right word.

"Small and unattractive?" Janis suggested.

"Resourceful," Olivia grinned, hurrying over to give her a hug. "Well done, Jools."

Wriggling free, desperate to escape all the attention, Julie ran back into the kitchen for more pizzas.

The hungry herd shuffled or staggered over and sat down, Jim helping Faye with Brian, Sophie helping Tel. They marvelled at the unexpected feast set before them.

"Hello?" Beth shouted from the other room. "Can someone help me up?"

* * *

Julie sat down after bringing out the last of the pizzas, eight in all. Before she started eating she said, "Is it alright if I stay then? My mum called and said I can go back because the bloke she met at bingo when she had a big win has gone, with her winnings, but I don't want to listen to my mum crying all over Christmas. So, can I, please?"

"If Beth doesn't mind," Olivia said, glancing across the table.

"I said she could stay, I ain't bovvered."

Jim said, "It's all in the past now and we're just looking forward, ain't we, babes. It was just a fling that meant nothing." He glanced at Julie. "No offence, Jools.

"S'okay, Jim." She looked at Beth with fawning eyes. "I don't know why you bothered with me when you've got someone like Beth. She's lovely."

"Oh," Beth said, surprised, "Thanks, Jools."

Julie put her chin in the palm of her hand and breathed, "You sing like a fairy."

They all looked at Julie, who was instantly embarrassed.

"Angel," Sophie said, sprinkling parmesan on her slices of pizza, "She means angel."

Beth picked up an empty pizza plate. "Blimey, you lot can knock 'em back. Come on, cough up, my little party piece didn't come free."

Olivia, smiling, took the plate and held it in front of their flummoxed faces. "Tomatoes," she said, "The pregnant woman wants your tomatoes."

"Two each," Beth said, "More than that will be gratefully received by my tomato starved babies."

As Olivia handed the full plate back, there was a snuffle and a cough from the other room.

"I suppose I'd better take Dick something."

She slapped two pizza slices onto a plate and, eschewing the salad spoons, grabbed a handful of salad, and stomped into the other room, thudding the plate down next to Richard's sleeping head on the coffee table. He snuffled again and lifted his face.

"Food," she said.

"Thank you," Richard croaked. As Olivia stomped back to the table he subconsciously muttered, "Love you."

"Bite me," Olivia snapped back.

"Are you into that kind of thing now?"

When there was no answer, just the sound of a group of people eating and chatting, he struggled to his feet and staggered behind the bar.

* * *

When they'd finished, Beth slowly leaned back in her chair and sighed in satisfaction. Then she quickly leaned forward in her chair and said, "Ow!"

"Braxton Hicks?" Sophie asked quickly. "Indigestion? Heartburn?" *Anything but actual labour pains*, she thought.

Beth winced, clutching her stomach. "I can let them wash over me when I'm lying down. It's when I'm sitting up, trying to lead a normal life, that they hit 'ard."

"Back to the sofa for you, babes."

"Thanks, Jim, but, if you all don't mind, I think I might go to bed."

"Of course!"

They all jumped to their feet, except for Brian and Tel, who staggered to theirs and hobbled forward. "We can only offer moral support and counselling services," Tel laughed, leaning against Brian, who was already struggling to balance on feet he still couldn't feel.

"Frostbite or drunkenness?" Tel asked him.

"Don't know and, at this point, don't really care."

"You'll care when you wake up in the morning and find ten toes lying in a pile at the bottom of your bed."

"Yes, but opening presents will distract me, and does anyone really need ten toes?"

They laughed.

As the group helped Beth to her feet and fussed around her, Janis poured all the dregs from the bottles of wine into her glass, red and white, and put her stilettoed feet up onto the chair Tel had vacated.

"Bit of a handsome chappie," she said to herself, feeling the warmth of his buttocks on her ankles. "Wonder if he's got any money."

Sophie's head was suddenly uncomfortably close to hers. Janis squeaked in alarm. "If you so much as look at my husband I'm taking your eyes out," Sophie hissed, "Is that clear?"

"Very."

Sophie stormed away and rejoined the human satellites circling around Beth. Janis quietly muttered, "If he's worth fighting for he must be worth something." She made a mental note to ask what he did for a living. It wouldn't be quite Olgivy status, obviously, but she was willing to let her standards slip a little for someone so good looking.

Julie bustled around her, clearing the table. Huffing, Janis wandered into the other room, swirling the dregs in her glass, and found the tall man – Robert, was it? – swaying behind the bar, trying to get the whisky optic to pour into a wine glass. She went to stand next to him.

"So," she said, taking down two tumblers and pushing them under the whisky, "Tell me everything you know about the Olgivys, and I might have a way of getting your ex-wife back for you. Consider it my Christmas gift."

Richard turned unsteady eyes towards her, and smiled.

CHAPTER 9

Once they'd all put Beth to bed, throwing cushions across the room at each other and laughing, they left her and Jim alone.

"Tel," Mark whispered, as Sophie, Brian and Faye made their way down the stairs, "Liv has something to show you."

"Do I?" Olivia laughed. "Pretty sure Tel doesn't want to see anything I've got."

"What's going on?" Sophie asked, stopping and turning on the staircase.

"Nothing," said Mark.

"Very unconvincing argument."

"It's to do with Christmas," Mark said. "It's a surprise."

"What's a surprise?"

"Wouldn't be a surprise if I told you."

"I don't like surprises. What are you three conspirators up to?"

"We claim our right to privacy," Tel declared, really feeling quite drunk – and full, and happy, very, very happy.

"As a husband you have no rights to privacy," Sophie grinned. "But I shall play my part and walk away as if nothing is going on."

She turned and followed Brian and Faye, who were dicing with death and tickling each other, down the stairs.

Mark bustled Olivia and Tel into their flat and whispered, "Tel hasn't got Sophie a Christmas present."

Olivia sucked in air.

"She said she didn't want one!" Tel said.

Olivia's eyes widened.

"Show him your stash," Mark said.

"Stash?" Tel laughed, "You have a *stash*, Liv? Might I enquire as to what the stash consists of? Nothing illegal, I hope, I am, after all, a lawyer."

Mark and Olivia stared at him with deadpan expressions.

"It's cocaine," Olivia said.

"What?" Tel was appalled. Even through his intoxication he was appalled. Olivia, dealing cocaine? Olivia, a crackhead? Or was it smackhead, he wasn't sure, it wasn't his area of expertise.

"Don't be daft," Mark said, "It's her present stash."

Olivia glared at Mark. "How do you know about that?"

"A woman *not* buying presents for Christmas? I wasn't born yesterday, Liv."

"I'm beginning to think the text message that I didn't send was a bad idea," Tel sighed.

Olivia looked awkward for a moment, then opened the door to the spare room behind her. It looked like a normal bedroom, with a single bed, wardrobe and a chest of drawers. There was a beautiful blanket on top of the duvet. Beneath the window was a table smothered in wrapping paper, gift bags, sticky tape dispensers and a pile of glittery stuff.

"Where are they then?" Mark asked, rubbing his hands together. "Your Christmas stash, where is it?"

Feeling like she'd been caught doing something naughty, Olivia knelt down by the bed and pulled out a banana box from underneath. The box contained prettily wrapped parcels, about twenty of them.

"You have been busy!"

Olivia gave a wan smile and leaned under the bed again, pulling out another banana box. The wrapped parcels were bigger in this one, just five or so.

Olivia got to her feet and walked over to the wardrobe. When she opened it, there were piles of Christmas presents inside of all shapes and sizes. Mark and Tel gasped in awe. Olivia remained stony-faced and moved over to the chest of drawers, opening the bottom one, the middle one and the top one. They, too, were full of presents.

"Blimey, Liv," Tel cried, running his hand over his head, "Did you buy for the whole village?"

"Not all of them," she said.

Mark's mouth fell open. "You bought for the village?"

"Only the people I know, I'm not Father Christmas." She bit her bottom lip. "Are you annoyed?" she asked.

"About?"

"Buying so many presents for everyone?"

He frowned. "No, why would I be annoyed?"

"Because we weren't supposed to buy presents, and I did get a bit carried away."

Mark took one step forward and pulled her into his arms. "Liv," he said, "I'm not Richard. You can do whatever you want, whenever and however you want. It's your life, I just want to share it with you. You never annoy me, ever."

She gave him her cute overbite smile and kissed him.

"Get a room," Tel laughed.

"We have one," Mark said, "You're in it. Get out."

Tel went to leave.

"I'm joking! Get back here. Do you have anything suitable amongst this ... festive frenzy, Liv?"

Olivia rushed back to the wardrobe and pulled out a wrapped box. "I got this for my mother – "

"Oh, I don't want to take anything from your mother, Liv."

"It's okay, she's in Uruguay, I can always get her another one before she gets back. It's a sandwich maker."

"What?" Mark chuckled, "Like a chef in a box who pops out to make you sandwiches?"

"No, silly."

Tel pulled a face. "I'm not sure Sophie would appreciate kitchen equipment, she's likely to throw it at me."

Olivia pulled out another wrapped box. "Selection of fine Scottish whiskies and a crystal tumbler?"

"I'm more the whisky drinker. Oh, is it for me?"

"My dad."

"You bought something for your dad?" Mark asked.

"On the off chance I might see him, but ... " She lifted it to Tel. " ... you can have it. Merry Christmas."

"Cheers, Liv."

"Have you bought something for Dick, too?" Mark said, a little too sharply.

Olivia snapped her head up. "No! Why would I? I didn't know he was coming."

"You bought your dad something, 'just in case'." He did air quotes. "I thought you might have – "

He stopped speaking when Olivia's eyes narrowed. He knew he should have avoided the air quotes.

"He's still my dad," she said.

"Yes, of course. I apologise."

Olivia pulled out several more parcels from the wardrobe, then started going through the boxes from under the bed, describing the contents. Tel kept shaking his head.

"Isn't there anything here you think Sophie would like?" Olivia asked, frustrated. "I've got some new gold earrings still in the box, would you like those?"

"Not taking your jewellery, Liv." He rested his elbow on his other arm and stroked at his stubble. "But there is something in this room she would absolutely love."

"Is it me?" Mark said, casually inspecting his nails.

Tel laughed even louder. "No, Mark, it's not you."

"Oh, that's a relief," Olivia puffed, "I couldn't possibly compete with someone like Sophie."

Mark started singing *Jolene*, changing the name to Sophie.

"What, then?" Olivia asked.

Tel lowered his eyes.

* * *

The table had been cleared, mostly by Julie.

"She's very good," Olivia whispered to Mark, as they watched her loading up the dishwasher, "She took the bags Tel and Brian brought back from the caravans upstairs to their rooms without me asking, and arranged all of Brian's presents under the Christmas tree."

"Where's my present?" he grinned.

"Hidden."

"Meanie. Should we offer her a job?"

"I might talk to Beth about it."

They joined the others in the *Friends* corner, who were fighting over the controls for the TV set on the wall. The men wanted to watch *Die Hard*.

"It's *not* a Christmas film!" the women argued.

"It *is*!" cried the men.

The women wanted to watch *The Holiday*.

"Romantic tosh," Brian said.

"I could write better myself," said Mark.

"Isn't that the one where they have racoons in the British countryside?"

"That's the one, *beyond* ridiculous."

Julie came through from the kitchen and stood awkwardly to the side, leaning on the back of a chair.

"Come and sit down, lass," Brian shouted over, "We don't bite."

"Bite me," Richard snorted from his slumped and semi-conscious position on the floor, leaning against Janis's armchair. She kept pushing his greasy head away with a taloned finger and grimacing.

"I'm a bit tired actually," Julie said.

"I'm not surprised after everything you've done," Faye said. "Hard worker, you are."

"Thank you so much for dinner," said Olivia.

"Yes, it was lovely," Beth said.

"Very innovative of you to feed eleven people on the spur like that," said Sophie.

Julie waved a hand in front of her, batting away their compliments. "I was just wondering if I was sleeping here tonight, or if I should go back in the shed?"

Olivia looked mortified. "Oh Jools, no, you're staying here with us."

Julie gave a relieved smile.

"I hadn't thought about sleeping arrangements," Olivia said, trying to concentrate. "We've got two spare guest rooms left and …" She bit her lip, looking from Julie, to Janis, to Richard. "… three people."

"Janis can share with Jools," Mark said.

"No, thank you very much," Janis snapped, "I don't share with anyone."

"No," Mark nodded, "You're more of a taker than a sharer, aren't you, but the alternative is to share with Richard."

"Absolutely not!" Janis sat up straight in her chair, knocking Richard over. He slumped to his side on the floor, clutching an empty bottle of wine.

"You could just throw a blanket over him," Tel suggested. "I don't think he's much bothered where he sleeps."

"I'll have the biggest room," Janis quickly said.

"Basement is big," Mark said. Turning his head to Olivia's ear he whispered, "We could lock her down there, keep her out of mischief."

"Don't tempt me," she giggled.

"Which room is the biggest?" Janis asked.

"Er, number five, on the left."

Janis stood up, glared at Julie, who took a step back, and stomped from the room swinging her hips. Mark followed her to make sure she didn't pick the lock on their flat and go snooping again. He watched as she bent down to pick up a bag from under the table in the hallway.

"Where d'you get that?" he asked, startling her.

"From the car."

"You had an overnight bag in the car?"

"I was … going to stay in a hotel tonight."

"Really?" He crossed his arms. "You planned this, didn't you, the whole thing. You came here to deliberately cause trouble, didn't you."

Without answering, she marched off up the stairs with her bag. Mark glared after her and muttered, "Should have pushed you down the basement steps."

"I heard that!"

"Good! If the room isn't to your liking we have a perfectly good coffin down there, layered with the dried husks of the people you've wronged. I'm sure you'll be very comfortable."

After watching her turn left at the top of the stairs towards the guest rooms he stormed back into the lounge hissing, "Bloody woman!"

Olivia sidled up to him and kissed his cheek. "At least you're not married to her any more, darling," she said, and the anger inside him instantly evaporated.

"I'm lucky to have you, Liv."

"You haven't … yet," she winked. Turning to the others she said, "I think we might go to bed."

Tel glanced at his watch. "It's only ten-thirty!"

"Bit tired," Mark said, yawning.

"Tired?" Sophie grinned.

Olivia turned puce. Turning to Julie she said, "You're in room four. There's toiletries in the ensuite and a spare pair of pyjamas in the chest of drawers."

"Thank you."

"Night, everyone."

"Night, Liv. Night, Mark."

While everyone was distracted, Brian pointed the remote control at the big screen on the wall and clicked on *Die Hard*.

Tel cheered.

Faye and Sophie crossed their arms and sighed.

Richard snored.

CHAPTER 10

Christmas Day

Brian opened his eyes and stared at the unfamiliar ceiling, trying to figure out where he was. Then he remembered why he was here and what day it was.

A huge smile split his beard in half.

Christmas Day!

He glanced at his mobile phone on the bedside table. It was 4am. Too early? Probably. He closed his eyes and tried to go back to sleep, but couldn't.

It was Christmas Day and he was already filled with childish excitement.

Presents! He hoped Faye liked hers. He hoped he liked Faye's. He hoped there was Buck's Fizz for breakfast. He started humming *Making Your Mind Up*.

The cloud of unconsciousness was long gone, there was no way he was getting it back. He looked at the clock again. 4.15am. The grandkids were usually rampaging through the house by now and screaming, "Father Christmas has been! He's been!" Sometimes there was vomiting if they'd chomped through more than one selection box, occasionally there were tears of over-excitement and lack of sleep. The split in his beard grew wider. This was a different kind of Christmas, a child-free Christmas with friends instead of family. He missed the kids, but he welcomed the peace and quiet too. It was a grown-up Christmas..

4.30am. Might as well get up.

He pulled the duvet back slowly and quietly so as not to disturb Faye. A rustle came from the foot of the bed. He didn't dare put the light on, so he reached down and had a feel. Two stockings filled with what felt and sounded like wrapped presents.

His smile broadened. He hadn't had a stocking the foot of his bed since he was … well, fifteen, because he'd whined to his mother at fourteen that there was no stocking. He smiled as he remembered his mother saying, "At what point does the stocking stop, when you're married with your own kids and I have to break into your house to put them at the foot of your bed?"

He put on his dressing gown and crept downstairs, went into the kitchen, made himself a coffee and sat down at the big table in the back lounge. The snowstorm still howled and lashed outside, creating a drift up the patio windows. The real fire had gone out, but the central heating kept it warm and cosy inside.

He put a couple of logs on the fire to stir it again, and wondered what time everyone would get up. Soon, he hoped.

He noticed the pile of presents Julie had put under the tree yesterday seemed a little bigger. Wishful thinking? He wandered over and sat on the floor in front of them, feeling a bit naughty as he lifted wrapped gifts one by one and gave them a little shake.

There were several from Faye to him, one was definitely a book, the others were soft, so probably pants and socks. There was only one from him to Faye, but it was a big one. Mark and Olivia had bought each other a little something, and there were quite a few for and from Jim and Beth. There was nothing from Sophie, but there was a big, squishy one to her from Tel. He thought the idea of a non-commercialised Christmas a bit silly, even grown-ups liked presents.

He stood up again and glanced over at Richard, lying on the floor underneath the coffee table in the *Friends* corner. Someone had thrown a blanket over him and pushed a cushion under his head. He was snoring and hugging an empty bottle of wine.

Brian went back to the table and glanced at the wall clock behind the bar. 5am. He lifted his eyes to the ceiling, listening for any sounds of somebody getting up. Nothing. He went into the kitchen to make another coffee, slamming down his mug and the tins and cupboard doors and drawers and coughing a lot. Listened.

Nothing.

What was wrong with these people? Didn't they know what day it was? Weren't they excited? How could they sleep on a day like this?

Idle, the lot of them.

He started singing a few lines of Wizzard's *I Wish It Could Be Christmas Every Day* in a deep baritone. Listened.

Nothing.

Impatient now, he took his coffee to the foot of the stairs and hollered Noddy Holder's famous line, "It's Chriiiiiiiiiiiiiiiiiistmaaaaaaas!" Listened.

Nothing.

He stood there for a minute, twitching his beard. Then he went into the lounge, stepped behind the bar and took an excruciating amount of time figuring out how to work the stereo system. Finally, Christmas music came out of the surround sound speakers, Brenda Lee's *Rockin' Around the Christmas Tree*.

Brian hurried to the bottom of the stairs. The music was loud but not overbearing, you could talk over it. Was it loud enough? Since no bodies appeared at the top of the stairs, he rushed back into the lounge and turned it up a little.

Still nothing, except for Richard muttering and turning over. Brian stepped over him and sat on the sofa, putting his feet up on the coffee table and *willing* someone to come and tell him off. He snugged into the leather. It was comfy. He put a cushion behind his head.

And drifted off to sleep to the sound of Bing Crosby's *I'm Dreaming of a White Christmas*.

***

Something hit his forehead, catapulting him from a dream about the Buck's Fizz girls having their skirts pulled off. He snuffled and started slipping into unconsciousness again, when something hit him again. Another something landed on his chest.

He snapped his lids open. His eyes roamed around the bright room. In the background, Christmas music played. In the foreground, in the armchair next to his sofa, Tel sat lobbing uncracked hazelnuts at him.

"Wakey, wakey, sleepyhead!"

Brian sat up, rested his arms on his knees and rubbed his face awake. His head felt fuggy. "What time is it?" he croaked.

"Seven-thirty, mate. We thought you were never going to wake up."

From the kitchen came the sound of multiple voices talking and laughing. He heard cooking and smelt bacon.

The kitchen door opened behind the bar and Julie poked her head out. "Oh good," she grinned, "You're awake. Are you hungry?"

They all laughed.

"Is the Pope Catholic?" Faye cried out. "You don't need to ask, you just need to feed. He's like a human waste disposal unit, sucks up anything with a calorie content."

A voice from the hallway cried, "Pregnant lady coming through!"

Beth, with Jim gently holding her arm, plodded into the lounge and made a beeline for the sofa. Brian jumped up and helped lower her down. He noticed Richard was no longer on the floor under the coffee table.

"BREAKFAST!" Sophie yelled from the back lounge.

Brian and Jim helped a puffing Beth to her feet again.

The table was a banquet of food, with everything in bain-maries running down the middle, help-yourself style. There were ready poured glasses of buck's fizz, and Brian thought he had never felt happier – the only time, apart from early airport flights, where he could legitimately drink alcohol for breakfast and not get moaned at. He downed a glass in one.

Faye came through from the kitchen with a jug of orange juice. Brian glared at her. "What are you wearing, woman?"

She stood with her hand on her hip and huffed. "This," she said, pointing down at her Christmas jumper and her baggy, muddy tracksuit bottoms, "is what you brought back from the caravan. I'm wearing a t-shirt with 'I'm Sexy and I Tow It' under this jumper."

"I grabbed what I could," Brian said. "It was dark and I was hypothermic."

"The only underwear you grabbed was a pair of thongs, Bri."

"Why do you have thongs in the caravan?" Sophie giggled.

Faye froze, unable to think of suitable answer.

"Is she buffering?" Tel asked.

Richard appeared from nowhere and thew himself into a chair, poured champagne into his glass, chugged it back, and filled the glass again. He looked horribly hungover, his hair in disarray, and he absolutely reeked.

"Where's Janis?" Sophie asked.

"The creature has not yet emerged from its pit," Mark replied. "Or she may have died in her sleep. Fingers crossed, eh?"

"Bit harsh," Tel laughed.

Mark shrugged.

"Beth," said Olivia, handing out warmed plates, "We have just the teensiest little problem."

"Oh?" Beth said. "Foxes have made off with the turkey? The veg has gone off? The gravy is a disaster area of lumps?"

"No, no. We've, er, run out of tomatoes."

Everyone around the table fell silent.

"Fresh ones?" Beth asked. Olivia shook her head. "Tinned?" Olivia shook her head again. "Bottled?"

"Yes, yes," Olivia beamed, pouring orange juice into her glass, "Just as soon as someone goes down and gets it from the cellar."

"The cellar!" Faye breathed. "I forgot there was a cellar. Where is it?"

"Through the door under the stairs," Mark said, putting down his knife and fork. "I'll go and get some."

"No, no," Beth laughed, waving his offer away, "You sit and eat your breakfast, I can wait."

Mark tucked into his fry-up again, and Beth breathed, "Wow, slow eater!"

"I'll go and – "

"No, no, I'm joking," she cackled. "Eat up, *quickly*!"

"Honestly, it won't take a minute."

"I'm winding you up, Mark. You enjoy your breakfast … *don't you worry about my poor, deprived babies.*"

Mark ate faster.

"Another buck's fizz, lass?"

"Oh," Faye said, holding out her glass, "I don't mind if I do."

"Is anyone photographing this for future reference?" Brian asked. "Someone get their phone out, quick!"

"Ahh, capturing memories," Olivia said, smiling.

They all picked up their phones. Faye put up victory fingers and pouted.

"Make sure you capture her *drinking at breakfast*," Brian said.

Olivia sat down and raised her glass. "Merry Christmas, everyone."

"Merry Christmas!"

"You've outdone yourself, Liv."

"Wait until you see lunch."

"Hmm," Brian said, scrunching up his face in anticipatory delight, "Can't wait."

"And you say this whilst stuffing your face with food?" Faye laughed.

"I've never eaten so well," he replied.

A hush fell over the table. Brian gulped, and slowly raised

his head to look at Faye, who was glaring at him with her lips pinched together very tightly. "Pardon?" she said.

He coughed. "I meant ... well, it's very ... I didn't mean – "

"Don't panic, Bri. Its Christmas, I'll let you off, just this once."

"Thank you, wife."

"You're welcome, husband. Consider it one of my Christmas gifts to you."

The eating and drinking resumed, interspersed with phonecalls from family and friends. They chatted and laughed and waved their hands at a stinky Richard. At one point, when Beth told them a joke and they all burst out laughing, Julie put her chin on her hand and said, "You're lovely."

"Oh," Beth said, surprised, "Thanks. Regret sleeping with my husband now?"

"Yeah."

"Good."

Jim looked stunned and embarrassed.

"When can we open the presents?" Brian asked.

Mark, stuffed to the gills, pushed his plate away and said, "After I've been down to the cellar for the tomato juice."

"Finished?" Julie asked, reaching out towards Richard's still full plate.

He handed her an empty bottle of champagne and said, "Yes, thank you, can you bring me another one?"

"I think you've had enough," Olivia said.

"Booze is the only thing that stops me thinking ... about you."

Mark sighed. "Thinking about everything you've lost, you mean."

"Yes. I lost Liv, and for that I will never forgive myself."

They all looked at him. He stared at his empty glass as if it was a crystal ball.

Mark looked at Olivia, who mouthed, 'Drunk?'

'Broke,' he mouthed back.

Richard came out of his reverie, slammed his hand down

on the table, and cried, "Where's my champagne?"

"Coming!" Julie yelled, running into the kitchen.

"And normal service is resumed," said Olivia, taking the bottle from a returning Julie and putting it on the back bar. Richard gasped in horror, then tried to take Faye's glass of Buck's Fizz. "Leave it," she growled, and Richard slumped back in his chair.

"Want to help me bring up bottles, Bri?" Mark asked.

"Yep. Jim?"

"What?"

"Want to help us carry up some tomato juice?"

Beth reached out and arm and pushed him off his chair. "Go on, babes. Hurry up, the babies are craving."

"I'll help," Tel said, getting up, "I'm not sure I've ever seen a basement before."

"Basement," Faye breathed, shuddering. "Shut the door behind you, I don't want any monsters escaping."

"There's no such thing as monsters," Sophie laughed.

"Isn't there?" Faye said, tapping the side of her nose.

Mark looked up at the ceiling and said, "I believe in monsters."

***

Mark opened the door to the cellar with some effort. It had a pretty tight spring fitted to it which squeaked like a trapped rat. Concrete steps dipped sharply, disappearing into an abyss of darkness.

"It's bloody freezing!" Jim cried.

"You don't heat a basement," Mark told him, "Not unless your customers particularly enjoy warm beer."

Tel sucked in air and gasped, "Is that ... howling?"

"Yes," Mark said.

Tel took a full step back and cried, "There's howling coming from the cellar?"

"It's the wind blowing through the vents," Mark explained.

"Blimey," said Brian, "Don't ever let Faye open this door, she'll have a fit."

"Epileptic?" Jim asked.

"Epic, with lots of screaming and running."

Mark reached out for the light switch. There was a brief moment of illumination, and then a ping from down below, plunging it into eerie darkness once more.

"Damn," said Mark, "Bulbs popped."

He turned and yelled, "LIV, DO WE HAVE ANY OF THOSE SPECIAL LED LIGHTBULBS FOR THE BASEMENT?"

They heard her high-pitched voice cry, "I forgot to get some."

"Ah," said Tel.

"Hmm," said Brian, stepping back to where Tel stood against the far wall.

Jim followed.

"Fear not," Mark said, moving away from the door and letting it slam shut, "I have just the thing."

He ran down the hallway and took the stairs two at a time.

"Just what you want to hear when you're standing at the entrance to Hades," Brian said, staring at the cellar door, "Heavy, plodding footsteps."

The footsteps thundered down the stairs again, and Mark appeared with a torch so large it had a heavy-duty handle on it. "One hundred-thousand lumens," he said proudly. "Brightest torch you can buy. It's what brought you home when you went to the caravans yesterday. Cover your eyes, men, I'm turning it on."

They covered their eyes. They waited. Nothing happened. When they uncovered their eyes Mark was shaking the torch and muttering, "Left the bloody thing on, didn't I. It's run out of charge."

"I'm not going down there without light," Tel declared, firmly shaking his head. "You should go, Jim."

"Me?"

"Beth needs tomato juice for *your* babies. Go on, and be

quick about it."

"I'm not going on my own!"

Brian pulled out his phone and turned on the torch, blinding himself. Mark pulled the door open and Brian aimed it down the stairs. It's puny light only illuminated the first four steps.

Tel added his phone torch, and then Jim and Mark. It was brighter, but still went no further than the four steps. Nobody moved.

"Are we men or mice?" Brian asked.

"Mice," Jim squeaked.

"Come on," he said, stepping forward. "Once more into the ..." He stopped. "Are you sure that's the wind coming through the vents, Mark?"

"Positive. Come on, you wimps, we have a quest."

"Find tomato juice or die," Jim cried.

"So, by that logic, if we don't find the tomato juice we're going to die?" Tel asked.

"No, I mean if I don't return with tomato juice *I'm* going to die, 'cos Beth will kill me."

"You're overthinking things," Brian said, grabbing hold of Jim's jumper and pulling him down, "We are the three musketeers, all for one and one for – "

"Fall," Tel gasped, as he stepped down, "We're going to fall and break our necks!"   "Think positive," Brian said.

"Bit difficult to do when we're plunging into the depths of the earth."

"It's just a basement," Mark said.

"With no lights and a sinister howling noise that sounds remarkably like a constipated werewolf trying to take a dump."

"It's the – "

"Vents, yes, I know, but it's bloody creepy?"

"Constipated werewolf taking a dump," Brian chuckled, "Very imaginative. We call it thretching in Yorkshire."

"Good to know!"

"It is, nobody gets offended if you say, 'I'm just off to the loo for a thretch'."

"Sounds disgusting."

"Well, it's certainly not pleasant."

"Could we concentrate on the task in hand?" Mark snapped, as the door closed shut behind them.

They reached the bottom of the stairs without tripping or screaming. They were in a bubble of light, surrounded by infinite blackness. It felt like they were floating in space. It felt like monsters were wating for them in the dark.

"Anyone seen *Riddick*?" Jim whispered. "Good film, a bit like this."

"Not now, Jim."

"Where's the tomato juice?" Tel breathed.

"Why are you all whispering?" Brian asked.

"Don't want to upset the thretching werewolf," Jim said.

"Oh for goodness – " Tel sucked in air. "What was that?"

"What was what?"

"I thought I heard something."

"It was probably a rat," said Mark.

"Christ, don't tell Sophie there's rats down here!"

"That's why the door's on a spring, to keep it shut."

"They climb up the stairs? This place is– There it is again!"

"Chill," said Brian. "Go back upstairs if you're that scared."

"I'm not *scared*." Tel's bulging eyeballs rolled in their sockets. "Anyway, everyone knows you should stick together in times of danger, it's always the one who wanders off alone who gets it first."

"Gets what first?" Jim asked.

"Killed!"

"I'll come with you," Jim offered.

He and Tel turned, and screamed.

There, on the periphery of their bubble of light, partially standing in the shadows, was a tall, dark figure.

"WHAT THE – !"

Brian instinctively raised his phone torch.

Richard stood there in his long, smelly coat, staring down at a bottle in his hands. "Olivia's forbidden me from using the optics," he mumbled, swaying slightly. "And the bottles, and the pumps. Bit mean, frankly. Is there anything down here I can have? Anything will do, I'm not fussy."

"RICHARD!" Mark yelled, "You scared the living – "

"Preferably something with a high alcohol content, otherwise what's the point?"

"Tomato juice?" Brian asked Mark, who lifted an arm and pointed into the blackness. He stepped forward, then stopped. "Where are my musketeers?"

"Scared, Bri?" Tel sniggered.

"Blind, Tel. If you could point your torches in this direction I'd be much obliged."

Jim, Mark and Tel stepped with him. Jim bumped into a barrel, as did Tel, and Brian. They made their way through them like balls in a pinball machine, feeling their way forward and feeling whisps of spiderwebs brushing against their skin.

"How big is this cellar?" Tel complained, as he skirted another keg.

"Not that big when the light is on. Pretty bloody massive in the dark."

"We could be stepping into another diversion," Jim breathed.

"Diversion?" Tel laughed. "Watch you don't trip over any 'Diverted Traffic' signs, Jim."

"What?"

Behind them, Richard whined, "Any alcohol content will do. Mouthwash, hand sanitiser, aftershave."

The barrels stopped and the boxes began.

"Look for ones with 'Tomato Juice' printed on the side," Mark said.

"I'd never have thought of that," Tel laughed.

Jim, a few steps ahead of them, yelled, "Found them!"

He picked one up and handed it back to Brian. He picked up another and handed it to Tel.

"You not carrying anything?" Mark asked, as Jim passed another one to him.

Jim picked one up and held it.

"Four boxes?" Tel gasped.

"Yeah, do you think that's enough? Beth's like a vampire with this stuff."

They turned with their boxes, and found Richard standing right behind them, still staring at the bottle in his hands.

"Bloody hell, Richard, stop creeping us out!"

"I ... I really need your help," Richard said quietly. "I'm ... I'm starting to feel ... sober."

"Sober?" Mark said. "We're frightened to light a match anywhere near you!"

"It's really quite a dreadful thing, losing everything, including the woman you love."

"You didn't –"

"If I could suggest we have this conversation somewhere a bit brighter?" Brian said. "Only I'm pretty sure a rat just ran over my shoe, and my phone's at ten percent."

They left the cellar a lot faster than they'd descended, clinking their boxes up the steps. Mark struggled to hold the box and pull down on the door handle. They backed up behind him, their phone lights pointing at their feet, darkness surrounding them.

"Come on, Mark."

"I'm trying." Finally, it opened and he threw himself against it.

Just as Faye, wondering where they were and telling herself it was stupid to be scared of a cellar door, was tentatively reaching out towards the rattling handle.

They burst through.

Faye, screaming like a victim in a *Hammer House of Horror* film, threw herself against the far wall with her eyes wide and her mouth hanging, absolutely terrified.

"Faye!" Brian cried, coming up last and quickly putting his

box on the floor. "Faye!"

She screamed again. He thought her eyes might actually pop out.

"Faye, it's okay, it's just us."

"Brian!" She clutched at him, panting off the adrenaline.

"Deep breaths, lass, deep breaths."

Jim came out of the kitchen and picked up Brian's box. When he took it back Mark was saying, "Not a word to the women about our yellow streaks."

They all nodded.

Tel looked around and said, "Where's Richard?"

* * *

"They left me!" Richard whined, after Brian had answered the frantic tapping on the cellar door. "They left me in the cellar, in the dark, all alone!"

"Never been so bloody scared in my life," Faye gasped. "I had flashbacks of every horror film I've ever watched."

"We didn't mean to leave him," Tel said. "We just ... forgot."

Richard screwed his face up into a fake cry. "I'm traumatised. I need brandy! No, whisky. Have I already tried the whisky? Can't remember. I'll have gin, definitely haven't had any gin yet."

Olivia got to her feet and went behind the bar, where she pushed a glass up against an optic. Richard suddenly found the strength to jump up and rush over. "Just the one shot?" he complained. "I could have been eaten alive by rats!"

"Rats?" Sophie cried, sitting up straight on the sofa next to a trembling Faye. "What rats?"

"There's no rats," Tel said.

"He said there were rats."

"He's drunk."

"Practically sober," Richard said, swigging back the gin before Olivia could add tonic and holding his glass out for more. "It's really quite a dreadful thing, losing – "

"Yeah, we've heard this one," Mark said.

Tel sat down next to Sophie and she gripped his arm tightly. "What rats, Tel?"

"He was hallucinating."

"No I wasn't!"

"Tell me, Tel."

"The big hairy guy said one ran over his shoe." Richard swigged back the finger of gin and held it out for more. Olivia huffed and filled it again.

"Ran over his shoe?" Sophie squealed. "Are there rats in the cellar, Mark? Tell me the truth!"

"There might be the odd one or two down there."

Sophie squealed again. "They could surge up!"

"It's okay, Sophs, we have a heavy spring on the door so it shuts itself."

"And that's enough to keep them out?" She lifted her legs up off the floor, her eyes everywhere.

"Unless they've learned how to turn a door handle," Jim laughed.

Tel glared at him. Sophie wrapped herself round him like a boa constrictor.

"Can they open doors?" she squeaked.

"What do you think?" Tel asked.

"I don't know, I've never really sat down with a rat and asked it in-depth questions about its ability to get places!"

"They can't get out."

"Are we talking about rats in the basement?" Olivia said, coming back over. "I've never seen one, or heard one."

"What about monsters?" Faye suddenly asked. "Are there any ... strange things down there?"

"There was when Jim was down there," Brian laughed.

"What do you mean?" Jim asked.

"Nothing, lad, just jesting."

Jim looked at Olivia. "Is this pub haunted?"

"Only by the spirits of Christmas past," she snapped, turning her head to Richard, who was sneakily helping himself to the optics.

Mark stared up at the ceiling. "Still no sign of the other one?"

"Not yet," Olivia said, "She's too late for breakfast now anyway."

"Talking about me?" said a grinning Janis, posed against the doorframe to the lounge and wearing an equally skin-tight, cleavage-plunging dress, this time in royal blue.

Mark sighed. Janis sauntered in and slithered onto the arm of his chair. He pushed her off with an elbow, pulling a face. She sidled up to Tel's armchair and he splayed his arms out like a dog anticipating a ball throw. She huffed and glowered at them all. Brian caved and stood up. "Here, lass, you can sit here."

"Eight seats for eleven people," she sniffed. "Not very good planning."

"Well, we weren't expecting to be gate-crashed by three extra visitors," Olivia said harshly.

"Where you going to sit, Bri?" Faye asked.

Brian pulled a dining chair from a nearby table, turned it around mid-air and straddled it. "Do I look sexy like this?" he winked at his wife.

"Like a cowboy," she grinned.

"Very Christine Keeler," said Tel.

"Bit before your time, wasn't it?" said Brian. "Bit before mine, too."

"What can I say, I read and I know things. Didn't she pose naked like that?"

"I don't think any of you are ready for that," Brian laughed.

"You don't look very comfortable," Mark remarked. "Are you comfortable?"

"Not really. I think I've split my jeans, it feels very *airy* back there."

"Take them off and I'll mend them for you," Olivia said, holding out her hand.

"That's my job," said Faye.

"I have a sewing machine upstairs."

"I have a shortbread biscuit tin full of sewing stuff."

"Oh, we've got one of those," Beth cried.

Brian looked at Mark. "They're arguing over who can get my jeans off."

"Enjoy."

"I am."

Janis coughed loudly. "What's on the menu for breakfast this morning?"

"Breakfast finishes at ten."

"Bit early, isn't it? Don't you cater for late risers?"

"Our customers generally have somewhere to go, it's not a holiday destination. We clearly state breakfast is eight until ten, otherwise we'd be cooking all morning."

"Well, it's not my fault I'm up late, I barely slept a wink all night."

"Out on your broomstick?" Mark laughed.

"The bed was *so* uncomfortable, it was like sleeping on rocks."

"Oh, ours is lovely, isn't it, Bri."

"Lucky you," Janis sneered. "I must have drawn the short straw. I nearly got up to look for the pea under the mattress."

"She thinks she's a princess!" Sophie whispered to Tel.

"All the mattresses in the guest rooms are new," Olivia said, slightly offended.

"I'd send them back," Janis huffed, "They're not fit for purpose. I'm pretty sure it's twisted my back. The pain, oh, the pain."

"Are you sure it wasn't the remains of all the people you've sucked dry under the mattress?" Mark asked.

"Ooh," said Faye, "Do you think so?"

"Stop watching horror films, lass."

"I won't, Bri."

"Your poor guests," Janis winced, thrusting out her chest as she rubbed the small of her back, "Having to sleep on those mattresses."

"You're not a guest," Mark said, "You're a grifter, here for a free ride because you've nowhere else to go."

"Nice," Janis sneered. "Character assassination at Christmas!"

"Consider the truth as my gift to you."

"You can help yourself to anything in the kitchen," Olivia offered.

"I'm not very good in the kitchen, am I, darling," she laughed at Mark.

"I wouldn't know, I've never seen you in one, *sweetheart*."

"I'll just have a cappuccino then."

Olivia threw an inviting arm towards the kitchen door behind the bar.

"I have to make it myself?"

Julie jumped up from the arm of the sofa next to Beth and cried, "I'll do it. Anyone else?"

They all rubbed their tummies.

"Full as an egg," said Tel.

"Couldn't fit anything else in," said Sophie.

"Got you all beat on the bulging belly," Beth laughed, running a hand over hers.

Janis reached out to Julie as she walked towards the kitchen. "Could you make me an eggs benedict while you're in there? Over-easy on the eggs and the bacon soft, not crispy."

"Just make the coffee," Olivia told Julie with a wink.

"What, denied breakfast?" Janis chided. "I won't be giving your pub a very good rating on TripAdvisor."

"We won't be giving a very good response if you do," said Mark. "Oh, the things I could write about our annoying, uninvited guest."

Brian coughed to break up the sudden hostility. "Merry Christmas," he boomed. "May it be full of peace, joy and happiness."

"May we always be blessed by the kindness of strangers," Faye said.

"God bless us, everyone," said Jim.

"Despite the fact that we're all atheists," Sophie laughed.

"And yet here you are," said Mark, "Celebrating Christmas."

"December 25th used to be a pagan festival celebrating winter solstice," she said, "Until the Romans stole it."

"Bit like they stole our money for a bath we don't have," said Tel.

Behind the bar, Richard raised his glass, emptied it, and filled it up from a bottle of crème de menthe. Olivia hurried over and took it from him. He looked crestfallen. When Olivia turned her back, he picked up another random bottle and, beneath the cover of the counter, filled his glass with absinthe. When he drank it he gagged.

Janis looked over at the Christmas tree and sighed heavily. "So, there's nothing under there for me?"

"Haven't we just had this conversation?"

"No spare present for anyone who turns up unexpectedly? Not very forward thinking of you. Way to make someone feel welcome."

"You're *not* welcome."

"Can we open the pressies now?" Brian asked. "Can we? Can we?"

The mounting tension exploded into a frisson of excitement. Brian and Faye led the surge to the Christmas tree. Mark and Olivia followed at a slower pace. Sophie and Tel tried to be casual but eventually succumbed to their inner child and threw themselves down on the floor with the others.

Beth said, "Just lob stuff at me."

"I'll have anything you don't want," Janis shouted, "Unless it's cheap crap, which it probably is."

"If it's crap she wants," Mark breathed, "I could – "

"Mark!" Olivia snapped.

Jim hurried over and picked up a couple of wrapped parcels. He took them back to Beth with a huge smile. They all restrained themselves and turned to watch her open them. A breast pump and baby clothes. Beth kissed Jim's cheek.

PITCHING UP AT CHRISTMAS!

"Yours are wrapped in blue glitter paper," she told him.

"Ooh," said Faye, "Blue? Coincidence, or a hint of things to come?"

"No," Beth laughed, "It's just pretty paper."

Jim came bounding back to the tree like an excited Labrador and picked up his parcels, flopping to the floor to open them. A shirt, some socks, and a book.

"What's this, babes?" he asked.

"It's a book, babes."

"I don't read books, babes."

"Why am I not surprised," Tel chuckled.

"Read the title, babes."

Jim muttered, "*How to Become a Perfect Dad*. Oh, that's great, babes."

"Glad you like it, babes."

"Babes, babes, babes," Janis sighed. "Almost as bad as darling, darling, darling."

Mark opened his mouth. Olivia gave him a warning look and he snapped it shut again.

Julie came back with mug of coffee and placed it on the table in front of Janis.

"A mug?" she gasped.

"Yeah," Mark said, before he could stop himself, "I was."

"I've basted the turkey," Julie said to Olivia.

"Lovely, thank you."

"Smells delicious," Mark said, giving her a kiss on the cheek.

"Can't wait," Brian said.

"Because all your other Christmas dinners have been so horrible?" Faye snapped.

"No, love." He sighed heavily, and Faye gave him a little smile and reached out for his hand. He smiled back and said, "Aren't you going to open your present from me?"

Faye pulled a huge, wrapped box from under the Christmas tree, making lots of excited noises.

Brian warmed up his smile, ready for the gratitude that

would soon pour forth from his wife.

She tore off the paper. Underneath, a box with a drawing of a pair of boots on it. Brian's smile widened in anticipated.

Faye seemed to hesitate for just the briefest moment. Delight, Brian thought, she was overcome with delight.

Faye took the lid off the box, pulled back the tissue paper, and said nothing. He'd blown her away, he'd literally rendered her speechless. His beard exposed teeth. Faye took a breath. Here it comes, he thought; best present ever, blah, blah, blah.

But it didn't go quite as he expected.

CHAPTER 11

"Brian."

"Yes, my love?"

"What are these?"

Sophie put her hand over her mouth to stifle a giggle. Olivia sucked her lips in, widening her eyes at Mark, whose mouth had fallen open.

"They're boots, lass."

"Yes, I can see they're boots."

"The ones you liked in Selfridges. You sent me a picture."

"I did."

"Show us the picture, Bri," Sophie sniggered.

Brian took his phone out of his jeans pocket, flicked through it, and turned it around for everyone to see.

There were two pairs of boots in the photograph. The ones on the left were a burgundy colour, with low heels and a zip down the side.

The ones on the right were half cut out of the picture and were bright red, with four inch stiletto heels and black laces running up the front.

They sat with hands clamped over their mouths, Sophie's shoulders silently hitching up and down. Tears were filling Olivia's eyes. Mark and Tel made snorting noises.

Faye turned to look at Brian. "I said the burgundy ones, Bri."

"Burgundy is red, isn't it?"

"No, Bri, burgundy isn't red."

"Oh." Where was the gratitude, the hugs, the kisses? "I

thought it was."

Sophie tentatively took her hand away from her mouth and, struggling to control herself, said, "Burgundy is ... a dark red and ... " A squeak escaped. "... purple colour."

"So, red then."

"No, Bri, not red."

He looked at Faye, his smile now gone. "You don't like them?"

"Only if she wants to take up pole dancing," Mark sniggered. "Do you want to take up pole dancing, Faye? Has it been a lifelong ambition of yours?"

Mark and Tel fell against each other, howling with amusement.

"Let me see," Beth called over.

Faye held up one long, bright red boot. Sophie and Olivia lost control, tears rolled down their faces. Beth said, "Oh," but not in a good way.

"Red, burgundy, what's the difference?" Brian asked, confused.

"The difference between being happily married and hastily divorced," Mark cried, wiping tears from his eyes.

"The difference between happy wife and happy hooker!" Tel laughed, falling backwards.

"I like them," Sophie forced herself to say.

Tel shot up into a sitting position and said, "What size are they?"

"Five," Faye said.

"*Foive*," Tel cried, falling back again.

"I'm a five," Janis called over, "I'll have them."

"To draw in more customers?" Mark asked.

Olivia tutted, trying to contain the smile pulling on her lips.

Brian remained straight-faced beneath his beard, his hopes and dreams about Faye smothering him with love and gratitude now gone. Faye continued to hold one boot up, staring at it like it was an alien artifact.

"What – " Olivia began, halting to contain a ball of giggles inside her, "What made you buy the half-pictured boots and not the boots in the middle, Bri?"

"I thought the boots in the middle were wellies."

"They do look a bit welly-ish," Sophie conceded. "But … are the red boots really Faye's *style*."

Brian shrugged. "I thought she wanted to try something different."

"Like stripping?" Mark howled.

"Can you even walk in heels that big?" Olivia asked.

"I dunno," Faye said, "I've never gone above two inches before."

Tel could barely breathe as he rolled on the floor, clutching at his stomach.

"Put them on, Faye."

"Yes, try them on."

"Ooh, I don't know."

"We'll help you," Mark gasped. "Tel, bring the crash mattresses in."

"Stop," Tel gasped, "I can't breathe."

Faye took off her fluffy slippers and they all fell silent. She unzipped one red stiletto boot – the zip seemed to go on forever – and slipped her foot into it. She pulled. And pulled some more. She eventually got it on, zipped it up – another lengthy process – and did the same with the other one.

She prepared to stand.

"Careful, Faye."

"Give us a hand, Bri."

"Are you sure you want to do this?"

"They're on now. Come on, lift me up."

Brian stood up, put his hands underneath her armpits and pulled her to her splaying feet, inches higher than she'd ever stood before. Her knees touched and she hunched over, trying to find her centre of gravity.

"Very elegant manoeuvring," Mark laughed.

Faye straightened up unsteadily with her arms out to the

side. "Okay, Bri, let me go."

"Release the woman!" Tel cried.

Brian unhooked himself from his wife and stepped back, his arms ready to catch her.

Faye's ankles wobbled, but she looked down at them and smiled. "It's quite nice up here," she said.

"Try taking a few steps."

Faye stared down at the red things on her legs.

"Look up, Faye."

Faye lifted her head, and one foot. The other foot went from side to side, but she managed to keep her balance and take a step forward, wobbling on both feet before lifting and stepping again. Brian followed an inch behind her.

"You look like Bambi on ice," Sophie giggled.

In a deep, slow voice, Mark said, "And here she is, a woman of indeterminate age, walking in high heels for the first time."

"Taken out of her natural habitat of low heels," Tel said, "Faye struggles to maintain her balance."

"Stop it, you two," Olivia said.

"I'm doing it, Bri, I'm doing it!"

"You are, lass, and my heart's in my mouth."

"I think I know how this ends," Mark said.

Another step. Wobbling, arms struggling to maintain balance, Brian bouncing from foot to foot, trying to anticipate when and in which direction she would fall.

"I'm turning round," Faye said, biting her bottom lip in concentration.

"Head up, Faye."

"You're doing it, Faye."

"Well done, you look marvellous."

"She looks like a marionette with its strings cut," Mark breathed.

"Aaand there she goes."

Brian was ready to catch her when one foot tipped completely over, throwing her off balance and flinging her sideways. He hoped she hadn't broken anything as he hooked his hands under her armpits and gently lowered her to the floor.

"That was fun," Faye grinned, unzipping them. "I felt like a supermodel."

"Didn't look like one," Janis said, sipping her mug of coffee. "You looked like – "

"Are you going to keep them?" Sophie quickly asked.

"No, I'll take them back and get the burgundy ones."

"I'll have them," Janis said again.

"No, I'll take them back."

"I'm a natural in high heels." She lifted a stiletto shoe. "Wear them all the time. You can't wear high heels if you're heavy."

There was a beat of silence.

"Heavy?" Faye eventually said, turning to look at her. "What do you mean, heavy?"

"It's a trap," Mark said, "Don't take the bait."

"I'm just saying," Janis said, "You have to be quite light on your feet to wear something like those, and you're not light, are you."

Faye looked at Brian. "Is she saying I'm fat?"

"You're not fat, lass."

"You're normal," Sophie said.

"Oh," said Brian, "I wouldn't go that far."

They all turned back to the Christmas tree, laughing, and continued opening presents. Janis tutted and sipped her coffee, pulling a face.

Faye gave Brian a bundle of socks, underpants, a hardback book about guns, a beard kit, and an unusual book of vouchers: "Don't read them out loud," she said, "They're not for company, they're, you know, a bit ... racy."

"Read them out," Tel heckled.

Brian flicked through them, his eyes widening with each page. "Looking forward to this one," he said. "If you could all leave the room for a few minutes."

"A few minutes?" Faye scolded.

"Moving briskly on," Olivia said.

Brian winked at Faye, and she giggled.

Sophie was surprised when Tel handed her a big, squishy package. "I thought we weren't doing gifts?"

"As per your 'not participating in an overly-commercialised Christmas' text," said Mark.

"That we didn't get," said Faye.

"Yes, well there is a tiny flaw in my logic. I hadn't factored in the bitter disappointment element."

Smiling, Sophie tore the paper off. It was a beautiful, multi-coloured blanket. "Oh, it's *gorgeous*!" she cried, hugging it and kissing his cheek, "Thank you."

Tel looked at Olivia and mouthed, 'Thanks."

Olivia lifted a thumb.

Sophie said, "I haven't got you anything."

"And there's the bitter disappointed element I was talking about," Tel sighed.

Olivia got up and went over to Julie, sitting down next to her on the sofa. "This is for you," she said, handing her a soft package. "It's just something to say thank you for all your hard work."

Julie beamed.

"Yeah, you did good," said Beth, and Julie beamed even more.

She tore the paper off. It was a pale blue jumper. Olivia had bought it for Sue, the barmaid who couldn't make it in on Christmas Eve – she'd have to go shopping before the pub staff came back. She briefly wondered if her mother could stop off in Mexico on her way home to buy a replacement blanket for the spare room.

"It's lovely," Julie said, putting the jumper on over her crop top and bursting into tears.

Beth put an arm round her shoulders and pulled her close. She gave Jim a dirty look, and he held out his hands, palms up, totally confused.

"Oh, nothing for me then?" Janis whined.

"We didn't expect you," Olivia said, annoyed but also feeling a little mean. There was a beautiful notebook and pen she'd bought for her friend in the village upstairs, but she hadn't wanted to give it to Janis. She felt bad about it now.

"You weren't expecting *her* either," Janis said, nodding at Julie, "So how come she gets a present and I don't?"

"Because she's not a nasty-mouthed, spiteful little cow," Mark called over.

"Some Christmas this is," Janis said, huffing. "Where you don't even get a present on Christmas Day."

"You *weren't* invited!" Mark cried, a little too high-pitched. "You're only here because Liv very kindly let you stay."

"Huh, lucky me, unwanted and un-presented."

"Turning up unannounced at Christmas is unprecedented, even for you."

Janis nonchalantly sipped her coffee, pulling a face and looking over at Julie, huddled up to Beth. "This is cold," she said, "Could you do me another one?"

"Kitchen's over there," Olivia said. "Help yourself."

"I don't know how to work the coffee machine."

"Oh, I used the sachets," Julie said, "You just open it, put it in the cup and –"

"*Sachets?*" Janis gasped, staring down at her mug and then up at Olivia. "You don't have a proper coffee machine?"

"We do," Olivia said, "But I don't think Jools knows how to work it."

Julie shook her head.

The others came back to the *Friends* corner with their presents. Richard stumbled over and flopped to the floor next to Janis's armchair with a glass and a bottle. Olivia leaned forward and snatched the bottle from his hands.

"Oh," he cried, looking lost and bottle-less.

Janis put a hand on his shoulder, lifted it, looked at it, pulled a face, and put the hand back again. "Poor you," she said.

"Poor me?"

"Yes, poor you, deprived of your only enjoyment in life by

people who've already taken everything you had."

"Excuse me?" Mark gasped.

"Look at him," said Janis. "A man, down on his luck, who *literally* has nothing, and you treat him with such disdain. It's not as if you can't afford to help him out, is it."

"He had a very generous divorce settlement!" Olivia said.

"You don't have to explain yourself, Liv," Mark said, "Especially not to her."

"Poor me," said Richard.

"To think," Janis said, staring at him pitifully, "He used to be part of the very wealthy Olgivy family."

Olivia's head spun round to Mark. "How does she know that?"

Mark sighed. "I found her going through our paperwork upstairs."

"Going through …?" She glared at Janis, who, with a tiny smile playing on her lips, whined, "Oh Mark, you didn't have to tell her."

"Of course I did, I tell Liv everything."

"Do you?"

"Yes," he snarled, "We don't keep secrets from each other."

"Don't you?"

"No."

Beyond annoyed, Olivia reached down and snatched Janis's handbag up off the floor, throwing it onto her lap and opening it up. "Searching through my personal belongings?" she growled, opening the bag, "Let's see how you like it."

"No, stop," Janis said, with no real emotion, adding, "Search away, I have nothing to hide."

Olivia was disappointed to find only a mobile phone and a lipstick inside the bag.

"Nothing to hide, eh?" Olivia said, taking out the phone and turning it on. She glanced at Janis, who seemed remarkably unbothered.

Sophie's skin prickled. Something didn't feel right. She looked at Janis and saw that she was struggling not to smile. She watched as Janis turned her head to give Richard an exaggerated wink, and Richard suddenly perked up. Sophie felt a sudden sense of doom. Co-conspirators, she thought. She'd seen that look before, in her office and in court. Janis and Richard were up to something.

"Maybe you shouldn't, Liv," she said.

"No, no, she's obviously not big into privacy, let's see what personal items she has in her phone."

Tel picked up on Sophie's nervousness and sat up a little straighter. He noticed both Janis and Richard were fizzing with anticipation. He didn't like it.

"Oh!" Olivia suddenly cried. "There's … there's messages from you on here, Mark."

"What?"

She stared at him, confused. "You've been texting Janis?"

"I bloody haven't. Why would I?"

Olivia tapped a finger on the screen. "Oh, Mark," she breathed, "What have you done?"

"Nothing!" He leaned over to look at the screen. Text messages. Lots of them, all from 'Mark'. "I never sent those," he gasped, "It must be another Mark."

Olivia carried on reading, her hand slowly rising to her mouth, tears filling her eyes.

"It's not me!" he insisted, "I haven't heard from her in *years*."

"Mark," Janis said softly, reaching out to touch his arm. He reacted like he'd been burned and snatched it away. "Maybe it's best that she knows."

"Knows what?" he barked.

"I can't keep up the pretence any longer, darling."

Brian put a hand on Mark's shoulder and could feel the vibrations of rage coming off him.

"What do they say?" Faye asked.

As the tears spilled down her cheeks, Olivia said, "He says he loves her."

"I do not! Quite the opposite."

"He says he misses her and can't wait to see her again."

"I never sent that! I've *never* texted her!"

"Mark," said Janis, "It's time."

"He says he's bored with me," Olivia wailed, "and wants to be with her."

"Liv! It's not true!"

Brian tightened his grip on Mark's shoulder.

Olivia sniffed, "She says she can't live without him, has to be with him, and … and he invited her here for Christmas!"

"I didn't! I bloody didn't!"

She threw the phone down on the coffee table and burst into tears. Mark tried to comfort her, but she pushed him away. Faye wrapped her arms around her and held her tight. "It's okay, Liv. It must be a mistake. Mark would never say anything like that. He loves you."

"I do." Mark's mouth opened and closed. "I … I don't know what's going on here."

"Calm yourself, lad."

"I'm sure there's a perfectly reasonable explanation," Tel said, "There has to be."

"We're in love," Janis announced. "We never stopped loving each other."

Sophie leaned forward and picked the phone off the table.

Richard looked up at Janis. "Is this where I get my wife back, like you said?"

"Shush," she told him, sweeping her eyes over Olivia, sobbing into Faye, and Mark, who was blustering and confused.

"Oh Liv," Beth breathed softly, "It can't be true."

"It is," Janis grinned.

"No, it's not!"

"Let me call the number," Sophie said, "It might be one of those apps that send out fake – "

A phone started ringing somewhere. Sophie stood up, Janis's phone in her hand, and followed the sound.

She walked up to the coat stand at the end of the bar, near the door. She rifled through the coats, feeling the pockets, until she came to a padded jacket. She picked a phone up out of the pocket and looked at it, then across at Mark.

"Is this your jacket?" she asked.

He nodded, saying, "But that's not my phone. I've never seen that before in my life."

"A likely story," Janis grinned, "That's his secret phone, the one he uses to keep in touch with me."

Sophie looked from one phone to the other. "They're the same texts," she said, "But they've all been sent in the last three days."

"We were worried Olivia would find out," Janis said, inspecting her painted talons, "So he got another one, his 'love phone', he called it."

"That's not true!" Mark cried, "She's lying!"

"You've got it all worked out, haven't you," Sophie said, narrowing her eyes. "But there's something not right about this, apart from knowing Mark well enough to know he wouldn't do this to Liv."

"Wouldn't he?" Janis grinned. "Are you sure about that? Don't you have the evidence right there in your hands."

Sophie shook her head, looking at the texts on both phones and saying, "I can't quite put my finger on it."

Tel leaned forward and said, "Mark, give me your phone."

Mark did without hesitation. He felt his world had just turned on his axis. Life without Liv was inconceivable, a black hole waiting to swallow him up.

Tel sat back and started prodding the screen.

Janis looked pleadingly at Mark and said, "It had to come out sometime, darling."

"Shut up, Janis. I've done nothing and you know it."

"Is it happening?" Richard asked Janis, turning to smile at Olivia, who was still sobbing and being comforted by Faye. "Is it happening now?"

"There's no texts on Mark's phone," Tel said.

"Of course not," said Janis, "He told me he was very careful to delete them all."

Sophie hurried over and leaned on the back of Tel's chair. "You tap here," he told her, "Tap Edit, then Show Recently Deleted. See? Nothing on his phone."

Sophie straightened up. "Wait a minute," she said, "*Janis* bought the phone. *She* texted from her phone to this one, and made up Mark's replies herself."

"No," Janis said firmly, "Mark sent them."

"And then," Sophie said, still thinking, "She dropped the new phone into Mark's jacket pocket."

Olivia raised her head, wiping at her eyes. "Really?"

"She's had ample time to deposit it," Tel said.

"And she wasn't bothered when Liv went through her bag and found her phone."

"Janis *wanted* Liv to find it," Faye gasped. "She set it all up."

"Why?" Mark pleaded. "Why did you do it, Janis?"

"I didn't."

"Now?" Richard asked. "Can I have her back now?"

"What are you talking about?" Brian asked.

Janis pushed the hand on his shoulder, tipping him sideways. "Say nothing," she hissed. "Keep your mouth shut, this is none of your business."

"Did Janis tell you that you'd get Liv back?" Faye asked.

Richard looked perplexed. "I don't know, I can't think straight with you all staring at me."

Sophie quickly moved behind the bar, putting the two phones on the counter. She filled a tumbler with whisky, and hurried back, kneeling in front of Richard and holding the glass in both hands. "If you tell me," she breathed, "You can have this."

"Stay quiet," Janis spat.

"Never mind what she says," Sophie smiled, as Richard licked his lips, "You can tell me, and then you can have this."

There was complete and utter silence.

Then Richard reached a hand out towards the glass.

"Uh-uh," Sophie chided softly, "Not until you tell me. What did Janis say, Richard? Tell me." She moved the glass closer to him, holding it tight, letting him smell it and watching his eyes widen as he stared at the amber liquid.

"Richard," Janis growled, "Don't say anything, they're trying to trick you."

"Come on, Richard. You can tell me."

"Don't you – !"

Richard's hands moved towards the glass. "She said she'd get Olivia back for me as a Christmas present. She said she had the perfect plan and that we wouldn't be alone any more."

There was a huge, collective gasp. Nobody moved, nobody spoke. The only sound was Richard slurping back the whisky.

Olivia looked at Mark. He opened his arms towards her and she fell into them.

"Oh Mark," she cried. "I'm so sorry I doubted you."

"I'd never do anything to hurt you, Liv, *never*." He held her tight and kissed the top of her head.

"I'm so sorry."

She looked over at Janis, who was languidly staring out of the window, and stood up. There was a look in her eye that nobody, not even Mark, had seen before. Pure rage.

"Get up," she hissed, "And get out."

"I can't go out in this," Janis sniffed. "Look at it, it's a blizzard out there."

"*Get up*," Olivia said again, taking a step towards her, "And get out." She glanced down at Richard, staring into his empty glass with a sad face. "You too, *Dick*."

"Me?" He wobbled his head up towards her. "Why? I haven't done anything!"

"Get the hell out of my pub, the pair of you."

"You're being ridiculous," Janis said. "You wouldn't send a dog out in this."

"Mark," Olivia said.

"On it," he cried, jumping up.

"Don't you touch me," Janis said, alarmed as he stepped towards her, "Don't you *dare* touch me."

"Brian?" Mark said, grabbing hold of Janis's arm.

Brian peeled himself off the dining chair like an old cowboy getting off a horse. He suddenly remembered the tear in the back of his trousers and threw a hand behind him. Bow-legged and with one arm behind his back he approached Richard, who squealed and shuffled back across the floor, crying, "I didn't do anything!"

Brian grabbed him by the collar of his smelly coat and hauled him to his feet in one swift movement.

Mark was dragging a very resistant Janis out of the room by her arm. Tel, Sophie and Faye followed.

Olivia ran ahead, into the hallway, and opened the front door. Snow and wind howled into the pub. Their clothes flapped, their hair whipped.

"You can't be serious!" Janis cried, spluttering against the snow flying into her face.

"Where are we going?" whined Richard.

"*Out!*" said Olivia, throwing an arm towards the swirling snowstorm. "*Get out!*"

Brian hauled Richard to the doorstep and gave him a hefty push. Richard lurched forward, slipped on the snow, lost his footing, attempted the splits and a sliding pose that Michael Jackson would have been proud of, and fell on his back.

"No!" Janis screamed, as Mark tried to push her out and she desperately gripped onto him. "You can't do this!"

"Watch me."

"I'll call the police!"

"They'll never make it through this snow, and they'll just tell you that licensees have the right to refuse entry to their premises."

"You're banned!" Olivia said, "For life! Never come here again!"

Mark swiftly pulled her hands away from Janis's clutches and forced her over the doorstep, holding up his palms to stop her stepping back inside.

"Where am I supposed to go?" she screamed. "It's *freezing*

out here!"

Olivia took her long camel coat and scarf off the stand by the door and threw them out into the snow. "Cover your baps up, love. Mark," she said, holding a hand out towards him, "Give me the key to the utility shed."

"Shed?" Janis screeched. "What kind of barbarians are you?"

Mark searched his pockets. "I don't have them. JULIE!"

A tiny voice from the other room cried, "What?"

"DO YOU STILL HAVE THE KEY TO THE UTILITY SHED?"

Julie came running into the hallway, her hand deep in the jeans of her pocket. She handed him the key and, in a small voice, said, "Do you want me to go too?"

"No," Olivia told her, "We don't."

"Oh, so she gets to stay," Janis hissed, "But not us?"

Mark tossed the key outside. It landed on top of a pile of snow.

"No!" Janis screamed above the howling gale. "You can't do this!"

"We can and we are."

"No!"

"What's happening?" Richard asked, lurching unsteadily to his feet and slipping over again.

"They're kicking us out in *this*!" Janis screamed again. "On Christmas Day!"

"Enough!" Olivia shouted, urging Brian and Mark to step back. "No more."

With a final look at Richard, confused, and Janis, furious as she pulled on her coat, Olivia slammed the door shut, pulled the bolt across, smiled and brushed her hands together.

"That's the rubbish taken out," she said, heaving a sigh of relief.

Janis pounded on the door for quite a while. When they went back into the lounge she appeared outside the window, frantically tapping on the glass. Richard stood behind her, still looking confused. Mark let the curtains drop from their restraints and she was gone. The tapping moved on to other windows. They ignored it. Then all was silent, except for the howling wind ... until glass tapping started up in the back lounge.

Mark hurried through. Janis and Richard were pressed against the patio windows.

"Let us in!" she cried.

Mark tutted and pushed the switch on the wall. A slatted security shutter hummed its way down. Richard and Janis's head followed it, their mouths opening and closing as they bent lower and lower. The shutter didn't reach the bottom, it got wedged in the snow drift. Mark left it, and was about to turn away when he heard a scooping snow sound. When he turned back, Richard was scraping the snow away from the bottom of the door and yelling, "Can you just slip a few bottles out?"

Mark rejoined the group.

* * *

"You okay, Liv?" Sophie asked.

Olivia gave her beaming, overbite smile, and said, "Yes, actually. Quite a relief to have them gone, to be honest."

"Are you sure?"

"Yes, quite sure. I should never have let them in."

Mark came over and hugged her. Sophie hugged her. Faye got up and hugged her too.

"Mine's a virtual hug," Beth said. "Quite an eventful Christmas, Liv. It's like being part of a live soap opera."

"Sorry," Olivia said. "Sorry, everyone."

"Don't apologise," Sophie said, "None of it was your fault."

"It was quite entertaining," said Beth, "Took my mind off the squirming children for a bit. Did you see the look on their faces?"

"No," said Mark, "I was too busy ejecting."

"They looked like rabbits caught in the headlights of a speeding train," Beth laughed. "The big boobed one couldn't believe you were chucking her out."

Smiles appeared on faces. Hands were held. Looks were exchanged.

"Let's just enjoy the rest of Christmas," Oliva said.

An alarm sounded on her phone. "Oh! The turkey!" she cried, and ran into the kitchen, closely followed by Julie, and then Faye.

Sophie looked at Mark. "Should I?" she asked, nodding towards the kitchen door.

"I think everyone would much rather you didn't," he said.

"Perhaps *you* should offer to help? Cooking isn't just a woman's job, you know."

"I'll be in the way," he winked.

Sophie thought for a moment, then got up and went into the kitchen.

CHAPTER 12

In the kitchen, Olivia was basting a beast of a turkey in the oven, Julie was peeling vegetables, and Faye was unloading the dishwasher of breakfast things.

"Anything I can do to help?" Sophie asked, loosely swinging her arms.

Olivia stood up, brushing her hair away from her face with the back of her hand. "You could make the bread sauce, if you like?"

"O-kay."

Sophie headed towards a counter that had a fresh loaf on top of a chopping board. She stood and stared at it. "So, bread," she said to herself, giving it a pat. "And what else? Milk? I'm guessing milk. Yes, milk sounds quite saucy."

She turned to look for a fridge, and found them all standing still, staring at her and grinning.

"Have you never made bread sauce before?" Olivia asked

"Made it?" Sophie huffed, "Never even heard of it."

"You've never heard of bread sauce?" Faye laughed.

"No, and it sounds … well, pretty disgusting actually."

"I'll do it," Julie said, bounding over and releasing Sophie from the bread board.

"What *are* you good at?" Faye asked.

"My job," Sophie said, "My arguments in court are pretty good. Hopefully I'm a good wife." She briefly wondered if she'd still be considered a good wife once she'd told Tel that they were now celibate.

"I meant in the kitchen," Faye said.

"Oh."

"The prolonged silence tells me you're not familiar with a kitchen," Olivia giggled.

Sophie shrugged. "No, not really."

"How do you survive?" Faye asked.

"If we're not out with a client we have lunch delivered to the office every day from a local delicatessen. We eat out a lot, and we have a lot of cereal in our cupboards."

"You never cook?" Olivia asked, shaking her head.

"No."

"Wow," said Julie. "I want your life."

"Yes, well, just study law for six to eight years and you're there."

"Oh. I failed my GCSEs."

"Take them again."

"Oh yeah, I could!"

"You should."

"You can stir," Olivia said, handing her a collection of wooden spoons.

Sophie stared at them. "Stir what?"

"Anything that's in a saucepan."

Sophie looked around. "I don't see any saucepans."

"Because we haven't started cooking yet."

"Right. I'll just stand here with my spoons and wait until stirring is required."

"That's right. Alexa, play some Christmas cooking music."

"There's Christmas cooking music?" Sophie gasped, as Michael Buble singing *It's Beginning to Look a Lot Like Christmas* filled the kitchen.

"Of course," Olivia laughed.

"Is there a 'definitely guilty, m'lud' playlist?"

She asked Alexa.

There wasn't.

***

In the lounge, Beth and Jim were playing a game of Dobble and screaming a lot. Every now and then Beth would clutch her baby bump and wince.

"You okay there, Beth?" Tel asked.

"Yeah, the babies are having a fight. Hope they're not like this when they come out. Oh, *cactus*!" she cried, slamming a card down.

"Anyone fancy a drink?" Tel asked, getting up and going behind the bar. "I haven't actually poured my own pint yet."

"Nah, I'm alright," Brian said.

"You don't want a drink?" Tel put a glass under a spout and slowly pulled the pump handle towards him.

"No," said Brian, "On account of me *not* being an alcoholic, despite rumours to the contrary."

Tel laughed. "It's Christmas."

"I don't generally drink during the day," Brian said, "Sends me to sleep."

"Or are you afraid of … da-da-DA, the wife?"

Now it was Brian's turn to laugh. "Could be."

"I won't tell if you don't."

"I'm fine, Tel."

"Suit yourself. Mark? Jim?"

They both shook their heads.

"Lightweights, the lot of you," Tel muttered, coming back to the *Friends* corner with a pint of foam. Brian shook his head and took it off him, went back behind the bar and pulled a half pint of foam.

"Not much of an improvement," Tel laughed, taking it.

"At least mine has some liquid in the bottom."

With Christmas music gently playing in the background, they talked about cars, caravans, the best campsites, the worst campsites, guns, work and the weather. Beth thrashed Jim at Dobble.

The fire roared. Outside, the snow fell.

It was very, very cosy.

***

The women toiled away in the kitchen, cooking dinner, listening to music and occasionally singing along. Every now and then one of them would shout, "Spoon!" and Sophie would rush over and enthusiastically start stirring something.

"I almost feel like I'm helping," she grinned.

"You are. Don't let the gravy burn."

Julie dashed in and out, preparing the table in the back lounge; condiments, sauces, glasses, bottles of wine, and the cutest centrepiece depicting a glittering, white-felted caravan made entirely out of wooden twigs.

Eventually, when steam was rising from everything, Olivia took the foil off the rested bird and cried, "Stand back, I'm carving the turkey."

"She's carving the turkey!" Julie yelled.

"Carving!" shouted Faye.

"Does it need stirring?" Sophie asked, holding up a fresh wooden spoon.

"No, Sophs."

Julie helped Olivia lift the bird onto a serving tray, and they watched as Olivia meticulously carved the breast into slices.

"Electric knife," Sophie said, amazed.

"You've heard of electric knives before, haven't you?" Faye asked.

"Oh yes, just never seen one in action before. It's quite clever, isn't it."

"Julie," said Olivia, "Bring me a couple of plastic containers from that cupboard above you."

Julie did, and Olivia threw turkey meat into the bottom of each, taking them over to the bubbling hob and scooping small portions from each of the vegetables with a slotted spoon. She opened the oven and tonged out roast potatoes and parsnips, used a ladle to add gravy, spooned in cranberry sauce, threw a couple of stuffing balls and a giant Yorkshire pudding on top, and slapped on the lids, forcing them down and squashing everything inside.

"Christmas dinner bricks," Julie laughed.

"It's more than they deserve," Olivia said, taking her phone from the pocket of her apron. "Richard, dinner is ready. Come to the kitchen window at the side of the pub and we'll pass them out. Come now." She hung up before he had a chance to say anything.

Julie picked up the two plastic containers, a knife and a fork, and put them on the windowsill.

"Prepare to plate up!" Olivia bellowed.

"Plate up!" yelled Faye.

"Yes, chef," Sophie cried, having watched Gordon Ramsay a few times.

Lids were removed from simmering saucepans and various vegetables were drained, tipped into serving bowls and covered over. A pile of perfectly roasted potatoes and parsnips were put into two large trays. Three gravy boats were filled and, the pièce de resistance, the turkey was garnished with roasted garlic and orange slices, sage leaves, cranberries and stuffing balls.

Julie used oven gloves to take the warmed plates from the second oven and rushed them out to the back lounge, just as Olivia slammed her palm onto a bell on the counter and yelled, "MEN! BARKIN' SERVICE!"

There was a tap on the kitchen window and Julie rushed over, opened it, and handed out the plastic boxes and cutlery.

"Can we come – ?"

Julie closed the window again and dashed back to the great serve-up.

"You handled that well," Olivia said.

"Used to work at MacDonalds," she giggled.

The men hurried into the kitchen. Their eyes bulged at the masses of steaming food on the counter.

"Grab a towel each," Olivia ordered, whipping off her

apron. "Grab something and take it through to the table. Don't spill or drop anything."

"We wouldn't dare," Mark laughed, picking up trays of potatoes and parsnips. "Bit of a bossy boots in the kitchen, aren't you?"

"Got to get things done," she puffed, smiling, "Now get going."

Brian flexed his biceps and picked up the turkey, straining a little as he took it through to the other room. The table was filled. Beth was helped over, and they all sat down.

"Bit dark in here," Olivia said. "Open the shutters, would you, Mark?"

Mark pressed the electric button and the shutters lifted. Outside, in the garden, standing in the whipping snowstorm and huddled together like lost children, were Richard and Janis. Richard was holding the two plastic cartons in one hand, with the other he tapped on the patio window.

"Can we come in?" he shouted.

"Open the bloody door," Janis screamed, "And hurry up about it."

Mark turned to Olivia, who rolled her eyes and said, "Let them in."

"Are you sure?"

"We can hardly eat Christmas dinner with those two standing there like a couple of starving urchins."

Mark tutted, but got up and opened a patio door. Richard skittered in, holding the collar of his ragged coat and the plastic containers.

Janis marched in, sternly eyeballing them all and hissing, "How *dare* you – !"

"Any table over there," Olivia said, pointing towards the front lounge.

Richard hurried off and disappeared behind the front bar.

"LEAVE IT!" Olivia yelled, surprisingly loud.

"But I just want – "

"*LEAVE IT!*"

Richard reappeared, his head hanging.

"Not here with you?" Janis sniffed, taking off her coat and lifting up her assets.

"You're not welcome at our table," Mark said.

Julie jumped up and ran into the kitchen, returning with two plates. She put them on a table in the front lounge. Olivia stood up, marched over to Richard, snatched the containers from him, took them over to the table, peeled off the lids and firmly upended each one. Layers of Christmas dinner sat squarely on the plate.

"Dinner," she said, "Is served."

Janis slowly sat down and peered at her squashed, oblong-shaped meal. She looked up at Olivia and, with a big smile, said, "I'm vegan."

"What?"

"Since when?" Mark shouted over.

"Since … forever."

"Weren't you eating pork pies yesterday," Brian asked.

"I thought they were mince pies," said Janis.

"They had pickle on them."

"And mince pies are made with beef suet," Faye said.

"Oh, are they? I just assumed everything would be vegan friendly."

"Why?" Tel said, "None of us are vegan."

"A pub is supposed to cater for everyone, isn't it?"

"Didn't you ask Julie to make you eggs benedict this morning, with soft bacon?" Sophie said.

"I meant vegan bacon, obviously."

"And the eggs?"

Janis shrugged. "Anyway, I'm just telling you I'm vegan."

"You could have mentioned it before," Olivia huffed.

"I thought I did. I must have forgotten. Silly me."

"Just eat the vegetables then."

"They're covered in meat and gravy."

"Just scrape off what you can."

"It's against my ethical commitment to eat any foods

containing animal products."

"You don't have any ethics," Mark yelled, "And you certainly don't have any commitment."

"I could do you a sandwich?" Olivia offered.

"A sandwich! On Christmas Day!"

"You'll have nothing if you carry on," said Mark. "Just be grateful for what you've got."

"I've got a cold dinner full of …" She picked out a piece. "… *dry* turkey."

"Dry!" Olivia gasped.

"Liv," Mark called, "Come back to us before you get caught up in her mad mind games."

As Olivia turned, Richard reached out and gently touched her arm. "I'd much prefer a liquid lunch, can I – ?"

"No," Olivia snapped, and stormed off.

She sat down and the goodwill around the table immediately poured forth, warming and soothing her.

"Born appetite," said Brian.

"This looks *wonderful*."

"You've really outdone yourself, Liv."

"This is a feast fit for kings."

"Help yourselves," she smiled proudly.

And they did.

* * *

Twice Olivia looked over at the front lounge and saw Richard down on all fours, trying to crawl behind the bar.

"Don't touch my stock," she cried, but she asked Julie to take them some glasses and a bottle of champagne – it was Christmas, after all.

"There's no condiments over here," Janis yelled. "And we don't have any crackers."

"You want to see crackers?" Mark said, "Pull out a mirror."

"Is there any more champagne, Olivia?" Richard whined.

"Is this cranberry sauce *fresh*?" Janis shrieked, "Tastes off to me."

"Olivia, my glass is empty."

"It's like having rowdy children at a kiddies table," Brian laughed, handing round the roast potatoes. "Should we put a cartoon on the telly for them or something?"

"It'll just overexcite them," Mark said. "Best just to ignore them."

"Olivia?" Richard cried, "More champagne? Maybe a brandy for my broken, frost-bitten heart." He pounded fiercely on his chest and coughed.

"Your roast potatoes aren't a patch on my roast potatoes," Janis complained.

Mark laughed. "When have you *ever* cooked anything?"

Brian held up a potato on his fork and turned it. "This isn't just any roast potato," he said in a deep, husky voice, "This is Olivia's roast potato."

Tel held his up. "The most perfect roast potato in the history of roast potatoes."

"All hail Liv's spuds!" Jim cried, holding up his pronged roastie.

Olivia laughed, then glanced at Beth. "You're not eating much? Are you okay?"

"The kids are pummelling my – " She glanced at Sophie, who was already starting to put her fork down. "I had one too many mince pies this morning," she lied instead, "The food is lovely."

"It must taste better when it's *warm*," Janis snapped.

Faye noticed that Beth was grimacing and trying not to show it. "Are you okay?" she asked.

Beth rubbed her bulge. "Yeah, bit of indigestion, I think."

Jim put his hand on hers. "You okay, babes?"

"Yeah, yeah, don't make a fuss." She raised her glass of tomato juice. "To Liv," she toasted, "Best cook in the Cotswolds."

"In the world!" Mark cheered.

"To Liv."

"Maybe not *the* best cook," Janis muttered, loud enough for them to hear.

"Fancy yourself a good cook then?" Tel asked, and Mark burst out laughing.

"I thought you said you didn't cook?" said Faye.

"I don't, but I know it all in theory."

"I bet you do," Mark mumbled, "Just too lazy to put it into practice."

"Kitchen duties are beneath me."

Faye's eyes were incredulous.

"Shut up, Janis," Mark shouted.

"Make me."

Mark stood up, ready to kick her out again, but Olivia put a calming hand on his arm and whispered, "Just ignore her, darling!"

"Crackers!" Brian boomed, holding one out to Faye.

Suddenly the table was filled with snapping and flying plastic objects and paper hats. They read out the terrible jokes and laughed anyway, drowning out Janis's litany of complaints, and also missing Richard shooting behind the front bar to fill a half pint glass with vodka, hoping it would be mistaken for water.

"Brian's hat's too small!" Sophie giggled.

"Bah humbug," he grumped, the hat perched on top of his head.

"We could stick a few together?" Julie suggested, making Brian splutter, "A *few*? How big do you think my head is?"

"It's big, Bri," Faye laughed.

"A *few* though? Come on, be honest." He turned his head to the side and lifted his chin. "Is my head big?"

"Silhouette of a Sasquatch," Olivia giggled.

"King Kong," Tel said, "Dead ringer."

Faye reached up and put her hands at the side of his sulky face, placing a kiss in the middle of his beard. "I love you anyway."

"Despite having an abnormally large head?" said Brian.

"No, because that giant head is filled with wisdom and great intelligence."

"And you say that after he gave you hooker boots for Christmas?" Sophie sniggered.

"He's not perfect," Faye said, turning back to her dinner, "But he's close."

Jim lifted his glass of beer and said, "Here's to Brian's big head!"

They all cheered.

"Are you sure this turkey's cooked?" Janis asked, when they'd quietened down.

Olivia opened her mouth to speak, but Tel wriggled a finger in his ear and grimaced. "Can anyone hear that high-pitched whining, or is it just me?"

"Kind of a scratchy, irritating noise, you mean?" Mark asked.

"Yeah, that's it."

"I think the boiler's on the blink."

"You should get that seen to."

"I will."

"I am here, you know," Janis snapped.

"There it is again!" Tel said. "Do you have the number for a good plumber, Mark?"

"No, but there's a leaflet in the hall for pest control."

Janis huffed, "I've never been so insulted in my life!"

"I find that hard to believe," said Mark. "Maybe you just didn't realise you were being insulted."

Richard tried to sneak behind the bar again.

"LEAVE IT!" Olivia yelled, and he slinked back to the table.

"Worst Christmas ever," said Janis.

"Wait a minute," Olivia suddenly cried, jumping up with a smile. "I forgot about this!"

She headed towards the space between the front lounge and the back, and pulled something out from the wall, dragging it across until the front and the back lounges were completely separated by a folding door.

"Didn't know that was there," Mark gasped.

"Neither did I until yesterday. A customer's kid found it

and wouldn't stop playing with it. It's for functions."

"Works pretty well at shutting out the riff-raff, too."

"I heard that!"

"Not soundproof, I'm afraid," Olivia said. "More champagne, anyone?"

"Yes, please," Richard cried.

Tel looked at Mark and shook his head. "Different noise altogether now, isn't it."

"More of a droning radiator problem," said Mark.

"You should bleed them."

Mark burst out laughing and cried, "Oh, don't tempt me!"

When they were full to bursting point and sitting back in their chairs, chatting and laughing, Mark skipped through tracks on Alexa's Christmas playlist until a xylophone started playing.

"This one!" Beth cried, "I love this one!"

As the xylophone faded out, Beth started to sing *All I Want For Christmas is You*, Mariah Carey style, and they instantly fell silent – even Janis. Her voice was pitch-perfect and filled the room, making them sway together at the table, clapping and joining in with the chorus. When she reached the final high notes she pointed at each of them in turn, coming to rest on Jim and glancing down at her baby bulge.

Jim started crying. The women wiped tears from their eyes. They all applauded and cheered.

When their appreciation died down, Janis said, "Was that the fat one?"

"Is that the one with the blow-up boobs who doesn't actually do anything but complain because of her low self-esteem problem?" Beth shot back, lifting her head and listening for an answer.

There was a heavy silence, and then, "Yes."

"I'd keep your mouth shut if I were you, love, I'm full of hormones and I'm bloody tetchy from carrying two babies around with me all day, every day."

More silence, and then, "Yes."

Mark threw his arms out towards her and gasped,

"Woman's a genius!"

Beth flicked back her blonde hair. "Well, I wouldn't go that far."

"The Ex Whisperer," Faye giggled.

"The Silencer," laughed Tel.

"Beth!" Jim cried, holding his hands towards her.

"To Beth," they all cried, raising their glasses.

"I'd like to make a speech," came Richard's voice.

"But you don't have a drink?" Mark guessed.

"No."

"Make a dry speech," Brian suggested. "What's your contribution to the party, Dick?"

There was the sound of someone shuffling awkwardly in a chair, and then, very quietly, Richard slowly said, "I'd like to thank Olivia for her hospitality, despite me being so horrible to her. I'd like to thank her for her years of putting up with me and for the devotion she's shown, which, to my eternal shame, I never returned." A hitch in his voice. "I'd like to thank Mark for putting up with me to please Olivia, and the rest of you for not belittling the sad, downtrodden man I've become."

They all looked at each other. Then Olivia said, "Help yourself, Richard."

There was the sound of a chair being hastily pushed back, followed by the loud clink of bottles.

"Get me one," Janis said.

"Get your own."

"You're already there, just pour me something."

"I don't want to. You were mean to Olivia."

"She's mean to everyone," Mark called over, "Liv doesn't take it personally, do you, Liv?"

Olivia shook her head, smiling.

"Pudding?" said Brian.

* * *

The clearing of the table was a carefully choreographed operation, each of them carrying things into the kitchen.

"I'm sure I've gained multiple pounds since we arrived," Sophie complained, scraping her almost empty plate into the bin, rinsing it under the tap and putting it in the dishwasher.

"I've eaten at least three days' worth of food in one sitting," Tel puffed, doing the same.

Brian popped the last couple of roast potatoes into his mouth as he scrubbed serving bowls under a hot tap. When Jim brought in the remains of the Yorkshire puddings he felt obligated to polish those off too.

"Are you ever full?" Faye admonished.

"Not wasting good food, lass."

Olivia and Julie wiped down countertops. Faye cleaned the hobs. Julie brought in glasses and condiments, leaving the paper hats in case anyone wanted to put theirs back on. She meant to collect the spent crackers littering the table, but forgot. The kitchen was where all the action was, and that's where she stayed. She felt very happy, the best Christmas she'd ever had. She felt useful and ... wanted.

"Right," Mark shouted, when everything had been cleared away, "My bit now. Everyone leave the kitchen!"

"What's your bit?" Faye asked.

Olivia giggled and said, "He's doing his Alpha Male bit, you know, like they chest beat over barbecues – *'Men are here, we burn burgers'*. He's heating the Christmas pudding brandy."

"Oh, big job," Brian gasped, "Think you can manage to warm up a bit of brandy on your own, Mark, or will you need assistance?"

"I volunteer to taste test at regular intervals to ensure he doesn't burn it," Tel laughed.

"Don't you think you've had enough to drink?" Sophie asked.

"It's Christmas Day!"

Sophie shrugged, figuring he was a grown-up, he could do what he wanted.

Olivia put the giant Christmas pudding into the microwave and turned it on. Julie took warmed bowls out of the oven and took them through. Faye took a bowl of whipped cream out of the fridge and followed her. Olivia grabbed spoons.

"Get out," Mark ordered, "I need to concentrate, it's a very complex operation."

"Don't forget the cinnamon stick," Olivia said, following the others through to the back lounge.

"I won't."

"And the star anise, just one."

"I've got it all written down."

"Written down," Tel howled from the other room.

"Orange zest is on the chopping board," Olivia said.

"Pith off," Brian laughed.

"Oh," she cried, putting her hand to her mouth as Mark pulled a saucepan from a cupboard, "You'll need a smaller – "

"Out!" he cried, happily glugging brandy into a stainless steel pot.

* * *

They were all seated excitedly round the table. The shutters were down again and the lights had been turned off. It was quite dark, except for the glow of the log fire and a shaft from the open door of the kitchen.

Mark appeared with a large Christmas pudding on a plate in one hand and a towel wrapped round the handle of the saucepan in the other.

"Don't drop it!" Olivia fretted.

He put them carefully at the head of the table, beaming with pride.

"The pudding," he announced, "Is done."

They cheered.

"Blimey," Tel said, peering into the saucepan. "How much brandy have you used?"

"All of it," Mark said proudly.

"It was a new bottle!" Olivia gasped.

"Yep. No point scrimping at Christmas. Ready?"

"As we'll ever be."

Mark picked up the saucepan with some effort, holding it unsteadily in one hand as he fished a kitchen lighter from his jeans pocket. He set the brandy alight and they all cheered. With two hands he gently poured it over the pudding, setting it aflame. They cheered again.

Mark's paper hat gently floated down from his head and set alight. Startled by the fire burning in front of his face, Mark's hand twitched, which shifted the towel wrapped around the hot, stainless steel handle. He cried out in pain as the skin on his thumb scorched and …

… he dropped the saucepan

A river of burning of brandy poured out of the pan and cascaded over the pudding, surging over the edge of the serving plate and across the table. Everyone jumped up, flapping at the flames and fanning its growth. It crept across the table, setting light to paper hats and empty crackers, the glitter design on the tablecloth and festive paper napkins.

The partition door flew open and Janis stood there, laughing.

Brian tossed the remnants of champagne from his glass, as did the others, but it barely doused the fingers of flames.

Richard ran over with his full champagne glass and emptied it across the table. The flames surged. Brian glanced at Richard. "Was that champagne?"

"Brandy."

"You threw *brandy* on a brandy burning table?"

"Well, I ran out of champagne."

Brian glared at him, dumbfounded.

Behind them, Janis cackled. Tel took off his Christmas jumper and started beating the table with it. Bright embers exploded into the air. Jim tried to fan them away from the Christmas tree.

Julie ran into the kitchen for a jug of water. When she rushed back in the fire was alighting the centrepiece caravan made of glittered sticks, and it burst into flames like it contained an incendiary device. She put it out with the water.

Tel carried on beating with his jumper, despite it making everything worse, until Brian put a quick hand on his arm to stop him before thundering into the kitchen.

Julie was blowing, the others were fanning their hands, trying to pat down the flames and crying out in alarm. Jim was frantically trying to help Beth to her feet, pulling and tugging, to no avail. Tel rushed over and grabbed the back of her seat, tilted it back and used all his strength to pull her away from the table. Mark helped drag her into the front lounge, passing Janis, who was in a fit of hysterics.

"She giggles while home burns," Sophie hissed furiously.

The fire was dripping to the floor when Brian burst out of the kitchen, his head tilted as he read the instructions on the side of a fire extinguisher.

"BRIAN! BE CAREFUL!" Faye screamed.

"STAND BACK!"

They stood back. Brian aimed the nozzle. Nothing happened.

"TAKE OUT THE PIN!" Mark cried.

"IT'S NOT A GRENADE!"

"*TAKE OUT THE PIN!*"

Brian took out the pin, pressed something, and the room was instantly filled with white powder.

After a few seconds the fire went out. Nobody moved as the powder slowly filtered down to the floor, leaving seven white bodies standing around the blackened table.

There was a shocked silence as they surveyed the carnage.

And then Mark said, "Would anyone like cream with theirs?"

* * *

"Jim!" Beth cried, gripping his hand.

"Are you alright, babes? You're not hurt, are you?"

"No. I need the loo."

The women hurried over, gathering around her and helping her to her feet. They'd gone three steps when Beth suddenly cried out loud, and stopped, bending forward with her mouth open.

"Too late?" Faye said, hearing the sound of running water.

"It's fine," said Olivia, "It's not a problem, we'll just get you to – "

"My water's broke," Beth breathed.

"What?" cried Sophie.

"My water's just broke."

"Now?"

"Sorry if it's a bit inconvenient, like."

"No, no, I didn't mean that, but ... *now*?"

The women looked down. They were standing in a puddle of spreading liquid.

Faye screamed, "*BRIAN!*"

He was there in an instant, running through from the back room like a giant bear. He assessed the situation in an instant, carefully putting his huge hands across Beth's back and bending to scoop up her legs. He lifted her in his arms and carried her to a sofa. Beth gasped, wide-eyed, and clutched at her bump.

Sophie clutched onto Tel, her eyes equally wide.

"Are you having contractions?" Faye asked, kneeling on the floor next to her.

"All day."

"*All day*?" Jim cried, "Why didn't you say something, babes?"

She laughed, then gave a strangle cry as another contraction took her. "Didn't want ... to spoil ... Christmas," she gasped.

"Think the arrival of the exes did that," said Brian.

"The fire just added to the general ... maelstrom," Tel said, glancing back at the blackened table as he held a trembling Sophie in his arms.

"Are the babies coming now?" Faye asked nervously.

Beth panted. "I think so, or I might just need a really big poo."

"Which is it?" Sophie snapped, "Babies or poo? You've had babies, Faye, are they coming now?"

"I was at the other end, screaming, Sophs. I don't know what was going on at the bottom end."

Beth cried out in pain and writhed on the sofa. Sophie clutched Tel. Julie started crying and Mark hugged her close to his side. Olivia was already on the phone.

Richard stood behind the bar, filling a glass with a shaky hand. "To early to wet the baby's head."

"Plural," Tel snapped, picking up on the rising anxiety, "There's two of them."

Richard looked around the room. "Two pregnant women? Where's the other one?"

Jim stood at the end of the sofa, his palms up, his face a twisted mask of horror. "Maybe …? What if …? T-t-try crossing your legs," he said, hyperventilating.

"Oh, I'm crossing my legs from now on," Beth growled.

"What do you mean, babes?"

Brian touched his arm. "Don't argue with a woman giving birth," he said, "Trust me on this, they'll say the most terrible things and won't remember any of it afterwards."

Faye was about to say something, when Beth cried out again.

"Breathe, Beth."

"Somebody call an ambulance," Faye said, covering Beth with the faux fur blanket.

"I have," Olivia cried, taking the phone from her ear, "They can't come."

"They can't come?" Sophie squealed.

"Why not?"

"The roads are blocked."

Brian dashed to a window. Outside, the snow was coming down in thick clumps and coming fast. Richard and Janis's recent leg tracks across the car park were almost filled in.

"What do we do, Bri?"

Beth screamed again, letting her knees fall apart. Jim

took one look and fainted dead away, falling to the floor in a heavy heap. Sophie started whimpering. Tel looked stunned, his mouth hanging open.

"Bri?"

Brian turned away from the window and saw Jim, just coming round on the floor, being helped to his feet by Olivia.

Sophie was sobbing hysterically against Tel, whose eyes were wide to the point of popping, and Julie had her head buried in Mark's chest.

Faye was soothing Beth and looking up at him with wide, desperate eyes.

"Mark," he said.

"Yes, Bri?"

"Do you have any snow shovels?"

"It's three miles of lanes to the main road, we can't shovel snow for three miles, Bri."

"What else do you suggest?"

"I'll get the shovels from the basement."

"Close the door after you," Faye shouted as he raced from the room, "And lock it."

"I'll call the hospital again," Olivia said, tapping her phone, "I'll tell them we'll clear the road for the ambulance, and I'll see if Jay-Zee's dad can bring the tractor out."

"Good thinking," Brian said. "Faye, are you alright with Beth?"

"We're good."

"Jim, stay up this end and stay conscious."

Jim staggered over to the armchair next to Beth, taking her hand from Faye and kissing it. "It'll be alright, babes."

There was a sudden thudding noise and a cry of pain from the hallway.

"I'm okay," Mark said, "Tripped over the sodding shovels."

"Lock the door!"

"There are no monsters, Faye!"

"Don't risk it!"

They heard the sound of a lock, and then Beth crying out

again.

Brian pointed at her as Mark came running into the room with four snow shovels. "Don't push," he winked. "Whatever you do, resist the urge to push."

Beth nodded and started panting heavily.

"She could be hours yet," Faye told him.

"It won't be hours," Beth puffed. "My mum said she coughed with … me and my brother and we … flew out, midwives had to … catch us in mid-air."

Sophie squealed with her hands at her face.

Brian boomed, "Tel, Mark, with me."

They took their jackets from the stand at the bar, pulled on scarves and gloves and woolly hats, grabbed a snow shovel each and headed for the front door.

Sophie pulled on her jacket.

"You stay here," Tel said.

She glanced at Beth on the sofa. "I can wield a shovel as good as any man. I'm certainly no good in here."

Mark handed her a shovel.

Olivia finished her phonecall, grabbed her coat, went into the kitchen, then followed them all outside.

CHAPTER 13

Outside

It was still blowing a gale. The snow whipped at their faces, the wind whipped at their clothes. They could barely see five feet in front of them. Brian had to shout to be heard.

"Let's just do what we can to clear a path for the ambulance."

Olivia said something, but it was swallowed up by the wind. She told Mark, who told Brian, who yelled, "Pete, Jay-Zee's dad, the farmer who lives down the road, is on his way in his tractor. He'll start clearing down to the main road from his house and then come up here."

They started half way across the car park, clearing a path towards the lane. They shovelled fast, tossing the snow to the side and swinging back for another scoop. It took three scoops before they could even see the gravel below, and each one felt as heavy as concrete.

Olivia used a kitchen bucket, scooping up the snow and tipping it to her left in a rhythmic swing. It took four buckets before she saw gravel.

It seemed hopeless, but they kept on shovelling.

It took twenty minutes to clear a path across the car park. The lane they could see beyond the falling snow seemed endless.

And it was getting dark.

"Come on," Brian said, as they all stood puffing. "We can do this."

"How far to the farmer's place?" Tel asked.

"About a mile and a half," Mark said.

"And so far we've cleared?"

They looked behind them.

"About a hundred yards?" Mark sighed.

"Do you not have a flame thrower?" Sophie asked.

"Oddly, no."

"How about one of those snow plough tractors?" asked Tel.

"No, because this is the Cotswolds, not Canada."

"What if we tie something behind a car?" Olivia said. "Like the sledge, and drive the car through the snow and use the sledge to push the snow – "

"Car won't drive though this, Liv."

"Oh. It was just a thought."

Mark hugged her. She was shivering. "You should go back inside."

"No, I want to help."

"Help with the women's stuff."

"I'll stay out here," Sophie said quickly, shivering herself, not only from the cold but also from the sheer horror of what was happening inside the pub.

"We're wasting time," Brian said, trudging off and plunging his shovel into the snow, again and again. The others followed behind, shovelling as one, except for Olivia, who kept getting the snow stuck in her bucket.

Inside

Beth's contractions were coming more regularly. Jim sat on the floor next to her, holding her hand. Every time she had a contraction he gurned his way through the pain of his crushed fingers.

Richard stayed behind the bar, holding a glass but not drinking from it. His eyes were very big as he stared at the woman on the sofa.

Janis sat at a table next to the *Friends* corner, glancing

over occasionally as she sipped on a large and slightly shaky G&T.

Julie was furiously chewing her nails, perched on the edge of the other sofa.

Faye had moved the coffee table out of the way and pulled up an armchair, struggling to stay calm and hide the panic that was building up inside her. She rang 999 and explained what was happening.

"Has the baby crowned?" the operator asked.

Faye looked at Beth, squirming and sweating and tossing her head from side to side. The faux fur blanket was draped over her parted legs.

"I don't know," she said.

"Can you have a look and see what's happening down there?"

"Have a look?"

"Yes, see if you can see the baby's head yet."

Faye started whining. She looked at Jim. "You do it."

"I ain't doing it." He started fanning himself with his free, unbroken hand. "I'm … I'm just a man, how am I supposed to know what it's supposed to look like?"

Faye looked at Beth. "I could give you a mirror and you could –"

Beth's face scrunched up with another contraction and she started panting heavily. "I struggle to wipe myself," she gasped, "Ain't got no chance with a mirror."

"I'll do it," Julie suddenly said, jumping to her feet and moving to the end of the sofa. "If you don't mind, Beth?"

"Uuughhaaargh," she replied.

Faye said, "I'm not sure you –"

"It's okay," Julie beamed, "My dog's had puppies a couple of times."

"That makes you our expert," Janis sighed. "God help us."

"Shut up!" Faye hissed.

"Ooh, tetchy."

"I'll be fighty if you don't keep your gob shut. Can't you

see we're busy?"

"She's *just* having a baby. It's the most natural thing in the –"

"Bring her over here so I can punch her face," Beth hissed.

Faye nodded at Julie and she went to the end of the sofa, gently lifted the blanket, and grimaced. "Can't see much." She reached into her back pocket and pulled out her phone, turned on the torch and aimed it inside.

"Oh," Beth cried, "Not quite ready for my close-up yet, Mr DeMille."

"What?"

"Nothing. The spotlight just caught me unaware."

Julie bent slightly to peer under the blanket. "Ugh," she said.

"Spare us the details," Janis tutted.

Julie moved the torch around, tipped her head from one side to the other, and stood up again. "Can't see anything," she announced.

"Should we get a bigger light?" Faye asked.

"Nah, there just ain't nothing there yet, as in, no baby head."

"Thanks, Jools!"

"No probs, Faye. I'll get some towels to – "

"Not another word!" Janis cried, wincing and holding up her glass like a barrier.   Julie raced from the room.

Janis raised a hand to her heaving chest and breathed, "I almost feel traumatised."

"'Ow do you think I feel?" Beth snarled.

"I can hardly bear to look at you," Janis said, looking.

"Go in the back lounge if you're squeamish," Jim told her.

"Says the man who fainted. No, I'll stay here, I'm comfortable here."

"How you feeling, Beth?" Faye asked.

"Ah, you know," she said, waving a hand in the air, "Worse pain ever. In fact," she said, turning her head towards Jim, "I think I've changed my mind, I don't want kids after aaaaargggh!"

"What can you see?" the operator asked, making them all wonder where the voice was coming from for a moment.

"There's nothing there yet."

"Thank God," Janis sighed.

"Beth, try not to push."

"I can't *not* push!" she snapped. "All I want to do is *push*!"

"Take deep breaths," said the operator.

"*I AM!*"

"Try and stay calm."

"You stay calm, I'm going for a full meltdo-aaaaaargh!"

Julie came back with an arm full of towels, and she and Faye spread them out on the sofa around Beth. Janis wandered over with her glass and bent over the back of the sofa. In a sickly sweet voice she said, "Is there anything *I* can do?"

"You can put your fluffin' baps away for a start!" Beth barked, "I don't want my babies mistaking, argh, you for their, ow, mother."

"Heaven forbid," Janis said, pulling a face.

Julie jumped up and ran to the coat stand at the end of the bar, pulled off a long scarf and came running back, flinging it around Janis's neck like a lasso and tying it in a knot. Janis choked and scrambled to pull it loose.

"What the hell do you think you're doing?" she snarled.

"I was just cover–"

"Are you trying to kill me?"

"No, Beth said to cov–"

"Should have pulled it tighter," Jim said, "She's still talking."

Janis pulled the scarf off with a huff and moved back to her table, flinging herself into the chair. She lifted her empty glass at Richard, still standing stock-still behind the bar with his eyes and mouth hanging.

"Drinkypoo," she trilled.

Richard didn't move, he was transfixed by the woman giving birth on the sofa.

"Hey, ex-husband, whatever your name is, I need a refill."

Richard, still unable to tear his eyes away, slowly raised a wine bottle to his lips and took a couple of deep slugs.

Janis huffed and got up to get her own.

Just as Beth started screaming in earnest.

Outside

Brian started yelling, "One, two, one, two," to keep up a rhythmic movement, but soon ran out of breath. Instead of bending to plunge the shovel into the show and then standing to toss it to the side, he stayed bent, shovelling and flinging, shovelling and flinging. His back hurt, and he could feel the Christmas dinner hanging heavy in his stomach.

Tel wondered why the hell he paid gym fees when he clearly wasn't as fit as he'd imagined. His lungs were burning, his legs were trembling from exertion and cold, and lifting the snow was harder than the weights he pulled. All his muscles screamed, but he didn't stop, couldn't stop, not in front of the others. He thought of the pain Beth must be experiencing, and ploughed on regardless. Up ahead, Brian seemed unstoppable.

Mark vaguely thought he should maybe join a gym. Gardening and lugging heavy plants around obviously wasn't enough. He should take up swimming when the weather got warmer. He should definitely start lifting weights, perhaps do some cardiovascular exercise, if his heart ever survived this gruelling endurance test. Until then, he would just carry on slicing and flinging the snow using the same rhythm as Brian.

Olivia wished she'd picked up a saucepan instead of a bucket, that big one with two handles that Tony used to make stocks. Stainless steel sides that snow would easily slip from, instead of this plastic bucket that seemed determined to keep hold of its contents. Sometimes she had to jerk it three times before the snow fell out, making her lag behind the others … except for Sophie.

Sophie could no longer feel her fingers or her toes. The scarf across her face just captured the vapour she exhaled and froze it against her skin. She was worried her nose might drop off. Despite the discomfort, she valiantly tried to keep up with the men, disappointed to find she could barely keep up with Olivia and her constantly jerking bucket.

The snow fell. The wind howled.

And the sun slowly slipped from the sky, plunging them into darkness.

Inside

"How much longer?" Faye yelled at her phone.

"The ambulance is on its way," said the operator.

"How long?"

"It's hard to say in this weather."

"Give me a rough estimate."

"I really can't, but it's definitely on its way. It's just leaving now."

"NOW?" screamed Faye, and Beth, and Julie.

"But we called twenty minutes ago, *longer*!" Faye said. "They're only just this minute leaving the hospital?"

"They had to clear the snow away from the doors first."

"Away from the …? I've got – " She quickly counted them in her head, " – five people out there clearing deep snow from a very long lane, and it's taken you twenty minutes to – !"

Jim snatched up the phone and yelled, "GET THEM HERE FAST! THE BABIES ARE COMING, *THE BABIES ARE COMING*!"

Julie looked under the blanket with her phone torch and shook her head at Beth and Faye. "We're gonna need more towels though," she said.

"Go get some, every towel you can find."

"On it."

Behind the bar, Janis rolled her eyes and turned to the tall man in the dark coat to say something witty and sarcastic, but he suddenly dropped like a rock and lay in a crumpled heap on the floor with the wine bottle glugging onto his open-mouthed face.

Outside

Brian was now muttering, 'One, two … one, two." He felt exhausted, but when he looked back he couldn't see how far they'd come because the falling snow blocked everything. Where was the tractor? Would the ambulance make it? Had they cleared enough snow?

There was no way to tell how far they'd come, he just knew he felt very, very tired.

And there was a pain in his chest.

Inside

Faye wondered how they were getting on outside. The snow outside the windows looked thicker and clumpier than ever. She hoped Brian had put his thermal underwear on. She fervently hoped the ambulance would get here before she had to deliver two babies on her own. She felt very stressed.

Julie, wiping Beth's brow with a damp cloth, thought this was very exciting. Beth was so pretty and clever, had a beautiful singing voice, and was about to have two babies. She wished she'd never met Jim, but then, if she hadn't, she'd have never met Beth, who was lovely. She hoped delivering puppies would be similar to delivering babies.

Jim wanted to cry. He wanted to scream. He wanted to hug Beth and take all her pain away – she was so brave, so strong. He loved her very much, never more than now. He wanted to jump up and yell 'THEY'RE COMING, MY BABIES ARE COMING! to the whole world. He was both excited and terrified. He barely noticed the pain from the crushed remains of his hand as another contraction hit.

Beth could think of nothing except the contractions. Her whole world now revolved around her pain. How close were they now, every few minutes? She'd lost track of time. She wondered if this would ever stop.

Janis thought they were making a mountain out of a

molehill. Women had given birth for millennia, why were they making such a fuss over this one? She was stealing her limelight. She felt very undervalued.

Richard thought nothing. He lay in a shocked and inebriated tangle of limbs on the floor behind the counter.

Outside

"Is this tractor ever coming?" Sophie screeched from the back. By the time it reached the front it was like a mouse squeak in the wind.

"Where's this tractor?" Brian yelled over his shoulder – *one, two, one two.*

"It's quite a way to the main road."

"Maybe it's got stuck?" Tel hollered.

"All … the more reason … to keep … digging."

"What if the tractor doesn't make it?" Tel stood up. Every muscle in his body was killing him.

"Tractors can get through anything," Mark yelled, coming to stand next to Tel, both of them leaning on the handles of their snow shovels and breathing heavily. "It's the ambulance getting through I'm worried about."

"Then keep clearing!" Brian bawled – *one, two, one, two.*

"Is everything alright?" Olivia asked, running up to them and shouting against the wind.

Behind them, Sophie slipped and fell face-first into the virgin snow on the other side of the lane.

"You okay?" Tel yelled.

She lifted her head and spat out snow. "I'm fine."

Brian stood up straight, turned, and glared at them.

"Why have you stopped?" he boomed.

"Just needed a breather, Bri."

"There's no time to take *rests*, get back to it!"

"Pretty tired, Bri."

"The ambulance could be here at any minute, we have to be …"

"Brian?"

"BRIAN?"

Inside

"NO, DON'T PUSH!"

Beth screamed and strained, lifting her head up off the cushions.

Faye stood up, shaking her hands, not knowing what the hell she should do.

Janis tutted.

The operator on the phone just kept saying, "Stay calm and breathe, stay calm and breathe."

Richard came round and scrambled to his feet, his wobbly head popping up behind the counter. When he was fully upright, albeit woozy, Janis held her empty glass out to him and said, "Gin and tonic."

Julie peeked under the blanket with her phone torch and shook her head.

Faye tucked in the blanket.

The operator said, "Stay calm and breathe."

Outside

Brian clutched a hand to his chest and fell to his knees. He tipped forward onto his head, and keeled over onto his side.

He lay there, breathing heavily, feeling pain stabbing through his chest.

Inside

"WHERE'S THE BLOODY AMBULANCE?"

Outside

"BRIAN! SPEAK TO US, BRIAN!"

Inside

"WHAT DO WE DO? *WHAT DO WE DO?*"

Outside

"WHAT SHOULD WE DO?" Tel cried.

Sophie fell to her knees in the snow beside him. "Brian?"

"Pain," he gasped.

"Roll him onto his back!" she yelled. "Hurry!"

It took all four of them, puffing and panting and slipping on the snow, to move him. He stared up at them with wide eyes, his hands still at his chest, his mouth opening and closing.

Sophie pulled his arms away and began chest compressions.

Inside

"Does that look like a head to you?" Julie asked.

Faye jumped to her feet and stood next to Julie at the end of the sofa. She looked. Squinted. Leaned forward. Took the phone torch off Julie and peered under the blanket.

"No," she said, "I think … I think it's a cushion."

CHAPTER 14

Outside

An orange light pierced through the white-flecked darkness and flashed across the hedgerows around them.

Olivia stood up and jumped up and down, waving her arms in the air, as a tractor slowly trundled around the corner of the lane. Its bucket was down and set at a jaunty angle, pushing the snow to the side as it went. It came to a standstill a short distance from where Brian lay in the road.

A blue flashing light merged with the flashing orange light as an ambulance pulled up behind the tractor.

"Oh thank God!" Olivia cried. "Help us!"

A paramedic jumped from the ambulance with a bag and hurried over, crashing to his knees next to Brian.

"Hello?" he said, "What's your name, buddy?"

"He's Brian. He's been helping clear the – "

"We think he's had a heart attack!" Sophie cried.

"Do something!"

Mark turned to Pete, the farmer sitting up in his tractor. "Can you clear through to the pub? There's a lady having a baby inside."

"I can," said Pete, "Only there's a man lying in the middle of the road."

Mark turned back to Brian and the paramedic. "Can we move him?"

The paramedic pushed instruments back into his bag. "Help me get him into the back of the ambulance."

They tried to lift him.

They couldn't.

Tel and Mark grabbed an arm each and began sliding him down the road.

"Sorry, Bri," Mark yelled.

Brian muttered something but they couldn't hear.

They hauled on his jacket to pull him up the embankment of snow they had created. When he was clear of the road, splayed out like a frozen starfish, Pete put his tractor into gear and drove on.

"Are you okay, Bri?"

Brian's beard twitched. "I've just seen a shooting star," he said. "Or maybe it was an angel."

They dragged him to the back of the ambulance, where a lowered stretcher stood waiting. It took all of them to push and wriggle him sideways onto it, but they couldn't pull the stretcher back up again.

Brian, clutching his chest with one hand, rolled onto his side and held up an arm. They heaved and pulled him to his feet. The driver threw the stretcher into the back of the ambulance, and they helped Brian clamber inside. He lay down on the stretcher, looked up at the red-faced paramedic and said, "Is it a heart attack?"

"I'm just checking your vitals now, buddy."

"If this is it, tell my wife, Faye, that I loved her very much."

"It's okay, Bri, it's going to be okay."

"And my kids, and the grandkids, tell them I loved them all."

"We won't have to," Sophie sniffed.

The paramedic prodded and poked, wrapped a band around his arm, looked at instruments and asked him a few questions. The others stood outside, shivering, their faces frozen with anxiety. Sophie and Olivia were clutching onto one another, wiping tears from their eyes.

"Will ... will he be alright?" Tel asked.

"Just give me a minute, buddy."

Mark climbed inside and sat on the patient chair. "Can you drive up to the pub?" he asked the driver, "There's a lady having twins."

"Close the doors," the paramedic shouted.

They did, and the ambulance slowly began to drive forward. Tel, Sophie and Olivia hurried along behind it.

"How you feeling, Bri?" Mark asked.

"I've felt better."

"Is he going to be alright?"

The paramedic smiled. "He's going to be fine."

"Oh, thank God!"

The paramedic popped something into Brian's mouth and said, "Chew this slowly."

"Isn't modern medicine brilliant," Mark gushed, patting Brian's giant arm.

Inside

Julie rushed to open the front door when she saw orange and blue lights flashing in the car park.

A paramedic hurried into the room.

"ONE!" Faye screamed, "There's only one of you? There's two babies waiting to be – "

"My colleague is in the ambulance with another patient," the paramedic said, kneeling next to Beth.

"You picked up patients along the way?" Janis said, coming from behind the bar and sidling up to the paramedic. "How very 'time and motion' of you."

"There was a big man in the road," the paramedic said.

"Big man?" said Faye. "Big man in the road?"

Outside

Afterwards, Faye couldn't remember running from the room, running down the hallway, or running and falling on the cleared but icy patio outside. Or colliding with the paramedic who had jumped out of the driver's seat and was running up the steps, bag in hand, into the pub.

She didn't remember falling down the last two steps and jumping up, running towards the ambulance that stood in the middle of the car park and shouting out his name.

She didn't remember Tel and Sophie and Olivia running up behind her, or how she pounded on the back doors of the ambulance crying, "BRIAN! BRIAN!"

A door swung open as if in slow motion. She saw Brian lying on a stretcher, Mark sitting on the chair opposite.

"BRIAN!"

Brian lifted up his head and peered at her through his parted feet. He smiled.

Confused, she looked at Mark, who was also smiling.

"Is he alright?" Tel asked, puffing up outside the doors along with Sophie and Olivia.

"He's fine," said the paramedic, picking up a bag.

Faye clambered inside the ambulance. "BRIAN!" she cried, throwing herself across him. "OH BRIAN!"

"Careful, lass."

He gently pushed her back with his arm and tried to sit up.

"Is he okay to sit up?" Faye gasped at the departing paramedic.

The paramedic grinned and said, "Probably the best thing for him."

Brian sat on the edge of the stretcher, leaning forward so his head didn't touch the cupboards above.

Mark laughed. *Laughed!* "We thought he had a heart attack."

"WHAT?" Faye gasped, beyond confused. This was no laughing matter. What was wrong with him?

Was she dreaming? Had she gone mad?

"Turns out," Mark added, as he looked first at Faye and then at the others standing outside, "That he had heartburn."

"Joking!" Tel cried, as Sophie and Olivia hugged each other.

"Not," said Mark. "One too many Yorkshire puddings, apparently."

Brian, now sitting up with his head bent against the upper cupboards, burped long and loud and hard. He burped like Homer Simpson. He burped like he'd been saving it up for a very long time.

"They gave me – " He burped again. " – an indigestion tablet. Seems to have done the trick." And he burped again.

"You gave *me* a heart attack," Faye cried, swatting him, "because you ate too much Christmas dinner?"

Burp.

"Beth!" Olivia cried.

They turned and ran inside.

Except for Brian, who plodded along, pounding his chest with a fist and burping a lot.

And Faye, who shuffled alongside, admonishing him, both furious and weak with relief.

Inside

"You do an excellent job," Janis said to the paramedic, as she leaned provocatively over the back of the sofa.

"Thank you." The paramedic didn't look up, he was concentrating solely on Beth, who was sweating and panting heavily.

"And you look so handsome in your uniform," Janis giggled, clinking the ice in her glass.

The paramedic briefly looked up, but said nothing. She let her smile drop and slugged back the last of her drink. Standing up again, she staggered back to the bar for another.

"Can I get you one?" she tinkled at the paramedic.

He didn't answer.

"This is a pub, after all, and it is Christmas."

"Are you having another one?" the paramedic asked, wrapping a blood pressure monitor around Beth's arm.

"Yes," Janis beamed, "You want the same?"

Beth screamed and lifted her head up off the cushion, pushing.

Another paramedic raced in and kneeled down next to his colleague, both talking and asking Beth questions.

"Oh!" Janis cried in delight, "Can I offer you a drink, young man?"

No reply.

Her glass full, Janis slinked like a cat over to the sofa and leaned over the back once more. "You lovely men let me know if you need anything," she simpered, her marshmallows hanging dangerously low. "I've taken a First Aid course. Well, just the one lesson, it was boring, but I picked up enough to help out if you need assistance in any way. I've not helped deliver a baby before –"

"Bab*ies*!" Jim snapped.

"– but how hard can it be, eh?"

"Pretty … bloody … hard!" Beth gasped.

Mark and Olivia burst into the room. "How is she?" they asked.

Jim, huddled around Beth's head at the top of the sofa, looked terrified and strangely angry as he glanced at Janis's swinging melons.

"She's doing alright, I think," Julie said.

"Of course she is," Janis sighed, rolling her eyes, "She's *just* having a baby."

"Bab*ies*!" Jim growled.

"Are you sure I can't get you lovely men a drink?"

Tel came into the room, closely followed by Sophie. Brian and Faye were right behind them, Faye still complaining at Brian for scaring her. They both stopped abruptly as Beth gave a long, howling cry.

"Surely there's no need for that much noise?" Janis tutted.

"Can we do anything?" Mark asked.

"You can get rid of *her*!" Jim snarled, furiously pointing at Janis.

Mark immediately pulled Janis off the back of the sofa by

her shoulders and frogmarched her into the back lounge.

"Get off me," she cried, "What are you doing? Don't touch me. Ouch!"

Mark returned, sans Janis, who continued to yell from the other room. "It's just a *baby*, for goodness sakes, I don't know what all the fuss – "

"BE QUIET!" Brian hollered, and the room went totally silent. Even the paramedic stopped pumping up the blood pressure.

Into the silence, Beth quietly whispered, "How about me, Bri? Am I okay to – ?"

"Yes, yes, of course, carry on."

Beth gave a strained, strangled cry that seemed to go on forever. Julie mopped her brow. Jim held her hand and kissed her face.

"We need to get her into hospital," one of the paramedics said, "She's close."

They quickly began packing away their equipment.

***

"Interesting Christmas Day," Tel said, as they sat slumped in the *Friends* corner, huddled onto two armchairs and one sofa, the other pushed away and covered with a sheet. Brian straddled the dining chair once more, no longer concerned about the rip in his jeans.

"Yes, it's been very … different," said Sophie.

"I don't know how you managed to pull it off, Liv," Brian said. "Must have taken *months* of planning."

"Nine months, to be exact," said Tel.

"Exes, fires and births," Mark laughed. "Almost sounds like the title to a song, doesn't it?"

"Or a horror film," said Faye.

"Well, *technically*," Olivia said, "There was only one small fire, but thank you, I tried my best to give you all a Christmas to remember."

"Oh, you've certainly done that," Tel said.

"I may never recover," said Sophie. "Seriously, I'm going to hire a therapist in the New Year to work through my trauma."

Mark stood up, sighing and stretching. "I'm as stiff as a board."

"Hear that, Liv?" Brian chuckled, "Nice surprise for you later."

Olivia blushed puce, and giggled.

"I'll make a start on the back lounge," Mark said.

"We'll help."

They all groaned and stood up and moved towards the other room.

They stopped at the entrance, and stared.

Two of the tables from the six-table assembly were slightly fire damaged, but everything else had been cleared away. An air freshener can stood on top and they could smell the scent of lavender – except Faye, who could smell nothing, ever.

A rhythmic brushing sound came from beneath. They bent as one and peered under.

Richard was on his hands and knees, diligently brushing the last few specs of dirt off the carpet and humming contentedly to himself.

Brian coughed. Richard's head snapped up and pounded against the underside of the table. He smiled and said, "How's the pregnant lady?"

"Still pregnant," Faye told him, "Thank God."

"But not for long," Sophie added. "I heard the paramedics saying they got here just in time."

"Thanks to Pete and his tractor," Olivia said.

"And you lot," said Julie. "I wish I had friends like you."

"You have friends like us," Mark said, giving her a sideways hug. "You have us."

Julie beamed.

"Have *you* done all this?" Brian asked, standing up straight and surveying the room. It was immaculate.

"I couldn't stand to look at it," Richard said. "I hate seeing things untidy."

"Oh," Olivia cried, "I forgot, Richard has OCD."

"You've done a good job," Tel nodded.

"Thanks." Richard scrambled to his feet, running the sleeve of his coat over the surface of a table.

"I supervised," Janis slurred.

They turned and saw her slumped at a table in the far corner.

"You couldn't supervise a piss up in a brewery," Mark said.

Janis raised her glass. "Hey, landlady, get me another drink, would you?"

Olivia ignored her and opened the door to the kitchen. Rinsed bowls and spoons were piled up near the sink, ready to go in the dishwasher. Everything was clean and tidy.

Richard came up behind her and said, "Can I have a drink now?"

"Yes, Richard, you can have a drink now."

He hurried off, grinning.

"Get me one?" Janis called after him, but he took no notice. "I'm starting to feel unseen and unheard."

"Who said that?" Brian asked.

Sophie put a hand on his shoulder. "How you feeling, Bri?"

"Okay. A little bloated and the chest still hurts, but another few burps should do it."

"I suspect there may be other, more pungent emissions later," Mark laughed. "Talking of pungent," he added, sniffing and striding through to the other lounge. "Richard."

"Yes?"

"Can you please, for the love of God, take off that stinky coat."

Richard put down the bottle and glass he was holding and clutched the collar of his coat with both hands. "I'm ... I'm cold."

"It's like a greenhouse in here," Faye said, glancing at the roaring fire.

"I must have caught a chill when I was sleeping rough, or pneumonia." He stepped back, away from where they were all gathered at the end of the bar. "I feel naked without my coat. It's seen me through many a dark, cold night."

"You don't need it on in here, surely," Olivia said.

"Honestly, it stinks to high heaven," said Mark.

"Have you been sleeping with dogs, or wolves?" Tel asked, wafting a hand in front of his face.

"They kept me warm," Richard croaked.

"Ahh," said Faye.

"You don't like dogs," Olivia said.

"They were my only friends." His bottom lip quivered.

"Just take it off."

"I can't. I won't."

"Here," said Brian, pulling off his Christmas jumper depicting a man's naked torso covered in festive tattoos, "Put this on instead."

"No."

"It might be a bit big but it'll keep you warm."

Mark took a step behind the bar and Richard snatched up a fancy cocktail stick and held it in front of him like a knife.

"Perhaps you should leave it," Olivia whispered. "He seems very attached to it."

"But it *stinks*!"

"I'll put an air-freshener round his neck."

Mark sighed and stepped away. Richard put down the cocktail stick.

"I'm bored!" Janis shouted.

"Boring, you mean," said Sophie.

Janis stood up and tottered over on her high heels, the hem of her dress sliding up her thighs and her marshmallow mounds wobbling with each step she took.

"You know what?" Olivia suddenly said, snatching Brian's Christmas jumper off the bar, "I am sick to death of seeing this woman's mammaries bouncing around my pub." She lifted the jumper and thrust it down over Janis's head, dislodging her carefully pinned hair and one false eyelash. "Cover the bloody things up!"

Janis cried out and began to pull the jumper off again, but Olivia pointed a finger in her face and said, "If you take that off you're out, do you hear me? I've done it before and I'm more than happy to do it again."

"Okay, okay," Janis whined, pushing her hands down the woolly arms.

"Oh, the relief," said Brian. "My eyeballs ache from the effort of not looking at them."

Janis huffed, standing there in her naked man with Christmas tattoos jumper.

"I think it suits you," Faye giggled.

"It's certainly an improvement," said Mark.

Janis stormed back to her corner.

Olivia's mobile rang and she raced to the coffee table to answer it. "Hello?"

"Is it Jim?"

"Has she had the babies?"

"What did she have?"

"Are they all okay?"

"Shh," Olivia said, walking away from them and saying, "Hello, mummy, where are you?"

They flopped into their seats – except Brian, who carefully straddled his chair.

* * *

They chomped their way through a tub of Quality Street as they watched a re-run of the *King's Christmas Broadcast*, and fought over which film to watch, all the time checking their phones, the tension exploding each time one made a noise. First it was Olivia's dad, Harry, which was awkward and short. A WhatsApp video call from Brian and Faye's daughter, Ellie, who was clearly drunk and enjoying herself at a party. Sophie's highly-excited mother called from the cruise ship, also drunk and partying. Then Julie's mother rang, saying she was sorry about Bingo Man and could Julie come home and cook the turkey.

"I can't, mom, it's still snowing outside."

"What should I do then?"

"Make toast."

Janis was slumped and fast asleep in the far corner of the back lounge, still wearing the naked man jumper. Richard was curled up and snoring underneath the Christmas tree.

"Should we wake them?" Olivia asked.

"Must we?" Mark groaned. "It's so peaceful, and if Richard moves he'll spread that awful smell around." He picked up the can of air freshener from the coffee table and sprayed it towards the Christmas tree. "We can't break the barrier."

They watched *Scrooged* with Bill Murray, and hauled themselves off to bed.

"If anyone gets a call from Jim, wake us up," Faye said, as she reached the top of the stairs.

They all nodded in agreement, except Janis, who was dragging herself up the banister rail with her eyes still closed.

They left Richard under the tree.

* * *

When Brian came out of the ensuite bathroom he found Faye, sitting on the edge of the bed trying on the red boots.

"I thought you didn't like them?"

"I don't know," she grinned, looking up at him beneath lowered lids, "I think they're growing on me."

"Are they?" He laughed. "You'll never be able to walk in them."

"You should have thought of that before you bought them."

"My brain doesn't do Christmas shopping."

"Clearly." She turned a leg this way and that. "They do make my legs look good though, longer. I thought maybe I would ... keep them."

"What for?"

Faye gave a little grin.

"Oh," said Brian, breaking into a smile and launching

himself onto the bed.

* * *

"Say something, Tel."
"I ... I don't know what to say."
"You understand what I'm telling you though?"
"I'm not sure."
"I don't want children."
"No, not yet, but later – "
"I never want children, Tel."
"So, what are you saying?"
"I can't risk getting pregnant. Ever."
"Ever?"
"Poor Beth was in so much pain."
"It passes."
"Oh, suddenly you're the expert on childbirth?"
"So, again, what are you saying, Sophie?"
"I was thinking that perhaps we could try ... celibacy?"

* * *

"What was that?" Olivia whispered.

Mark stopped what he was doing. "It sounded like someone yelling 'what'."

A muffled but angry voice filtered into their bedroom. A man, yelling, "You want to try *what*?"

"It could be Jim," Olivia fretted.

"We wouldn't be able to hear him from here, Liv, the hospital's at least sixteen miles away."

Olivia pushed him away. "No, silly, it could be someone talking to Jim."

"In what context would one of us say 'You want to try *what*?' to Jim?"

Olivia shrugged. Mark snuggled up to her again.

The man's voice yelled, "We've only been married for ten minutes!"

"Ah," Olivia said, "It's Tel. They must be arguing."

"Let's give them their privacy," Mark breathed, "And enjoy

our own."

CHAPTER 15

Boxing Day

Mark was dragged from his sleep by the sound of his phone. At first he tried to ignore it, then he remembered about Beth and the babies.

Peeling Olivia off his chest, he reached out to the bedside table and answered it, noting that it was just gone 4.15am.

"Hello?" he grunted.

"Mark! Mark!"

"Is that you, Jim?"

There was the sound of somebody sobbing and sniffing. "MARK!"

He sat up. Olivia stirred and mumbled, "Who is it?"

"Jim, is that you?"

Olivia quickly sat up and pressed her ear against his phone.

"MARK!"

"Is everything okay?"

"I'm ... I'm a dad! A dad, Mark! Me! A dad!"

Olivia was up on her knees, supressing a burst of excitement as she bounced up and down on the bed.

"Congratulations, Jim!"

"Ask him what he had, if they're all okay. Ask him – "

Before Mark could draw breath, there was a clatter on the other end and the line went dead.

Mark leapt out of bed as he dialled Jim's number. It was engaged. He tried again as he struggled to put on his dressing gown using one arm. Olivia jumped up to help him. Still engaged.

They ran down their hallway, threw open the door, and started running towards the guest rooms, when Mark suddenly glanced at Olivia and cried, "Liv!"

"What?"

"You're naked!"

She screamed and ran back to their flat. Mark started banging on guest room doors, staring at his phone and willing it to ring. Brian and Faye were the first to emerge.

Mark's phone rang. He answered and put it on speakerphone. Olivia, now in a dressing gown, sprinted down the hallway, just as Tel and Sophie were coming out into the hallway.

"Jim, is that you?"

"I'm a dad, Mark, a dad!"

They all shouted their congratulations. Julie burst into tears.

"How are they?" Brian asked.

"What did you have?" said Faye.

"Is everyone okay?" Sophie said.

Jim sobbed hysterically, unable to speak.

"Jim," Tel urged, "Are Beth and the babies okay?"

"Yes." More sniffing. "They're ... they're beautiful, so beautiful."

"Take after their mum then," Mark laughed, as tears pricked his eyes.

"What did you have?" Faye asked again.

"A boy," Jim wailed, struggling to catch his breath, "And a girl."

"Ahh." They all nodded and smiled at each other, except for Tel and Sophie, who nodded and smiled but didn't look at each other and were standing on opposite sides of the hallway.

Olivia started sobbing. Faye hugged her.

"How's Beth doing?" Brian asked.

"She's ... she's *amazing*. They popped out at the end." His voice went high-pitched and unsteady. "One after the other."

"She said they would," Faye sniffed.

"It's the best thing I ever saw in my life," Jim spluttered, "Apart from all the gooey stuff."

Sophie winced.

"How heavy?" Tel asked. He felt quite emotional, and not just because of the babies.

"Not too heavy," Jim squeaked, "They're only small. Tiny little things they are."

"Pleased for you both, Jim, I really am."

"I gotta go, I have to ring the families."

"We're the first?" Olivia gasped, clutching a hand to her chest.

"Beth insisted," Jim said.

"Ahh," the women breathed.

"Give her our love."

"Will do. Catch ya later. Bye."

"Bye, Jim."

Mark hung up. There was an instant of silence as they glanced at each other, and then they started laughing and hugging each other.

"Twinnies!" Julie sobbed. "I bet they're gorgeous, just like their mum."

"A boy and a girl," said Brian, "How lovely."

"Baby campers!" Faye cried. "I've got two cream rompers with 'Happy Camper' on the front."

"Have you?" said Brian.

"And baby blankets," she added.

"Shocker!" said Mark.

"And I might have bought a couple of pairs of the cutest baby shoes you've ever seen."

"You'll have to show me," Olivia giggled. "And I'll show you mine."

"Aye-up," Brian laughed, "Women are getting broody already."

Tel looked at Sophie. Sophie glanced at him, and looked

away again.

Nobody noticed.

A door next to them opened and Janis stood there, her hair all over the place and her makeup smeared across her face. She was wearing a sheer negligee, which everyone avoided looking at. "What the bloody hell is going on?" she snapped. "Do you know what time it is?"

"Baby time," Julie said.

"What?"

"Beth's had her babies, a boy and a girl."

"Who's Beth?" Janis asked, and they all gaped.

"The pregnant one," Brian said, frowning.

"Oh," said Janis. "Well, can you keep the noise down, some of us are trying to sleep."

She stepped back and closed the door.

"She's just a ray of golden sunshine, isn't she," Mark said.

Brian stood in front of her door and started singing *We Wish You a Merry Christmas*, very loudly.

The others heartily joined in.

From downstairs, Richard yelled, "Is it Christmas Day again?"

"Yeah," Mark shouted over the banister, "It's like Groundhog Day but with more glitter."

Laughing, Faye cried, "This is ... *The Twilight Zone*, doo-doo-doo-doo."

"No!" Richard howled.

"Oh Christ," Mark gasped, stepping back and holding his nose, "I can smell him from here."

"Fresh air," Faye sang, as the others stopped singing and simply beamed at each other with relief and joy.

"Christmas babies," Julie grinned. "I can't wait to meet them."

"Me neither."

"Right, I'm off to my bed," Brian said. "Try not to trip over the red boots on your way back, Faye."

"Oh," Olivia jeered, "I did wonder why your hair was so

messy, Faye. Rough night?"

"You can talk," Faye said, pointing at her hair and making Olivia blush.

Sophie was suddenly acutely aware that her hair was immaculate, and that her husband was stoney-faced.

Mark laughed. Faye turned in her doorway and said, "Mark, are you sure, absolutely positive, the cellar door is locked?"

"Yep."

"The monsters won't come after you," Brian said, guiding her into the room, "You're much too chewy."

She punched her tiny hand against his giant arm and he laughed. "Come back to bed, my little minx."

Smiling, Mark and Olivia walked back to their flat.

Tel and Sophie wandered back to theirs, still on opposite sides of the hallway.

None of them heard the sound of a thud and a cry coming from Brian and Faye's room a moment later, or Faye muttering, "Maybe I should take them back."

Or Brian saying, "No, keep them."

**

The following morning they all slept in. By the time Tel and Sophie walked into the kitchen, determinedly not looking at each other, Faye was draped over the counter flicking through Christmas photos of the grandkids on her phone, Brian was juggling burning bread out of the toaster, and Julie was sipping on a cup of coffee and smiling dreamily.

"I'm not cooking today," Olivia declared, as she spread butter on crumpets. "Just help yourselves to anything."

Sophie went to the coffee machine. She didn't ask Tel if he wanted one.

Tel opened cupboards until he found the boxes of cereal, and poured himself a bowl.

"Good news about Beth and the babies, isn't it," Mark said, busy frying bacon.

"So glad they're okay," said Faye.

"Instant family," Brian said, "That'll take some getting used to."

"Beth can do it," Julie sighed, "She's amazing."

Faye glanced at Brian and whispered, "I think she's found a role model."

"Couldn't have picked anyone better."

Richard stumbled through from the lounge. Mark immediately raised his hands against the stench and cried, "Take off that coat and burn it!"

"Not in the pub," Olivia said. "Two fires would look suspicious if we have to make a claim on the insurance. They might mark us as pyromaniacs."

Mark opened a window. "Oh," he said, looking out, "The wind's died down and … it's stopped snowing."

"Yay!" Julie cried.

A heavy thudding came down the stairs and Janis hurried barefoot into the kitchen, her hair down and messy, makeup still smearing her face. Her tight blue dress looked decidedly baggy and everyone averted their eyes from her gaping cleavage.

"Have I missed breakfast?" she gasped, glancing at the clock on the wall.

"No fry up this morning," Olivia told her, "It's help-yourself day."

Janis sighed. "Bloody crap service in this pub."

"Don't come again then."

"Ever," Mark cried from the frying pan.

"Can you get me a coffee, at least?"

Olivia pointed over at the coffee machine. "I've put instructions on the wall."

"It's easy," Julie said from behind her steaming cup. "Cappuccino's nice."

Janis picked up a cup and glanced at the instructions. She put her cup down again and sighed.

Olivia went and made her a flat white.

"I wanted an expresso," Janis said.

Olivia tutted and took the coffee back to her crumpets.

Mark's phone rang on the counter, just as he was raising a bacon sandwich to his mouth.

"Mark?"

"I am he." He put the sandwich down. "Is everything alright, Jim?"

Everyone stopped what they were doing and turned.

"Is Beth okay?" Julie gasped, "And the babies?"

Mark put the phone on speaker.

"Is everything okay?" Faye asked.

"Yeah, yeah. Well …" They all stiffened. "It's Beth," he said, and there was a collective inhalation of breath.

"What's wrong?" Olivia quickly said.

"Nah, nuffing's wrong, it's just …"

"Spit it out, Jim, before we die of suspense."

"Her family can't make it up from London 'cos of the snow."

"Ahh," said Faye.

"She's a bit … miserable."

"That's normal after having a baby, Jim."

"Nah, she's feeling really happy, but … she's had the twins and doesn't have anyone to show them off to."

"Ahh."

"Can you come?" Jim asked.

"I'll get my coat," Julie cried, running into the hallway.

"I think she's fed up of me and needs some company."

Mark looked around the kitchen. They all nodded, smiling.

"Come *on*!" Julie shouted from the hallway.

"We'll be there as soon as we can, Jim."

"Thanks, Mark. Thanks, everyone, it'll really cheer her up."

"See you soon."

Mark hung up and said, "How?"

"My Range Rover?" Tel said.

"Probably better than my Kia," said Brian.

"How many seats?" Mark asked.

"Seven."

"There's nine of us," Richard said. "I used to be an accountant."

"Not a very good one," Olivia snapped. "More embezzling than accounting."

Julie came and stood at the kitchen door, coat on, hood up, scarf wrapped around her neck. "Are we going?"

"Hold your horses, lass."

"I don't have any horses. I wish I did, I'd be halfway to Oxford by now."

"We're just working out the logistics."

"The what?"

"My car's stuck in the snow though," Tel said, quickly chomping down the last of his cereal. "We'll need to dig it out."

"We only have to get it up to the car park," Brian said, "The lane might still be clear."

"The ambulance made it through," Faye said.

"It's snowed since then, lass."

Julie hurried into the front lounge and peered through the window. "Tracks are only a bit covered up."

Mark came through with his sandwich, followed by the others – except for Janis, who was still fiddling with the coffee machine, and Richard, who'd found a bottle of rice wine in a cupboard.

Mark looked at the thick white blanket outside and asked, "Can we do it?"

"Yes we can," Brian squeaked.

"I'll get the snow shovels. Oh," he said, standing still and holding his head.

"You alright, Mark?"

"Yeah, just a touch of déjà vu, there must be a glitch in the matrix."

Olivia rushed to check the back patio doors were locked.

"Bring salt, Liv!" Mark called to her, "And the exes."

She rushed into the kitchen, grabbed salt from a cupboard

and herded a disgruntled Richard and a whining Janis to the coat stand in the hallway.

"Why have we got to come?" Janis growled. "I don't even have anything on my *feet*!"

"I'm not leaving you alone in my pub," Olivia said. "Now put some wellies on." She pointed at a line of boots underneath the coat stand.

"They're all *green*, they won't match – "

"Put some on or go barefoot."

Janis pulled some on. "They're too big."

"They'll do. Come on."

Olivia bustled them out the front door, Richard clinging to his bottle of rice wine and Janis schlepping through the snow in her giant wellies, and locked the front door.

* * *

"Why do the women have to come?" Faye sulked, as they all trekked through the snow. "Anything to do with cars is men's stuff."

"Yeah," Janis hissed, "*Why?*"

"Equality Act 2010," Brian said, "It's the law. Wouldn't want you whingeing and whining about being left behind and missing out on all the fun."

"I wouldn't have whinged."

"You can't cherry pick what you're willing to do, Faye."

"No?"

"No."

"Damn."

It took them ages to make their way down to the far caravan area, with Janis moaning every floppy step of the way, until Sophie quickened her pace and strode past her, throwing out a hand as she did and pushing her into the snow.

"Hey!"

"Sorry."

"No you're not!"

"You're right, I'm not."

Tel's black Range Rover had snow up to its wheel trims on one side and wheel arches on the other. He unhitched it from the caravan, took a folding snow shovel out of his boot, and five of them started digging.

"You're doing great," Julie encouraged from the sidelines.

"Set those tyres free," Sophie yelled. "Here, Faye, let me have a go."

"I'm cold," Janis muttered.

"I'm thirsty," said Richard.

"Here," Mark said, handing Janis his shovel, "This'll warm you up."

"I don't shovel snow!"

"You do now."

Too cold to argue, Janis delicately started scraping at the snow, so slow that Mark snatched it back off her and started digging again.

"I'm thirsty," Richard said again.

Brian quickly made a loose snowball and threw it in his face. Richard licked it off his lips and said, "Needs more alcohol."

Fifteen minutes later the snow had released its hold on the car and they stood leaning against it, puffing like steam trains, knackered.

"We can't clear a path all the way up to the car park," Mark gasped. "I still ache from yesterday."

"We could make a line of snow angels," Faye said, and Brian gave a burst of amusement. "It would flatten the snow!" she snapped.

"She has a point," Sophie said.

"Might be plausible in a Disney film," said Tel.

"Shut up."

"No, you shut up."

"Will you two pack it in," Faye said. "What's the matter with you both?"

They both turned their heads away from each other with tight lips.

"Did you bring some salt, Liv?" Mark asked.

She reached into her jacket pocket and pulled out a small salt cellar. Mark looked at it, then at her, then back at the salt cellar.

Brian burst out laughing. "And what do you expect us to do with that?" he howled.

"You said bring salt," Olivia said to Mark. "I've brought salt."

Brian laughed louder.

"I meant a big catering tub, Liv."

"Oh. You didn't specify."

"Did you think we were going for a picnic?"

"Don't be facetious."

Mark took the salt cellar from her and, trying not to laugh, delicately sprinkled some on the snow in front of a tyre. "Pepper?" he called out.

Olivia pushed him. He fell onto his side, rolled onto his back, and sighed, "Clear blue sky."

"We could wait for the sun to melt the snow?" Faye suggested, as Mark scrambled to his feet, grinning at Olivia, who couldn't help but grin back.

"Yeah, let's give it a couple of months and then try again," Brian chuckled.

"Faye," Mark said, "I'm only asking this because you're Faye, bringer of endless blankets and cushions, but I don't suppose you've brought a bag of salt or cat litter with you, have you?"

"We don't have a cat," Faye said.

"Bag of salt for emergencies?"

"What emergency would require a bag of salt?" she asked.

Mark spread his arms out. Brian's shoulders were silently hitching up and down.

"Oh," she said. "No."

"Car mats," Tel said.

"I'll get mine," said Brian.

Floor mats were placed in front of each tyre. Tel straightened his wheels and slowly pulled forward. And backwards. And forwards again.

The tyres skidded.

They all went to the back and pushed.

"Keep the revs down, Tel."

"Take it slow."

"Argh," said Faye, slipping face first into the snow. Brian lifted her up with the hood of her jacket.

"Again!"

The engine purred. The car rocked.

It began to move, slowly crunching its way forward.

It stopped, wheels spinning.

They pushed, falling.

Inch by strenuous inch, with bodies regularly slipping and falling in its wake, they got it up the car park.

* * *

"Seven seats," Tel said, getting out of the car, "Nine people."

"As I think I mentioned earlier," said Richard.

Julie pulled a sad face and whimpered. Mark gave her a sideways hug and said, "Don't worry, you're coming."

"I'll stay here," Janis said, turning to walk up the steps of the pub.

"You're not," Mark said, "You'll be into everything."

"And he's definitely not getting in my car wearing that foul coat," said Tel.

"You still have the key for the utility shed?" Mark asked Richard.

Richard plunged hands into his pockets and rummaged around. They all took a step back as a foul stench assaulted them.

"Christ, has something died in there?" Sophie asked, covering her nose and mouth.

"I'm gonna gag," Mark said, bending forward.

"You okay, darling?"

"*Bleurgh.*"

"He's definitely not getting in my car."

"Utility shed," Mark gasped, straightening up again. "You can wait in there until we get back."

"What?" Janis screeched. "You're locking us in a *shed*?"

"Not locking," he told her, "You're free to come and go as you please. My preference would be for you to go."

Janis pulled a face, made worse by the makeup she still hadn't wiped off – she looked like a pouty panda.

"Load 'em up," Brian cried, "And move 'em out."

* * *

Tel slowly drove out of the car park and onto the lane, relieved to find that their efforts from yesterday still stood, with just a thin sprinkle of snow on top.

"It's fine," he told the others, "We're going to – "

The car slid sideways, mounting the piles of snow they'd shovelled the day before.

"It's frozen overnight," Brian said. "It's going to be slippy."

Tel reversed over the mound and back onto the road.

A few more feet. Another slide, this time into the embankment of snow the tractor had left in its wake, which was higher. The car wheels wedged on top, the back wheels spun on the ice.

They got out, trudged through the rough snow and pushed against the front of the car. Faye slid down the bank into a ditch, and again Brian had to pull her out using the hood of her coat.

Olivia went down next, followed by Julie.

Brian put his car mats behind the back wheels, and Tel finally managed to get back on the road again.

"It's really slick," Tel said, navigating a bend and slamming into tractor piled snow again.

"Want me to drive?" Brian asked.

Tel glanced at him, then nodded.

They swapped seats.

"Brace yourselves," Faye cried, as Brian backed onto the

road again, "It's gonna be a wild ride."

"Thank you for those kind words of encouragement, wife."

"You're welcome, husband. Try not to kill us."

"I'll do my best."

"Do your best*est*," Tel said, pressing himself into the passenger seat as the car navigated a corner and refused to turn.

They got out. They pushed. They got back in again.

"Where's Julie?" Sophie asked.

Julie's head appeared above the pile of snow she'd slipped down, and Tel jumped out to drag her over.

Everyone shivered in the car, their clothes wet, their teeth chattering like a bunch of castanets.

"Should we go back?" Olivia asked.

"No!" cried Julie, "I wanna see Beth and the babies!"

"It does seem dangerous," Tel said, as Brian slithered into another snow drift at the side of the lane. "Should we risk it?"

"Yes!" Julie howled.

"How much further to the main road, Mark?"

"About a mile, maybe less."

Brian looked at Tel. "It's your car, you decide."

"The only problem is," said Sophie, leaning forward in her seat, "There's nowhere to turn around."

"What about the farmer?" Faye suggested. "He must have a driveway, we could turn there, couldn't we?"

"Pete has a gate across his entrance," Mark said, "He's had a lot of trouble with travellers coming onto his land, so he keeps it locked."

Tel sighed. "Forward it is then."

* * *

They were in the waiting room of the John Radcliffe Maternity Ward in Oxford, seven of them huddled tight together around a radiator. Their coats gently steamed on the back of chairs.

Jim bounded in. "You made it!" he cried, giving Mark a

huge hug.

"Barely," said Brian. "Roads are terrible."

"Beth is going to be so pleased to see you. Come and meet the babies."

He turned, and bumped straight into a large, fierce-looking nurse. "It's two visitors to a bed," she said sternly.

"But there's no one else in there," Jim told her.

"Two visitors to a bed."

"We've risked life and limb to get here," said Tel. "We promise to be quiet and not stay long."

"I'm afraid I can't allow that, it's against the rules," the nurse said, "No exceptions."

Behind her, in the corridor, an Indian family walked past. Jim watched them disappear onto a ward, and pushed by the nurse. "There's at least eight of them," he said, and the others followed en masse.

"Beth!" Julie screamed, when she saw her sitting up in bed, "You look *amazing*!"

"Careful!" Beth laughed. "I'm still a bit sore." She looked at the others. "Oh, I'm so pleased to see you all."

"Told ya," said Jim.

"Couldn't keep us away," Brian said.

They hugged her, one after the other, and then Faye, Sophie and Olivia sat carefully on the edge of her bed while the men stood at the end looking awkward. There were three other new mothers on the ward, one of them asleep. Baby cots stood next to each one.

"Look at what I did!" Beth cried, nodding towards her two cots.

Faye, Olivia and Julie stood up and cooed around the sleeping babies. Sophie stayed with Beth, forcing a smile. She felt she could sense the pain and discomfort all around her. She was never going to do it, never.

She glanced over at Tel. He averted his eyes.

The women's voices reached a hushed crescendo of excitement.

"They're so gorgeous!"

"Oh Beth, you did good."

"Didn't I, though?"

"Did you contribute at all?" Mark grinned at Jim.

"Yeah, at the beginning, you know, when we made them."

"Did you manage to stay conscious long enough to watch them being born?" Tel asked.

"Yeah, after the initial shock of – "

"Please," Sophie said, raising a hand, "Don't go into detail."

"I was alright," Jim beamed, "Weren't I, babes."

"He was brilliant," Beth said.

"And look," he said, raising a hand and showing off a sturdy hand gauntlet with a line of Velcro straps, "They x-rayed it and there's no broken bones."

"Sorry, babes."

"That's alright, babes. Think I was in more pain than you."

Beth laughed. "You carry on thinking that, babes."

"How was it?" Faye asked.

"The birth? Oh, you know, worse pain ever."

Sophie flinched.

"Towards the end the midwife mentioned the C-word."

"Not very professional," Tel laughed.

"Caesarean section, babes. You better believed I pushed after that. Did it all by myself."

"Clever girl," said Olivia.

"I told the nurses to turn the light off, they babies keep coming," Jim howled.

"He did," Beth sighed. "Just what you want to hear when you're in excruciating agony, bad dad jokes."

"Can we pick them up?" Julie asked.

"Yeah, just try not to wake them, I've only just got them off."

Julie already had tears in her eyes as she reached down and very carefully picked up the baby wrapped in a pink blanket.

"That's Dotty," Beth said.

"Oh," Julie breathed softly, "She looks like a Dotty."

"That's what I thought. And that's Bryan," she said, as Faye picked up the baby snuggled into a blue blanket, "Bryan with a Y."

"Really?" Faye gasped, looking at Brian, who grinned like a Cheshire cat.

"I'm very honoured," he said.

"If he turns out anything like you, Bri, I'll be well pleased," she winked.

He stared up at the ceiling.

"You crying, Bri?" Mark asked.

"Little bit."

"Come and hold her," Julie whispered to Sophie.

"No, it's okay, I can see them from here."

Julie took a careful step towards her. Sophie stood up and stepped back, adamantly refusing to take the baby for a good four seconds, until Julie held out the pink bundle and her treacherous arms instinctively wrapped themselves around the tiny child.

She looked down at the perfect face and breathed in the scent, so powerful it took her by surprise. Her arms gently rocked, her voice went soft as she whispered to her. So beautiful. So perfect. What a miracle.

She looked up at Tel with tears running down her cheeks. For a brief moment he looked surprised, and then a knowing smile spread across his handsome face. He glanced at his watch. "We should be going soon," he said.

"We just got here," said Faye, carefully passing Bryan to Olivia.

"Got someplace to go?" Beth asked.

"What's your rush?" said Mark.

He looked at Sophie, holding the baby and crying. "I have something to work out with my wife."

"There's nothing to work out," Sophie breathed, hardly able to tear her eyes away from the beautiful creature in her arms. "I've changed my mind."

"All the more reason to leave Beth in peace," he grinned.

Julie guided Sophie to a chair and she sat down, totally rivetted on the newborn.

"Or not," said Tel.

Faye, now bereft of baby, went and stood at a respectful distance from the new mother in the next bed, who seemed delighted to have someone to talk to. Olivia gently handed Bryan to Mark, who held him like he'd been holding babies all his life. Olivia stared at him as he cooed. He glanced up and saw a look in her eyes.

"I want one," she sniffed.

"I do too, one day."

"One day soon?"

"We should probably get married first, Liv."

"The hormones are strong," Brian muttered to Tel. "Thankfully, Faye wouldn't dream of – " He looked over and caught a look on his wife's face. Terror ran through his veins.

"You were saying?" Tel laughed.

Olivia hurried over to help a new mother in the opposite bed, who had woken up and was struggling to sit up.

Faye, not wanting her to feel left out, sidled up to the fourth new mother in the far corner and spoke to her. After a few minutes, she hurried over to Olivia and whispered something in her ear. Olivia smiled and nodded, and they both walked towards the doors.

"Where you two sneaking off to?" Brian asked. "You don't have any babies hidden about your person, do you?"

"We're on a quest," Faye said.

"For?"

She glanced over her shoulder and said, "They've all got cravings, and the staff are busy."

"I would *kill* for a ham and salad sandwich," one mother said. "Extra mayo."

"Bring back all the mint Aeros you can find," said another.

"Pickled onions!" cried the mother in the corner,

sounding quite desperate. *"I need pickled onions!"*

"Oh," cried Beth, "If you're going to the shop downstairs, bring me back anything green, would ya? I could literally eat a raw cabbage, or sprouts."

"You must need it if you're feeding these two," Sophie said softly, still staring at the perfect face as Faye and Olivia took off down the corridor.

"They're giving me iron tablets, but they just ain't doing it for me."

Julie bent down and gently took the baby from Sophie, quietly humming as she carried her back to the cot. Sophie's arms now felt empty. She glanced over at Tel again, and he winked back. Mark was putting Bryan down in his cot.

Sophie turned her full attention to Beth. "Did it …?" she began. "Did it hurt very much?"

Beth smiled. "I ain't gonna lie, it was like passing two rugby balls, but, you know what? They're totally worth it, and they say you forget about the pain, though I'm not too sure about that, my flange feels like – "

Sophie threw up a hand.

"But look what we've got," Beth breathed, staring over at her children,. "Look what we made."

Sophie looked over at the babies, two little angels wrapped in blankets, and a hitch caught in her throat. It was indeed incredible, creating new lives.

Brian was saying to Mark, "You know when mothers bring their newborns into the office to show everyone, and you look at the thing they've brought in and force yourself to say, 'Oh aren't they beautiful,' but they're not?"

"Are you saying my kids are ugly?" Beth snapped.

"No, I'm saying we don't, in your case, have to lie. They are magnificent, Beth."

"Ta, Bri. I'm quite chuffed with them."

Beth suddenly screamed, as did the other three mothers on the ward.

"Occurring?" Mark gasped, wide-eyed and a bit terrified.

Faye and Olivia had returned carrying plastic bags, and excitement exploded as they emptied the contents onto beds, followed by a long period of contented humming as the mothers began consuming, one plunging her fingers into a jar of pickled onions and eating them with her eyes closed.

"No greens for you, I'm afraid," Olivia said to Beth, who frowned. "However," she added, reaching into her plastic bag, "They did sell ... cherry tomatoes!"

"Oh thank God," Beth cried, snatching at them and ripping off the plastic. "Just the one carton?" she chomped.

Olivia pulled out a second, and Beth screamed again.

As the mothers ate and chatted, Tel reached out to Sophie and pulled her up from the chair.

They sneaked out of the ward.

"What are we doing?" Sophie asked.

"You'll see," said Tel.

He opened a door down the corridor that had a CLEANERS ONLY sign on it. A store cupboard.

"How very Chandler and Monica," Sophie said, letting him pull her inside and close the door.

"Who?"

"From *Friends*."

She didn't say any more.

Neither did Tel.

* * *

"Where have you two been?" Faye asked, when Tel and Sophie eventually came sauntering back onto the ward wearing huge smiles and holding hands.

"Just went for a walk," Sophie sighed.

"Rough walk, was it?" Faye grinned.

Sophie brushed her hair down, noticing that Tel had his Christmas jumper on inside-out. Faye and Olivia laughed, then turned back to Beth.

"It was so nice of you to make the effort to come," she was saying. "I really appreciate it. You're good friends."

They hugged. They cooed their goodbyes to the two sleeping babies in their cots, and waved their way off the ward.

All the mothers waved back.

* * *

They stepped out of the hospital and shivered in their wet coats. The sky was no longer blue but battleship grey.

They raced across the car park and threw themselves into Tel's car. He immediately turned the heating on full blast. They still shivered.

"You okay to drive?" Brian asked, slipping into the passenger seat as Tel started up the engine.

"Yeah, I'll go slow."

Directly behind him, Sophie pushed his shoulder. When he turned to look at her she still had that glint in her eyes. "Not too slow," she said.

"Strap yourselves in," he cried, "It's gonna be a bumpy ride."

There was a huge crack of thunder from above, seemingly right above them, and then rain lashed down, creating a stream down the windscreen and across the car park.

"No aquaplaning," said Brian, as Tel pulled away. "I'd like to see in the New Year, if it's all the same to you."

* * *

By the time they got back to the Woodsman the snow had all but gone, except for the odd large mound. Rivers of water ran across roads and down the lanes, but they were passable.

Tel pulled up in the car park as close to the pub as possible, and they sat there in silence for a moment, glad to be back in one piece and feeling happy for Jim and Beth.

They pulled up their hoods and got out. They were instantly drenched.

Mark quickly opened the pub door and they poured inside. Olivia grabbed an umbrella from the coat stand. "Just going to check on the exes," she said, "Make sure they haven't froze to death or anything."

"I'll come with you," said Faye.

Tel held Sophie's hand and glanced up the stairs, smiling.

"We should go," she said, and he huffed.

Julie went into the kitchen, shouting, "I'll put the kettle on."

They ran through the rain and jumped up the wooden steps to the glass fronted shed, standing in a tight huddle underneath the overhanging roof. Richard's stinky coat hung from a hanging basket hook, half of it wet from the rain, and they pulled faces as the smell hit them. Mark tried the door, but it was locked from the inside.

They peered through the glass.

"I don't see them," Faye said, pressing her hands above her eyes.

"Are they gone?" Mark asked, crossing his fingers.

"No, there they are," said Sophie. "On the floor next to the open oven door. They appear to be … sharing the same sleeping bag. "

"Are they dead?" Faye asked.

"Wife, can you stop being so morbid?"

"I'm not morbid, I'm just curious."

Mark started tapping on the window. They all joined in.

The bodies in the sleeping bag didn't move.

"This will be a surprise for them," Sophie said, "Waking up and finding our faces peering in at them."

"You don't think they've … you know?" Olivia asked.

"I think it's quite possible," said Sophie.

"Ooh," Faye cried, "A budding romance."

"Or a desperate attempt to not be lonely," said Brian.

"Well, they certainly have a lot in common," Mark said, "They both have black, cold hearts."

"We don't know anything yet," Olivia said. "They could be just huddling together for warmth."

"The cold comes from the inside," Mark muttered. "There's no thawing the iciness of their dead souls."

Tel and Sophie glanced at each other. Tel put his tongue

in his right cheek and tipped his head towards the pub, jiggling his eyebrows up and down for greater emphasis. Sophie giggled silently, held up two fingers and mouthed, "Two minutes." Tel's face broke into a huge grin.

Finally, their tapping raised the sleeping couple, who looked first at each other and then, raising their heads, over at the window. They both visibly jolted when they saw the crowd outside, staring in at them.

"Open the door!" Mark cried.

Richard and Janis looked at each other again, then down at themselves inside the sleeping bag.

"Oh God," Mark sighed.

"What?"

"They're naked."

"They're not!"

"They're not leaping up to open the door, are they."

Richard dragged an arm out and undid the zip. Inside, they were still dressed but 'ruffled'. Janis pulled the dress around her like it was a second skin that had gotten twisted.

"That's an awfully nice jumper Dick's wearing," Tel said. "Is that … cashmere?"

"Expensive jeans, too," said Sophie, "They're just muddy at the bottom."

"Quite nice clothes for a street sleeper, don't you think?"

"I do think."

While Richard and Janis made a big show of searching for and putting on shoes and wellies, Mark sniffed and turned around, looking at the coat hanging from the basket hook. "What *does* he have rotting in his pockets?" he said.

Brian turned with him. Mark, with his head as far back as it would go, took a deep breath and plunged a hand into a pocket.

"Ugh," he said.

"Dead rat?" Brian asked.

"Oh, the smell is *rank*."

Brian put a hand on his arm. "This is a job for … a professional."

"A professional pickpocket?"

"No, someone with no sense of smell. Faye!"

"What?"

"We need you."

She stepped towards them, pleased as punch to be needed.

"Find out what Dick's got in his pockets," Brian said.

"Why me?"

"You can't smell."

"There could be something horrible in there, like a mouse or a rat. I could get bitten."

"I'll compensate you for any injuries," Mark said, glancing over his shoulder and watching the exes approaching the windows.

"You'll compensate me anyway," Faye said, keeping her hands firmly at her sides.

"You drive a hard bargain. Do it."

Faye slipped her hand into one pocket and brought out some cellophane wrapped mints, a mini toothbrush and paste, a coach ticket, and some damp tissues.

"The other one," Mark said, "Quick."

"Alright, alright, keep your hair on."

As Faye rummage around in the second pocket, Brian peered closer at the wool coat and said, "This looks almost new." He brushed at a dry patch of mud. "Don't you think these looks like muddy fingerprints, like he smeared the mud on himself, possibly to make it look like he's been sleeping rough?"

Mark looked, inspected, touched, and hissed, "The lying little –"

Faye pulled her hand out. A wallet and a tiny spray bottle. "Hell's Smells," she said, reading the label. Without thinking, she sprayed some into the air in front of them. Brian almost choked. Mark bent over and dry heaved. He straightened up quickly and took the wallet from Faye, still heaving. Inside were cards and cash. He quickly flicked through the money.

"How much?" Brian asked, as the glass doors to the utility shed opened and Richard cried, "Thank God you're back, I've had

nothing to drink!"
>Mark looked up at him and said, "A grand at least."
"I thought he was broke."
"Yeah, so did I."

CHAPTER 16

"What is *this*?" Mark snarled in Richard's face, holding up the wallet.

They'd returned to the pub and were now in the *Friends* corner, Mark furiously interrogating a remorseless Richard, who was sitting cross-legged and nonchalant on a dining chair. The others sat around.

"It looks like a wallet to me," he said smugly, "But it could be a trick question. Is it a trick question?"

"Don't be clever, Dick. Is it yours?"

"Do the credit cards have my name on them?"

"You know they do."

"Then you know it's my wallet."

"It's *full* of *money*!"

"Money?" Janis squeaked from the next table.

"You told us you were broke."

"I did. It may have been a slight exaggeration."

"You were lying?"

"I was."

"Why?"

Richard sighed. Mark wanted to punch that snide expression right off his face.

"I'd rather not say," Richard said.

"Are you even a heavy drinker?" Olivia asked from an armchair, "Or did you fake that, too?"

"Sadly, that bit's true, though not as bad as I might have led you to believe, maybe a few too many at weekends, but – " he said, twisting his head to look at the bar behind him, " – it was far too good an opportunity for me to pass. The rice wine was a new low, even for me, I tipped that out on the way to the glass shed. Most of the other drinks went in the Christmas tree pot or on the deplorable poinsettias."

They all looked at the poinsettias dotted around the room. They were limp and dying. The Christmas tree was turning brown and already shedding its needles.

"Not my favourite plant," Richard said, "Very gaudy, I always think."

"I didn't *buy them* for *you*," Olivia spat.

"I think we all need to stay calm," Brian said, noticing Mark balling his hands into fists and his face take on an expression of pure rage.

"Why?" Mark snarled. "Why did you do it?"

Richard shrugged. "Why not? Look, if you're going to continue asking me ridiculous questions I'd like a glass of wine to quench my thirst. A burgundy, not the rancid vinegar you've been passing off as wine."

Olivia nodded at Julie, who rushed to the bar.

"Why have you done this?" Sophie asked. "Why did you go to such elaborate lengths? Just to torment Liv?"

Richard stuck his tongue out and touched his neck. "My mouth is terribly dry, it needs lubrication."

"It needs a smack," Mark snapped.

"Steady," said Brian.

Julie handed a glass to Richard and he sipped at it slowly, nodding his head in approval.

"Tell us why," Olivia said.

The air around them was heavy with tension. They were all at various stages of shock and anger. Mark felt murderous, but Richard brushed at his pale blue jumper as if he didn't have a care in the world.

"Glad it's over, actually," he said. "Wearing that filthy coat was really starting to irritate me."

"Poor you," Faye sneered. "It must have been awful."

"It was. Hell's Smells," he laughed, "Very apt. Got it off

eBay, amazing what they sell. Wears off after a couple of hours, I had to keep respraying."

"Unbelievable," Tel said, shaking his head.

Mark stood up, growling, and started pacing up and down behind Richard, staring at the back of his head with his face twisted.

"Just tell us why," Brian said calmly.

"I keep telling you, why not?"

"Did you really lose your job and your flat?" Olivia asked.

"I did lose my job, yes, but I found another one, a better one. I still have the flat."

"So, you're not homeless?" Sophie asked.

"No."

"Absolutely unbelievable," Tel said.

"I don't understand why you would do something like this," Olivia said quietly.

"You ruined my life, I ruin your Christmas, it's as simple as that. It was almost too easy. You're very gullible, Olivia, very easy to manipulate, always have been, always will be."

"Shut your mouth!" Mark snarled, punching him in his shoulder.

"Ouch," Richard said calmly, "I could have you for assault."

"I'd rather be done for murder, you low-life little – "

"MARK!" Brian boomed. "Calm yourself. You're playing right into his hands."

"I might press charges," Richard said languidly, "Like you did with me last year."

"For something you'd done," Tel said.

"Yes, sending those motocross bikes onto the campsite was quite fun."

"Fun?"

"Wearing those handcuffs, not so much. I'd like to see you in handcuffs," he said, turning to Mark. "Do you want to hit me?"

"Very much, but I won't give you the satisfaction."

"Oh. Pity."

Richard took another sip and stared at the ceiling.

"Why go to such extremes, Dick?" Sophie asked. "There has to be more to it than you're telling us. It's an awful lot of effort for free meals and alcohol."

He took a deep breath and looked from one to the other. "My girlfriend –"

"You have a girlfriend?" Olivia gasped, as Janis cried, "Girlfriend?"

"Yes. I'm not completely without charm, you know."

"Can't say I've noticed," said Faye.

Mark shook his fists behind Richard's head, barely able to control himself. Brian shook his head and Mark stepped away with a snarl. Julie rushed to the bar and poured a brandy, handing it to him. He took it and walked to the far side of the room, where he paced and sipped and glanced at Richard with unrestrained hostility.

"My girlfriend went to spend Christmas with her family in France," Richard continued. "I was left alone. I don't like being alone. I was bored. Also, hungry, and Olivia is an exceptional cook, usually."

"You did this for a free meal?" Tel gasped.

"Several free meals, to be precise, although I have to say the boxed Christmas dinner was below par, but the endless free booze almost made up for it."

"Worth it, was it, to make yourself look homeless?" Sophie asked.

"Oh yes, looking down-and-out was imperative. Olivia wouldn't have let me in otherwise." He smirked over at Mark. "She does so like an underdog."

Mark slammed his glass down on a table and stormed up the room. Brian and Tel quickly jumped up and physically held him back. Richard sat on his chair, sipping his wine and grinning.

"Do *not* mistake my kindness for weakness," Olivia hissed.

Suddenly, as if in slow motion, they watched as Olivia

leapt up off the sofa, ball a fist, and, throwing all her weight behind a straight arm, she smashed it straight into the side of Richard's face. He yelped out in pain and surprise, lifting a hand up to his cheek.

Faye started clapping. "You get him, Livs, the bloody horrible creep."

"Olivia!" Tel gasped, half smiling in awe.

"Explain the black eye to your girlfriend," Olivia snarled at him.

"Easily," Richard said. "I walked into a door. You really are a silly little woman."

Olivia threw her fist at his face again, faster than he could react, straight into his nose. "Explain *two* black eyes," she snarled.

Richard, panting with pain, delicately checked his nose for blood and found none. Agitated, he pulled his phone from his front pocket. "Assault," he spat. "I'm calling the police and having you arrested."

"What for?" Brian asked, letting go of Mark, who rushed to Olivia's side. "Nothing happened."

Richard pointed at his face and snarled, "She *punched* me! *Twice!*"

"Did she?" Faye shrugged. "I didn't see anything."

"Me neither," said Sophie.

"You tripped over your own feet," said Tel. "Not surprising after all the alcohol you've consumed."

"I saw it, Rupert," Janis said. "I'll be your witness."

"How can you be his witness?" Sophie asked, frowning. "You were upstairs the whole time."

"Very unsociable woman," said Faye.

"Very rude," Brian said.

Richard pressed nine on his phone.

"I wouldn't do that if I were you," said Tel.

"I'm pressing charges."

"Really? For something you imagined? I think the police have better things to do than listen to the drunken ravings of a gatecrashing ex-husband?"

Richard pressed another nine.

"Don't you have a criminal record?" Sophie asked. "Weren't you arrested for instigating a motorbike riot on Liv's campsite last year, and breaching the conditions of your bail *and* a restraining order?"

Richard's finger hovered over his phone.

"Police will take one look at lovely Liv and laugh you right out of the pub," said Brian.

"You have a history of intimidation," Sophie said.

"Your word against ours," said Tel.

Richard let his hands drop to the arms of the chair and glared at them all. He opened his mouth to speak, but Mark said, "Get out. Get out now."

"Your coat's outside the front door," Olivia said. "Get it and go."

"I would, except your farmer boy still has my wallet."

Mark looked down at the wallet in his hand. "So I have!" he cried, opening it up. "Let's see, you've been here for two nights."

"On the floor!" Richard snapped.

"Plus meals and copious amounts of alcohol."

"Most of which I didn't drink."

Mark pulled a thick wad of money out of Richard's wallet and, shaking it in front of him, said, "This should cover it, I think."

"Take it, if it makes you feel better."

"I will, and it does."

Mark tossed the wallet at him. As Richard pushed it into his back pocket, his phone buzzed. He glanced at the screen.

"My girlfriend's on her way back," he grinned.

"Does she know what a low-life scumbag you are?" Olivia asked.

"Obviously not, if she's coming back to him," said Brian.

"I'm sure she'll find out soon enough," Sophie said. "The two black eyes might give her a clue, if she has any sense."

Richard tapped his screen with a thumb. "I really must be going now. I've ordered an Uber, it'll be here in fifteen minutes. I'll wait for it outside."

"Good choice, pal. Now sling your hook."

Standing up, Richard sauntered casually from the room.

Janis ran out after him and charged up the stairs to her room.

The group looked at each other. Julie stood watching from behind the bar, not really sure what had just happened but sensing it was something big and bad.

The front door opened, and closed again.

Olivia stomped into the kitchen. Julie followed her.

When the others saw her marching down the hallway carrying something in her hands, they jumped to their feet and followed her out of the pub.

Richard was standing at the bottom of the steps in the rain, brushing at his coat as if trying to clean off the mud. Olivia hurried down the steps, to the step above him, and, raising her arms, furiously plonked a large bowl of trifle on top of his head, wriggling the bowl until it gave a slurping sound and released its content.

"Bit of a waste," said Brian.

"I like trifle," said Faye.

Richard chuckled as jelly, blancmange and cream oozed down his face and across his shoulders, slithering over his coat before hitting the floor.

"Is that the best you can do?" he laughed.

Julie, on the step above, nudged Olivia. When she turned, Julie handed her a small, open can. Olivia smiled and picked out an anchovy, splatting it against the back of Richard's head. And another. And another.

Richard scraped at the trifle and the anchovies. "I can wash it all away," he said, "The rain's doing it already, but you'll never be able to get rid of me, Olivia. Never."

Faye suddenly left Brian's side and tottered down the steps, where she proceeded to spray Richard with the spray bottle of Hell's Smells she still had in her hand. "Taxi won't take you smelling like that though, will it," she snarled. "How dare you treat our friends like that, how *dare* you."

Faye gave him her most evil look before stomping back up the steps, dripping wet. She crossed Sophie coming down the steps with a huge blow-up snowman from the front of the pub in her arms, which she awkwardly used to bat Richard across the head. "You horrible little toad of a man," she cried, as Richard's laughing head bounced from side to side.

Tel, incensed that he was laughing at his angry, snowman-wielding wife, pulled an inflatable reindeer from its mooring and ran down the steps, whacking Richard front and back whilst Sophie whacked from side to side. Richard's head bounced like a pinball, until Sophie's snowman squeaked from her hands and went bouncing off across the car park

Faye bent down and, from an untouched pile of snow underneath the porch, picked up a handful of snow and fashioned it into a ball, which she threw at Richard, missing him by miles. Brian bent down and quickly pressed together an enormous snowball. He lobbed it and it thudded directly on the back of Richard's head, jolting him forward. He fell into a muddy, icy puddle.

He spluttered as he picked himself up, just as Julie came racing out of the pub, screaming like a banshee and holding something above her head. As Richard got to his feet, she leapt into the air and, in an impressive mid-air manoeuvre, plonked the substantial remains of the Christmas turkey over his head, bottom first.

Faye shrieked with laughter as Richard blindly stumbled around pulling at the carcass. When he got it off he threw it on the floor. His hair and face were covered in grease and bits of meat, and he looked absolutely furious. "I'll have you for this!" he raged. "You see if I don't!"

Janis came running out, wrapping a scarf around her neck with one hand and carrying an overnight bag in the other. "Wait for me, Rupert," she cried, "I can give you a lift somewhere."

"Are you leaving us?" Mark shouted after her, "So soon?" He gave a meaningful fist pump and breathed, "Yes!"

As Janis approached Richard, she stopped and took a step back, looking him up and down, at the unidentified stuff on his head and what looked like trifle all over his coat. Also, he stunk. "Have you been spraying yourself again?"

"You cretins!" he yelled, shaking a fist at the group. "You morons!"

"We're cretins," Mark shrugged.

"Morons, no less," said Tel.

"Happy little morons though," Brian grinned. "Which is more than can be said for Dick right now."

"Or ever," Olivia grinned.

"Are you rich enough to afford a full valeting of my car afterwards?" Janis was asking.

Apoplectic with rage, Richard kicked the turkey carcass across the car park. It broke into several pieces, the biggest of which bounced across the bonnet of Janis's car and came to a greasy rest against her windscreen.

Brian and Tel laughed so hard they were holding on to one another and choking. Faye and Sophie had to pat them on the back and tell them to calm down. They'd just managed to gather themselves together again when Janis, stomping to her car, caught a high heel on the gravel and went *skimming* across the ground.

She got up and wiped down the front of her camel coat, now filthy, and squealed in frustration. She turned to Richard and yelled, "Do you want a lift or not?"

With a furious look at them at the top of the stairs, he thundered over to Janis's car and got in. A second later he got out again and, to the sound of Janis screaming, "I can't bloody breathe!", he took off his coat and, staring at them with it hanging from his outstretched hand, dropped it to the floor.

"That'll keep the parasites away," Brian hollered.

"And the zombies," Tel laughed.

"Don't ever come back here again," Mark yelled.

Janis started her car up. They could see them arguing behind the turkey. Janis put her windscreen wipers on and it smeared the carcass across the glass.

As she drove by them, Richard wound down the passenger window and shook a fist at them. "I'll get you for this!" he yelled, "I'll be back!"

"No you won't," Olivia yelled back, still laughing, "You're barred, for life."

Mark suddenly bent down and made a snowball, which he lobbed at the open window. It splattered in Richard's face.

Suddenly, they were all bending and throwing snowballs, hitting him again and again as the window slowly closed. Snowballs pelted the car as it roared towards the exit.

The last thing Richard and Janis would have heard were their screams of laughter.

"So childish," Sophie giggled.

"But fun," said Tel, "And very, very satisfying."

"Celebratory drink?" Brian suggested, turning to go back inside.

"Could I just say – ?" Mark began.

"You can say anything you want," Tel said, "But can we go inside first? Only I'm drenched and freezing my nuts off."

"Oh!" Sophie squealed, "We can't have that!"

Tel winked and breathed, "Maybe you could – ?"

"Don't finish that sentence!" Faye cried, "I'm sure Sophie could, but we don't want to hear about it."

"I was just going to say maybe Sophie could run me a bath."

"Yeah, sure you was. Yours alright, Bri?"

"May need some attention later."

"Okay."

* * *

Tel and Sophie were halfway up the stairs when Mark said, "Can I have a quick word?" They reluctantly came down again and merged with the others in the lounge. Julie was quickly pouring out brandies to thaw them out.

"I'd just like to say," Mark began, and Tel said, "Make it quick."

"I will. I'd just like to say – "

"Is this like a toast?" said Faye, taking her glass from Julie.

"Are you hungry?" Julie asked, "I can make you some toast if you want?"

"Maybe later, I want a bath first."

"Me too," said Tel.

"Me three," said Sophie. Turning to Olivia, she added, "Can your hot water cope if we all take a bath at the same time?"

"I don't know."

"We'll have to share," Sophie said, winking at Tel.

"Ooh," said Faye, looking up at Brian. His beard parted in huge smile.

"Can I just say what I want to say?" Mark asked.

"Get on with it then."

"I'm trying!"

"We'll be quiet," Faye said.

"Thank you. I just wanted to express my gratitude for all your help this Christmas."

"You're welcome," Tel said, emptying his glass and slamming it down on the counter, before grabbing Sophie's hand and turning towards the door.

"I haven't finished yet," Mark said.

"Oh. Hurry up, I'm frozen."

"You love us," Sophie said, "We're brilliant people, and you're glad we were here to help you divest yourselves of the psychopaths, that about it?"

"Yeah." Mark shifted awkwardly on his feet. "Pretty much."

"Right," Tel said, "Catch you later."

"Wait!" They stopped hurrying towards the door. "Please, just listen."

Tel sighed and sat on a bar stool. Sophie stood next

to him. Brian had his arm across Faye's shoulders, and Olivia reached out to hold Mark's hand. They looked at him expectantly.

"I'm really grateful for everything you've done for Olivia and myself the last few days."

"We're really grateful for the food," said Brian.

"And the booze," Tel laughed.

"And the exceptional hospitality," said Sophie.

"It's been lovely," Faye said, "Really lovely."

"Best Christmas I've ever had," said Julie.

"Ahh."

"It's a Christmas I'm sure will stay in our memories for a long, long time," Brian said, and they all nodded, and glanced at the door.

"You're all very kind," said Olivia, glancing at her watch. "It's a bit late for lunch now, I was going to do some turkey sandwiches but the turkey is no more."

Brian put his hand on his chest. "It gave itself up for a good cause."

"Excellent turkey plopping, by the way, Jools," said Tel.

"Thanks. I used to play a lot of netball at school, it was my best subject."

"Wow, you had a netball court?" Faye sighed. "We just had beanbags to throw around the classroom."

"Wow," said Brian, "You had beanbags? We were just given a good thrashing and –"

"Okay, that's enough," Tel sniggered. "You'll be doing Monty Python's armless Black Knight next."

"It is but a scratch."

"I did ballet at school," Sophie said, twirling a strand of hair and staring off into the distance. "I was quite good at it."

"I didn't know that," said Tel.

"Ah, you don't know everything about me. Anyway, it was years ago."

"I give up," Mark said, flopping his arms at his sides.

"No, go on, Mark."

He looked from one to the other. "You're the best people I've ever met and I feel very honoured to be part of this group. It's good to know our backs are always covered by people who have our best interests at heart."

"We do," said Brian.

"No man gets left behind," said Faye.

"Jim would say, 'All for one and one for all'," Tel laughed.

"But seriously," Mark said, putting a hand on his chest, "Thank you, from the very bottom of my heart. Without you I'm not sure we could have coped with Dick and … what was her name again?"

Olivia laughed. "Jolene, was it?"

"Jennifer?" said Sophie, frowning.

"Definitely began with a J," Faye said. "Joy?"

"Joyless?"

"Anyway, whatever her name, she's gone," Mark said.

"Hopefully never to return, lad."

"Oh, she's never coming back here again," Olivia said, an edge to her voice.

"Nor Dick."

They all booed. Faye cried, "The *meanies*!"

There was some brief hugging and back patting. Mark stood back with tears in his eyes. Olivia held his hand and smiled.

"How about we nibble our way through the rest of the afternoon," she said, "And order a takeaway later?"

"Curry," said Brian.

"Ooh, yes," said Faye.

"Are we done now?" Tel said, standing up.

"Go, have your baths!"

Before he'd even finished his sentence, four sets of feet were thudding up the stairs.

* * *

They were gathered around the big table in the back lounge wearing pyjamas and dressing gowns, too lazy to get dressed after their afternoon 'naps'. Seven spoons scooped and sampled from the takeaway tins lined down the middle on banmaries. Poppadom and naan breads were handed around. The fire crackled.

"Finally, it feels like Christmas," Olivia was saying.

"It's quiet without them, isn't it," Faye said.

"Who, Beth and Jim, or Dick and Joyless?"

"All of them."

"Hopefully there'll be no more drama," Olivia sighed. "I need a couple of weeks to recover."

"Don't we all," said Brian. "The biriani is excellent, by the way."

"So is the jalfrezi."

"You decided against the vindaloo, Liv?"

"I don't want to risk starting the day with more drama," she laughed.

"Oh," Julie squeaked, "I forgot to tell you, I changed the vacant guest rooms while you were all busy giggling in yours."

A beat of silence, broken by Sophie sniggering and nudging Tel, who nudged her back.

"Thank you," Olivia beamed.

"S'okay, I like being useful."

"You certainly are."

"I found something under the bed in room five."

Julie jumped up and went behind the bar. She came back and splodged what look like a small, clear jellyfish on an empty part of the table. Faye dared to stick a finger out and prod it. It wobbled.

"What is it?" Olivia asked.

"Dunno."

"I know what it is," Sophie grinned. "Was it Janis's room?"

"Yeah."

"It's, erm …"

"Spit it out, Sophs."

"It's a cutlet."

They stared at it. "What kind of cutlet?"

"A chicken fillet."

They looked from the jellyfish to Sophie. "Radioactive chicken, was it?"

"It's a *gel insert*," she said, and they still looked blank. "You put it in your bra to make your boobs look bigger."

"Oh!"

Faye gingerly picked it up. "Bit big, innit?"

"Well, they were, weren't they." Brian weighed his hands in front of his chest.

"You mean, the freshly risen souffles weren't real?" Olivia gasped.

"There's nothing real about her," said Mark, "Even her boob job needs accessories."

"So," said Faye, squeezing it, "That must mean that Miss Joyless is currently living life with one enormous boob and one small one?"

Mark screamed with laughter, which set the others off. They stopped when his phone rang.

"Who could that be?" he muttered, pulling it out of his pocket.

"Answer it and all will be revealed," said Brian.

The screen read 'unknown number'.

"Could be important," Olivia whispered to him.

So he answered it, put it on speakerphone, and lay down it on the table.

"Mark?" came a familiar voice, and Mark dropped his head into his hands.

"The gall of the woman!" Olivia hissed.

"Mark, it's Janis. I'm … I'm stuck."

"I don't care."

"I'm in trouble."

"I don't care."

"I need your help, Mark."

"Not a chance."

"Richard insisted I drive him to Oxford to catch a train back to London. Pretty smelly journey, I can tell you, and cold, we had to have the windows open the entire time."

"I don't care."

"And then, when I asked him about meeting up again, he just laughed and left me."

"Still don't care."

"And I'm low on petrol. And money. And my cards are all maxed out."

"Couldn't give the tiniest."

"I've got just enough petrol to get back to the pub."

Olivia gasped out loud.

Mark snatched up the phone. "Hold on a minute," he told Janis.

"Yes, yes, of course."

He took it off speakerphone and marched into the kitchen, where they heard a tirade of loud and creatively used expletives.

"Never heard *that* word used six times in one sentence," Sophie said, impressed.

"Rhubarb," said Faye.

"What do you mean, you still want twenty barkin' grand!" Mark screamed. "Are you out of your fluffin' mind? You're not getting *anything*, not a single barkin' penny, not now, *not ever*!"

There followed a long, lingering silence. Mark eventually came through from the kitchen with a tired smile on his face. "She's not coming," he said.

"Oh," Sophie sighed, "That's a shame."

"What was the deciding factor?" Brian asked.

"It was either my threat to take her back to court to reclaim some of the divorce settlement, or Sophie."

"Me?"

"Told her you were skilled in martial arts, owned nunchucks and weren't afraid to use them."

"What's a nunchuck?" Sophie asked.

"A small, furry animal," said Faye.

"That's a chipmunk, lass."

"Oh."

Olivia's phone rang.

"She better not be ringing you," Mark growled.

"She doesn't have my number."

"She'll have snooped through your phone."

"It's password protected. Oh," she cried, looking at the screen, "It's Beth on a video call. Beth!"

Beth's smiling face appeared on the screen, pillows behind her, and a slither of Jim's face down the side. Olivia held it up for everyone to see. They all cried, "Hi, Beth."

"Is everything okay?" Faye asked.

"Everything's fine," she gushed. "I just wanted to show you ... *this*."

The picture on the screen turned and hovered over the twin cots, where the babies were peacefully sleeping. They all cooed.

"They're still gorgeous," Julie sighed.

"Are they bigger?" asked Brian.

"Probably, I've just fed them. Oh!" she suddenly cried, peering closer to the camera, "You're having a curry!"

Three women's voices in the background all cried, "*Curry!*"

"I would *kill* for a curry right now," Beth said. "First thing I'm having when I get home."

"When are they letting you out?" Sophie asked.

"Hopefully tomorrow, fingers crossed."

"Do you think you'll cope alright?" Faye asked.

"I don't think, I know," Beth laughed. "I took out a contract. Is that what you say, Tel, taking out a contract?"

"Depends on the context," Tel laughed. "Are you planning on having someone killed?"

"Nah, I've hired a nanny on a six month contract, just to ease us into twindom. We'll see how it goes after that."

"Good planning," said Faye.

"Wise decision," said Sophie.

"Anyway," Beth beamed, "Just wanted to say hi, thanks for visiting this afternoon, it really cheered me up, and enjoy your curry, you lucky people."

"Bye, Beth."

"Bye."

"Oh Beth," Olivia said, standing up and walking off with the phone, "I wanted to ask you something."

* * *

They were snuggled up on the sofa and armchairs, wrapped in blankets despite it being warm from the central heating and the open fire – it just seemed the right thing to do. There was an assortment of nibbles nobody was eating on the coffee table, and *It's a Wonderful Life* was playing on the giant TV screen.

"It's black and white," Julie said, pulling a face.

"Everything was black and white back in those days," Brian grinned.

"Was it?"

"No, Jools, it wasn't," Mark laughed. "Only the films were black and white."

"Oh."

"Jools," said Olivia, "I might have an extra Christmas present for you."

She sat up excitedly.

"Would you like a job? Working here, I mean?"

"Yes!" she gasped.

"I think you'd be a great asset to us."

"I think so too," said Mark.

Julie was shaking her fists in front of her. "Are you sure?"

"Yes, quite sure," Olivia smiled. "I checked with Beth and she's fine with it."

Julie shook her fists harder, her elbows nudging into Brian on the sofa next to her. "Thank you!"

"You're more than welcome."

Julie turned to Brian and said, "I've got a job."

"So I heard," he chuckled. "Now watch the film."

CHAPTER 18

The Day After Boxing Day

Tel got a phonecall as they were halfway through their bagels with smoked salmon and cream cheese breakfast, fresh from the mobile bakery van that supplied the local area.

It was their downstairs neighbour in London.

"Merry Christmas, Mrs Braddock."

"And to you, Mr Okenado. I'm calling to inform you that you've received a delivery of a very large box. It has a picture of a bathtub on the side."

"Tub's arrived!" he said to Sophie, who grinned excitedly. "Thank you for letting us know, Mrs Braddock."

"It's sitting outside, on the pavement."

"On the pavement?"

"What?" Sophie gasped.

"Can you take it in for us, Mrs Braddock?"

"I am seventy-six years old, Mr Okenado, how would you propose I do that?"

"Could you ask them to leave it in the downstairs foyer?"

"The delivery men have gone."

"Gone?" Tel thought for a moment. "I'll call building security, and maybe Mr Wilberforce from the top apartment, and they could –"

"Mr Okenado, it took six bulky men with tattoos up their arms to lift it out of the back of the van and carry it up to the building, where they discovered it would not fit through the main door. One of them fell to the ground afterwards and clutched at his chest for a moment or two, before being carried back to the van by the others."

"Somebody might take it," Tel said, mostly to himself.

"Only by a gang of six bodybuilding thieves, Mr Okenado, and, fortunately, you don't tend to see many of those wandering around Kensington."

"I'll sort it out, Mrs Braddock. Thanks for letting us know."

"You're most welcome."

As soon as he hung up, his phone rang again.

"Colin here from building security. There's a rather large box addressed to you currently sitting outside. Its partially blocking the main entrance."

"Could you and perhaps Mr Wilberforce move it into the foyer? We'll be back later."

"Not in my job description, hauling heavy items," Colin said.

"Okay, I'll sort something out."

"Sort it out quickly, Mr Okenado, it's upsetting some of our residents."

"Yes, of course."

He hung up and frantically dialled a number.

"I'm on 'oliday," the plumber said. "Not working until after New Year's Day."

"It's an emergency," Tel said.

"It always is. Call back on – "

"I'll pay double your normal rate."

There was a silence, except for Sophie gasping, "Tel!"

The silence continued.

"Triple," said Tel.

Sophie threw her hands in the air.

"Triple, you say?"

"Yes, but it has to be done today, and it's going to take at least six of you."

"Six triple pays?" asked the plumber.

Tel forced himself to say, "Yes." He gave him the details

and hung up.

"We have to go," he said, pushing the remaining bagel into his mouth.

"Us too," said Brian, standing up. "We've got the family coming round."

"Yay," Faye cried.

"Thank you, Mark and Liv, for ... "

Olivia sniggered. "A lovely time?" she suggested.

"A Christmas from hell?" Mark grinned.

"It's been fabulous, actually," Sophie said, getting up. "Talk about a crash course in human behaviour. Main character syndrome is now my favourite psychosis and I'll be diagnosing all my clients with it from now on."

"I have at least four," said Tel.

"I've enjoyed every minute," Faye said.

"Must do it again soon," Brian laughed.

"Yeah, I'll see if I can get them back for Easter or something," said Mark.

"Don't you dare!" snapped Olivia.

After collecting their belongings from the guest rooms, they hugged en masse in the hallway, and again outside the front door of The Woodsman.

Words like 'brilliant' and 'fantastic time' and 'thank you so much' were bandied about like verbal confetti as Brian, Faye, Tel and Sophie left the pub, waving and blowing kisses back at Mark and Olivia.

"Give us a lift?" Brian said, as Tel clambered into his car.

"What, back to Birmingham?"

"No, you dope, to the caravan."

They got in, still waving and blowing kisses.

"Pace yourself, woman," Brian said, as Faye's air-kissed hand flew backwards and forwards in front of his face, "We're driving past again in a few minutes, you'll get tennis elbow at this rate."

Brian helped Tel to hitch up his caravan. They hugged. They got into their cars, and Brian wound down his window and yelled, "Herd 'em up and move 'em out!"

They drove past Mark and Olivia, still standing outside with their arms around each other.

"Love you!"

"Talk soon!"

"Thanks for everything!"

"Bye."

Every single one of them, like all guests over the Christmas, breathed a hefty sigh of relief.

There was no place like home.

Mark and Olivia

They closed the front door behind them and locked it.

"Alone at last," Mark sighed.

"Until tomorrow, when we open up again."

"Spot of naked streaking round the pub, darling?"

"Yes please, darling."

Olivia ran up the stairs, tearing off her Christmas jumper. Mark followed, both of them giggling like children.

Brian and Faye

Just as they got to the main road, Faye turned round in her seat and spotted a thin, square present behind Brian.

"What's this?" she said, picking it up and grinning.

"Oh, forgot about that. Saw it when I went to the Bullring for your sexy boots, thought you might like it, bought it."

"What is it?"

"Open it and see."

She did. It was a large, full colour calendar featuring Chris Hemsworth in various stages of undress, flexing his muscles and moodily staring off into the distance.

She quietly flicked through the pages, one by one, two or three times, sighing a lot.

Brian was glad of the peace.

Tel and Sophie

The plumbers managed to get the bath out of the box and squeeze it, with millimetres to spare, through the front door of their building. It took all six of them, plus a security guard and Mr Wilberforce from the top floor, to get it up the staircase – fortunately wide enough to accommodate all of them, plus tub – to their apartment.

It wouldn't fit through the door.

One of the plumbers, under the intense scrutiny of the security guard, took out one side of the doorframe.

It took all day to fit it. Tel thought it might not have taken them all day if they weren't being paid by the hour.

Finally, it was done, and the plumbers collected their payment, which took all the cash they had stashed around the flat.

They were barely out the door before Sophie, shrieking with joy, raced into the bathroom and carefully cleaned the newly installed, bespoke, freestanding, marble, double-ended, roll top slipper bathtub with brushed brass feet and in-built jacuzzi. She turned the taps on full. Steam rose into the air.

Smirking, Tel watched her from the doorway as she lit incense sticks and candles and placed them around the room. She turned on some romantic music. When the water reached the jets, she poured a generous amount of specially bought, ridiculously expensive bubble bath into it and turned on the jacuzzi.

She was so excited!

"Wine, Tel."

He fetched a bottle from the fridge, noting that the M&S ready meal now had its own ecoclimate.

"It's alive!" he cried.

He took two wine glasses from a cupboard and placed them on the decorative glass table next to the tub.

Sophie dashed into the bedroom to change. Tel chased after her, closing the bathroom door behind him to contain the steam.

They got heavily distracted.

"Bath," Sophie kept saying.

"It's massive," he told her, "It'll take ages to fill."

A short while later, giggling like overexcited children, they raced naked into the bathroom.

Sophie opened the door.

The room was full of bubbles so dense that the door cut a swathe into the gleaming suds. They couldn't see the bath, or anything else.

"Too much bubble bath?" Tel asked.

"Possibly."

"We should turn the jacuzzi off before the apartment turns into a giant foam party. Where is it?"

"Where's what?"

"The switch for the jacuzzi."

"I don't know."

"You turned it on, didn't you?"

"I was too excited to take much notice, I just pressed a switch."

"Which was where?"

"I ... don't recall."

A little while later, with both of them covered in bubbles, Tel swung the pipe of a wet and dry vacuum cleaner around in the air until they finally located the tub and were able to turn off the jacuzzi. Tel knocked the bottle of wine and glasses off the decorative table with the nozzle, and stepped onto the broken glass.

They spent the rest of the evening in A&E, where a young nurse gave Tel three stitches and some advice about not adding bubble bath to a jacuzzi.

BOOKS IN THIS SERIES

PITCHING UP!

Pitching Up!

Pitching Up Again!

Pitching Up In Style!

Pitching Up In America!

Pitching Up At Christmas!

If you enjoyed this book, or any of my books, please leave a rating or, better still, a review on Amazon. I thank you.
Email: deborahaubrey01@gmail.com
Facebook: AuthorDebbieAubrey
Until next time, ta ta. Dx

Printed in Great Britain
by Amazon